Grandma's Secret Blessings

A Memoir with a Twist

By **JohnEgreek**

Book design by John E. Hodgkinson

Front Cover Image: © | 123rf
Image ID: 36792935 (Print Only Extended License)
Copyright attribution:
<a href='https://www.123rf.com/profile_tomsickova'>tomsickova / 123RF Stock Photo</a> Copyright: Tatyana Tomsickova
Redesign: Argjendd11@fiverr.com

Back Cover Image: © | 123rf
Image ID: 38829317 (Print Only Extended Licence)
Copyright attribution:
<ahref='https://www.123rf.com/profile_khomich'>khomich / 123RF Stock Photo</a>
Copyright: Yauheni Khomich
Back Page Author Photograph: John E. Hodgkinson

This is a Non-fiction Memoir with a Twist of Fiction
Written by JohnEgreek
Visit my website at www.JohnEgreek.com
Printed in the United States of America First Printing: October 2017
Published by: Sojourn Publishing, LLC

Hard Cover ISBN: 978-1-62747-101-5
Paperback ISBN: 978-1-62747-095-7
Ebook ISBN: 978-1-62747-099-5

Published for: Meta Home Publishing Company

Inspired by:
My granddaughter Aubrey Rose Mote, whom I have seen,
but never met. She inspired me to tell Grandma's Secret Blessings.

Dedicated to:
My Greek Family: Who believed in me from the very first day
I was born and loved our family "Unconditionally."
Christina and Lambro Meta – My Grandparents
Barbara Lambro Meta – My Mother
Genevieve Lambro Meta – My Aunt
Alexander Lambro Meta – My Uncle
Odysseus Lambro Meta – My Uncle
Victor Lambro Meta – My Uncle
Margarite Lambro Meta – My Aunt

Thankful for:
My daughter Natalie J. Hodgkinson,
who taught me about the "will to live."
My granddaughter: Kalista Rankin,
"with the most beautiful smile in the world."

My Son Roc Ivorrie and wife Tonika, who have done their part to erase
"prejudice" in the world, along with my
Step-Grand Children: Aniesa, Ronnie, Aaron and
Granddaughter Daisha.

My Son Ryan Mote and wife Kate, parents of Aubrey Rose.

The Charles Truax Family, who signify the love and admiration
that a family should have for each other.

My brother Donald Hodgkinson and his wife Suzy, along with my
nephews Robin & Dimitri, who showered me with their
love and their kindness.

My Dearest Friends - Bob Scott,
Phyllis House, Sherrie and Bob McRoberts.

The women I let get away:
Terry Gibson, Holly Richards Livesay,
Sandra Weber, Mary Spirkoff and
the misfortunate love of my life, Nalanie Kittel.

Cathy Curtis – Thank you for being
the Angel who helped to open my heart.

Dishonorable yet Honorable to Mention:

Raymond Roy Hodgkinson

My father who hated me from the very first day I was born, who has never wavered from his contract, someone whom I no longer consider as my worst enemy, but as my greatest teacher. With Understanding, I have empathy for his wounded child.

"He taught me how not to be, if there is any honor in that."

Special Endorsements and Acknowledgements

In his book, "Grandma's Secret Blessings," Author JohneEgreek, aka John Hodgkinson, brilliantly showcases how guided and determined self-healing processes can heal your inner, wounded-child. As he narrates and creatively paints beautiful and picturesque stories for the reader to experience his journey, you gain the power in affirmations, prayers, and visualizations. You also discover the secret to the ultimate reality that "we hold the key" to our own healing by releasing the traumas and pain. To find out how — I encourage you to read this book cover to cover and not stop unless done. This book is for anyone who deep in their core believes that there is a way out of the suffering, misery, and loneliness that you still have in your life. Talk about healing generations — John has made it his life purpose of guiding people how to tap into their powers to "transcend and go beyond." Trust me, you will be wonderfully inspired.

~ Gagan Sarkaria, High Achievement Wellness & Business Coach,
Chinese Astrology Master & Energy Healer
www.UnfoldYourSuccess.com

The Journey Home to Our Essence: reconnecting to our joy, creativity and love.

All of us have had experiences in our past where we didn't have the resources to handle them. It may have been emotions that were too overwhelming, situations in which we shut down, froze, adapted and survived. In doing so, Author JohnEgreek captured the disconnected essence and the fragmented lost connections to the core of his vitality, lifeforce and the authenticity of his being.

At our deepest level we know something is missing or holding us back. Our soul longs for full expression and we seek to heal the fragmentation that has occurred. We are the ones who regularly attend workshops, courses, seeking answers by reading books, doing therapy or taking on coaching. We may even know when we disconnected, which specific events from our past set in place the wounding, the beliefs and limitations that hold us back in life and yet discover we never seem to actually find the full solution to the emptiness or blocks inside. I know because that is my story.

In searching for my own healing, I have trained in many modalities and undergone a myriad of experiences. From shamanic rituals, to past life regression, leading edge neuropsychological training, trauma therapy and many body and mind-based therapies. My personal journey has been to overcome suicidal depression. Life circumstances, events from my past and from my lineage meant I was on high alert from a very early age. I had a constant sense of an ever-present threat which created an aching loneliness and sense of disconnection from life. All the trainings I have attended provided clues and some answers, but nothing seemed to offer the complete break through until I was led to uncover the fragmentation of my soul and bring home the pieces. It has been a most loving, healing and embracing process.

The healing of our wounded little self, the reclamation of our soul fragments, the healing of our traumas, those we carry as part of our ancestral lineage, our cultural traumas, past life events and the release of the painful patterns from the tissue memory of our body, leads to integrated healing and a return to our innate joy, wisdom and love for self and other. Our true joy, freedom, creativity and inner wisdom is finally free to be fully expressed.

I offer support as a peer, one who has travelled this path. Life changes when you have an embodied experience and regain connection with your soul's full essence. Find out more by contacting simoneengdahl@bigpond.com or visit my website www.simoneengdahl.com

Author JohnEgreek weaves tradition, love, abuse and the past in with the present like a painter bringing it all together with artful brush strokes. To edit "Grandma's Secret Blessings, A memoir with a Twist," I gained beautiful insight into Greek traditions and family life. I feel John's willingness as a writer to share his vulnerability makes his heart wrenching story all the more powerful.

~ Karen Collyer Intuitive Author and Editor

Contents

Chapter One

What a beautiful day to take a stroll through the park. Sitting under the old oak tree, I can't believe how much life slipped past me. The smell of the oak tree permeates the air. I'm thinking how different my life could've been if I knew then what I know now. Unfortunately, none of us get do-overs.

I watch the ripples of water rolling across the lake. I can hear the joyous sounds of children playing. The birds are chirping, ducks are quacking and people are talking. Someone's radio is playing nearby. I recognize the song. It paints a picture in my head that will most likely remain in my mind for most of the day, "This is dedicated to the one I love." I first heard the Shirelles sing it in the 60's. A few years later, the Mamas and the Papas sang it. I remember they were a popular 60's band.

For some reason, I change the words when I sing it in my head. I used to sing the oldies to my daughter. She would laugh at me because I twisted the lyrics. I can't believe how strongly this song resonates with me. Life can never be as happy as I want it to be. But, I would be satisfied to know somebody loves me. It's an upbeat song, with an air about it that resonates with thoughts of joy. I recognize the one thing I've missed most this lifetime is someone to love.

The song plays over and over in my head. I cast a glance at the far end of the park where three kids are playing "kickball". Seeing them laughing and playing makes me think about my brother and sister when we were about that age. The little girl is about three and the two boys might be five, six, or even seven. They're laughing and pushing each other around, while kicking the ball. A moment of sadness comes over me. I can only remember one time in my life at that age when my brother and I ever played together. With my sister, never. How awful is that?

I begin thinking about my granddaughter, Aubrey Rose. The little girl appears to be about her age. I hope she's laughing and having a fun time with life. I wonder what she's like? What would I tell her about my life if I ever got to meet her? I am her grandfather, sixty-seven years old and retired. A father's not supposed to be estranged from his family, especially his grandchildren. This is not how I envisioned my life. My grandparents were the most treasured people in my life. I adored them, loved them with all my heart and I am thankful they passed their wisdom to me.

Unfortunately, there's some unknown reason for this. I'm sure it's another lesson in life destined to haunt me. If only I knew why, or what it is that I did to deserve this. My father hated me from the very first day I was born. That's not me, so why is my son punishing me by pushing me away? I have no clue.

I love my children more than they'll ever know. I divorced their mother, not my children. My heart aches with pain. I feel like I'm Humpty-Dumpty with a broken heart and a broken soul. It feels so painful and it seems that nothing can put me back together again.

My brother tells me to reach out to him. He has no clue how many unanswered text messages, phone calls, and emails I've sent. How much rejection can one soul bear? I settle with the thought, ***"Life is what it is."***

While I'm watching these kids play, I jot down some words. I'm compelled to capture my thoughts about my life to share with Aubrey Rose even if we never meet.

While writing, the ball the kids are playing with comes rolling my way. The little girl runs after it. Hearing the boys tell her what to do makes me laugh and think, *Typical boys.*

I watch her run across the grass, her little pony tail swaying back and forth. She jumps across each lump of grass along the way. She has an aura befitting an angel. I no longer hear the song ringing in my head. The ball reaches me seconds before she does. What a beautiful little girl. She has deep brown eyes, brown hair, an olive complexion and a smile that lights up the world.

As I reach out to hand her the ball, she says with the cutest voice, "Hey mister, what are you writing on that paper?"

She turns to throw the ball back to the boys, then turns her attention back to me.

"Well, my beautiful angel, I was watching you kids play with the ball. I started thinking about my granddaughter; her name is Aubrey Rose and I'm guessing she might be about your age? What are you, three?"

"Yep, it was my birthday just last week."

"I've never met Aubrey Rose and seeing you made me start writing notes to her."

"How come you don't know her?"

Too ashamed to say, but not to ignore her question, "To be honest with you honey, I don't know. Her daddy stopped talking to me five years ago."

"Is she pretty?"

"I've only seen pictures of her on the computer or on Facebook. I got a Christmas picture two years ago. It's on my refrigerator. I think about her every day. She's an angel like you. The only difference is that she has blonde hair and blue or green eyes. I only hope she is as giggly and bubbly as you."

"Mister, are you going to send the notes to her?"

"No, I'm writing her a book, full of stories about my life, my family and our heritage. There's too much to say in one note."

"What's a heritage?"

I'm chuckling inside. It's been some time since I was around a little one at this age. I forget how inquisitive they can be. I tell her what a heritage is in the simplest way possible.

3

"I'm half Greek and my grandparents taught me all about my Greek Heritage. A heritage is where you and your present and past relatives come from. It's the place where our background comes from."

I find it difficult explaining this to a three-year-old. Somehow, she acts like she understands.

"Do I have a heritage?"

"We all have a heritage. That's a question you should ask your mommy and daddy, or even your grandparents."

"Oh, okay." Her next question catches me by surprise. "Will you tell me your stories?"

"Oh, you are a precious angel. I love your spirit. I would love to tell you my stories. You remind me of myself when I was your age. I was always listening to the stories the old folks were telling instead of playing with the kids. Their stories intrigued me. They were usually about coming to America and what they did to survive the Depression. I'm afraid it will take too long to tell you my stories. Some of them might make you sad, even make you cry. Your mommy and daddy may not like that."

"Why, are they scary stories?"

"No, mostly sad and lonely stories. It's too late to tell them to you today."

"No, it's not."

"I'll tell you what. I'll tell you my stories tomorrow afternoon around two o'clock, if you get permission from your mommy and daddy. They need to come to the park with you, or send you with a note saying that it's okay. How does that sound?"

"That sounds goody. I'll see you tomorrow mister." She turns to run and play. Seconds later, I look down and she's standing in front of me.

"Hey mister, what's your name?"

"You can call me by my Greek name, Yianni. And what's your name, precious?"

"No, not precious, my name is Christina." Without saying another word, she runs to catch up with the boys.

I have goose bumps all over my arms. Tears are rolling down my cheeks as I sit here baffled and confused by what has just transpired. This little girl is the same age as my granddaughter Aubrey Rose and has the same name as my grandmother. I can't help but think this is Grandma at work. She's sending me another secret blessing.

The following morning, I wake up excited to see if Christina shows up. I give gratitude to the universe for sending her in my direction. I have high hopes, with no expectations. It'll be different talking to a three-year old. I'll use tenderness and caution with my choice of words.

At two o'clock, I'm sitting on the bench under the big oak tree. I can smell the aroma of oak sap as I'm thankful for the shade it's providing. Looking out across the lawn, I'm anxious to see Christina appear. A few minutes pass when I see her heading my way. She's holding hands with her mother as they skip across the lawn.

When they're close enough for me to hear, Christina yells out, "Hi, Mr. Yianni."

I stand up to greet them. Christina says, "This is my Mommy."

Reaching out with both hands, I grasp hers. She says, "My daughter couldn't stop talking about you. She's so excited to hear your stories. I thought it would be best to check them out for myself. It's a pleasure to meet you, my name is Barbara."

She reminds me of my Aunt Genevieve. She's about the same height, five feet three inches tall and a body frame one size above petite. She's slender, but not frail. Her long brown hair matches the color of her eyes, which definitely are the avenue to her soul. Her olive complexion shines with the radiant beauty of both her eyes and her hair. Her smile lights up the world, exactly like Aunt Genevieve's did.

She spots the tears rolling down my cheeks, "Why the tears?"

"I'm so glad you came, and it's an honor to meet you."

I have got goosebumps and a bit of a lump in my throat as I continue.

"I find meeting your Christina mysterious, yet magical, and then along comes you. My stories are about very special people in my life. My grandmother, Christina, and my mother, Barbara. You remind me of my Aunt Genevieve. This is overwhelming." I wipe the tears from my eyes and brush aside the goosebumps from my arms.

"Christina tells me you have a granddaughter her age, whose name is Aubrey Rose. Such a beautiful name. Is it true you haven't met her?"

"Yes, it's true," I say, embarrassed and ashamed.

"What's up with that?"

"I don't know. My son pushed me away more than five years ago. I found out about my granddaughter on Facebook. Nobody even told me they were having a baby."

"Oh, Yianni, I'm sorry for your pain."

"Thank you. My life is empty and I'm all alone. When my son cast me out of his life, he ripped my heart clean out of my chest. One day you're holding them, and the next day they're throwing you away like a piece of trash."

"He's the one I thought we got right. He never judged anyone. He was the perfect angel, yet he judges me now and hasn't taken the time to know me. I have a deep hole burning inside. I'd be better off if he'd put a gun to my head. At least the misery and pain would be gone. I've died three times over since he pushed me away. No parent should have to suffer this kind of hell."

"There must be something you can do to change things, Yianni?"

"I've nothing but love for my kids and my grandkids. I did the best I knew how. I'm not perfect and there is no solution that I can find. It's hard to climb the mountain, when standing at the top is a monster, his evil and vindictive mother. She's done her best to put the knife in my back. It's in deep now. It's bleeding the life out of me."

"I respect my son's choices. He's an adult now. As an adult he gets to make his own decisions, no matter how much they hurt me, or himself for that matter. One thing for sure, I will never stop loving him, in spite of his decision. Parents always love their kids, no matter what."

"I can feel your pain."

"Thank you, Barbara. I'm not sure anyone can ever feel my pain, if they've never walked in my shoes."

"You know Yianni, people sometimes forget that their children one day grow up. And as they do, they start asking questions. Someday your granddaughter will find out she has a grandfather. When she does, she's going to be very angry with her parents for keeping you away."

"Interesting you say that Barbara. Last night I was watching a movie on Netflix. The title caught my attention. *An Unfinished Life*, starring Robert Redford, Jennifer Lopez and Morgan Freeman. But it's the childhood star, Becca Gardner, who grabbed my attention."

"What's it about Yianni?"

"Jennifer Lopez is beaten up by her boyfriend, as her daughter, Griff, watches. Not the first time, but definitely the last, as she makes the decision to take her daughter to Wyoming. On the way their car breaks down, they hitchhike to a bus terminal to take a bus the rest of the way. Once on a bus, Griff says to her mother, 'Where are we going?'"

"We're going to Wyoming, we're going to your grandfather's ranch."

"The response from Griff, seven years old, catches my attention. **'I have a grandfather? And you were going to tell me, when?'**"

Tears roll down my cheeks, as my thoughts drift to Aubrey Rose.

Barbara says, "See Yianni, that movie tells it all. One day your granddaughter is going to have a similar reaction. I hope it doesn't take too long. It's shameful what her parents have done. They shouldn't be keeping her away. A child needs a grandparent as much as they need a parent."

"You're right Barbara, they do grow up and ask questions. I only hope that if that day ever comes, she treats them with kindness."

"Kindness? Your son and his wife don't deserve kindness. They should pay for keeping you away. Why kindness? I don't get it?"

"Kindness because things have a way of repeating. I only hope she treats them with kindness, because I would never want them to feel the same pain that I'm feeling now."

"You're an amazing man, Yianni. I don't think I could treat anyone with kindness after they broke my heart, like your son has broken yours."

"Barbara, it wasn't easy for me to reach this conclusion. I've lived a lifetime with a father who has hated me since the very first day I was born. He still hates me even today. Now my son turns his back on me. It's only kindness and numbness that keeps me alive. I live the mantra, one of Grandma's important secret blessings, *'**Treat others how you would want them to treat you.**'* I treat others with kindness because it's the only way to close the gaping hole in my heart."

"Don't you think time heals all, Yianni?"

"I do believe time heals all. Unfortunately for some, time eventually runs out. I don't want my son to live with regret like I have. I regret not having a father love me. I regret even more what has transpired between my son and me. I realize I wasn't the greatest of fathers. I had no role model to show me. Having an ex-wife who doesn't encourage or support me as their father, makes it's an impossible hill to climb. Don't get me wrong. I've been a good provider, always there for my kids financially. But life isn't always about money. I realize more than ever that I wasn't there when they needed me most. That's what I regret."

"Yianni, it's hard to be there when you're divorced. Didn't their mother include you in family events?"

"Not once Barbara. Not one time did she extend an invitation to me. All she ever expected from me was money. She did a damn unrespectable job keeping me away. She succeeded in burying the knife in my back."

"But you love your kids, Yianni, I find it difficult to understand."

"Yes, I love my kids Barbara. But love is supposed to work both ways. There's an empty feeling inside. Not once did I ever hear my father tell me that he loves me. I always tell my kids from the deepest place in my heart, 'I love you.' They're not just words. When I say them, I mean them."

"I know you love your children, Yianni. I can feel the tenderness and the hurt in your voice, even though I only met you today."

"There's more than regret, there's anger, guilt, fear, and worse yet, sorrow. No one should live with any of these. They create dis-ease, which one day will manifest into a disease. Even though it hasn't yet, it's killing me slowly."

Before we say another word, Christina jumps in, "Tell me a story, tell me a story Mr. Yianni."

Her timing's perfect. She's a messenger sent from heaven telling me that it's time to let go, time to move on. "Yes, Christina, it's almost time. First, I need to tell your mommy about my stories. If she gives her approval, I promise I'll tell you a story. Why don't you go over to the swings for a few more minutes? We'll call you back when it's time?"

Without argument, she runs to the swings.

"Barbara, the stories about my life at times will be sad. They might make you cry or feel uncomfortable. They're truthful stories about my life. Some will be about my Greek family and some about me. You'll hear about the pain I've endured from the losses that I suffered throughout various times of my life."

"Did you say you were Greek?"

"I did."

"Now isn't that a coincidence, because I'm Greek too."

My heart leaps from my chest. I can't believe she's Greek. But I know there's no such thing as a coincidence.

"No wonder I thought you reminded me of my Aunt Genevieve. I see you as a reflection of her and your smile is a perfect match for hers. It lights up the world."

"There are happy stories, and some of them are quite magical. I'd like to tell them all. They will paint a picture of the person I was and the person I've become. You'll learn it's important to have an open heart. Life presented me with some great lessons and many challenges. You'll learn about many distinct aspects of life. If you're okay with this, we can start with a story today. You and Christina will enjoy this story, it is about my Greek grandmother, Christina."

"Great, just a synopsis each time will suffice."

"Of course. By the way, Christina's curious about her heritage. Now that I know you're Greek, there's no doubt she'll learn about her Greek heritage."

"Fabulous, that will be fabulous."

"My Grandma, in her infinite wisdom, shared many insights about life with me. I call these insights, *'Grandma's Secret Blessings.'* When I share them, I will preface them by saying this is one of *'Grandma's Secret Blessings.'*"

"It sounds like you had a very insightful grandmother!"

"I did. She shared her deepest secrets with me. She loved me without conditions, like grandparents are supposed to love you. She taught me how to play blackjack and solitaire with her. I loved her very much."

"One more thing before we start. There's a very important aspect to these stories that you should understand. Many of these stories have been in my mind for a very long time. Some might seem over-exaggerated. They contain the truth as I see the truth today, and how I saw the truth back then. Grandma used to say, '*Yianni, when you tell someone a story, always tell the truth because the truth will set you free.*'"

"That's awesome advice. I tell my kids, '*I'm telling you the truth, but the truth that I tell you is how I see it through my own eyes.*'"

"That's great advice Barbara. I'm going to remember that one."

"I'm excited to hear your stories, Yianni, especially the ones about your Greek heritage. Since I lost my father a little over a year ago, Christina and my boys haven't learned much from my mom. She's been in such a funk since the loss of my dad."

"I can relate to that. Let me assure you, my stories are about my family and friends. Not their failings or mistakes, as much as they are about my inner struggles, my inner beliefs and my way of being. They serve me well in what I call '**Life**.'"

"Would you like me to start the storytelling?"

"I'd like that, but my boys should be here. If you don't mind, I'd like to run home to get them. It's not too far away and we'll be back in less than twenty minutes."

"It would be my pleasure."

She calls for Christina to come over. She tells Christina it would be important for her brothers to be here. "Why don't we go get them? Mr. Yianni will be here waiting for us to come back."

"Oh goody, we'll see you in a minute, Mr. Yianni."

I wave goodbye, as I watch them run as fast they can, until they disappear into the parking lot.

Twenty minutes later I see them coming back. I see Christina running ahead of four other people. It looks like she brought the whole family. There's five of them, like my family. Two brothers and Christina. When they reach me, Barbara introduces me to her husband and then to her two boys.

"This is my husband, Ray, and my two sons, Charlie and Bobby."

We exchange kind words and handshakes. Ray has a striking resemblance to my dad. Same name and about the same age when I was the age of these kids. He even has the same rotten scowl on his face, the one that says, "I don't want to be here."

Charlie and Bobby have the same names as my two best friends. Charlie has a light complexion, blue eyes and is seven. He reminds me of my older brother Donald. He looks more like his dad, as my brother did. The middle child, Bobby, has an olive complexion, brown eyes, brown hair. Reminds me of myself at that age. He looks like his mom. I can see the Greek in him, like everyone could see the Greek in me. He's five.

This is unreal, yet there must be some irony in it. I can't help but wonder how this will play out. I know Grandma's behind sending this family to me, but why?

Finished with the introductions, Christina is asking, "Hey Mr. Yianni, what story are you going to tell?"

Chapter Two

Grandma, you will always be the
Queen of my heart.

~John Egreek

"Today I'm going to tell you a story about Grandma being on TV."

"Your Grandma was on TV? I wish my grandma was on TV!"

"In the late winter of 1956, my grandma receives a letter from Hollywood. Grandma didn't read. She spoke broken English, accented by a deep Greek accent. Uncle Victor, almost thirteen years old and the only uncle living at home, reads her letter. It's a confirmation letter telling her she's been chosen to be a contestant on the famous TV show in July called 'Queen for a Day.'"

Christina interrupts, "Your grandma was a Queen?"

"Grandma, if she wins the show, will be 'Queen for a Day.' If she wins, she'll be granted one wish."

"Did she win, did she win? What did she wish, what did she wish?" Christina asks, with extreme anxiousness. She has a cute way of saying things twice.

"You'll find out soon Christina."

"Okay. Okay."

Her dad, mean scowl on his face, his right hand raised in the air, says "Christina, keep your mouth shut and let him tell the story. You kids need to be seen, but not heard."

I gasp, then take a second to catch my breath. My dad used to say the same thing. His scowl not only looks exactly like my dad's, but his demeanor is a perfect match. I shake my head in disgust. Without saying a word, I turn my attention to the story.

"In 1956, a couple of days after celebrating our birthdays, Grandma comes down to the Faith Street house to find me. I'm living with Uncle Alex and my Auntie Joanne at the time."

"You're living with your aunt and uncle, why not with your family? Where were they living?"

"I'm sad to say Barbara, but my brother and sister Chrissy were living with my aunt and uncle from my dad's side. It was a small two-bedroom house located on the south side of San Francisco. For now, you should know that my mom was in the hospital with a broken back and neck from a car accident. This will all come out in another story. Fair enough?"

"Fair enough."

Christina says, "Hey, your sister's name is like mine."

"Yes, she's named after Grandma, but they changed it to Christine instead of Christina. Dad didn't care for Grandma, so he made sure Chrissy didn't have her name."

"I like my name better."

Chuckling inside, I continue.

"Grandma walks down to the Faith Street house to find me. She wants me to go downtown, into San Francisco with her, to find a dress for her special day on 'Queen for a Day.'"

"My grandparents never drove cars. They were too afraid to learn. 'In the Old Country, we walk and in this country, we walk,' they'd say. So, we walked downtown."

"Grandma usually tells me stories about the Old Country when we're walking. She's so proud of where she came from. I didn't even know where the Old Country was. She or Papa (my grandfather) would point it out to me on an old globe of the earth that Uncle Victor had. But I couldn't pinpoint the exact location of the Old Country back then. They would point to the southwest side of Greece."

"When we reach downtown, we walk into The Emporium, a mid-line department store built in the 50's. Inside were shops much like the malls of today. As Grandma searches for a dress, I stand by the window to watch the people as they walk by. I'm a people watcher. I love looking at people, their different get-ups, and each of their unique, yet beautiful faces. San Francisco's well known for its diverse collection of people who wear the garb of their culture."

"It takes Grandma just a few minutes to find a dress. It's a black-and-white flowery dress with a hint of purple. In those days, black and white is the main color of most clothes. Grandma pays for the dress, puts it in her brown paper bag, grabs me by the hand and together we walk home."

"On the way, Grandma's very quiet. 'Grandma, mhat's the matter myth you, why are you so quiet?' I ask."

"Grandma laughs because I'm talking like her. 'Oh Yianni, my little Yianni Capedoni, you're always asking Grandma mhat she's thinking.' Grandma called me Yianni, Yianni Capedoni. As did most of my Greek family. My Uncle Victor still calls me that today." (Grandma never could say 'what' or 'with', always she said 'mhat' or 'myth,' which might look like typos, they're not. I chose to write it just as Grandma said it.)

"'Grandma, what does that mean when you call me Yianni, Yianni Capedoni?'"

"It means you are the captain of your own ship."

"I didn't realize it then, but many years later I recognize this was another one of Grandma's secret blessings. Then I go back to my original question and I ask Grandma what she's thinking."

"She tells me she's thinking about the day she'll be on TV. It was only two weeks away."

"Grandma, what do you want if you're 'Queen for a Day?'"

"Oh Yianni, that's a secret. You have to wait until you see me on TV, I'm not telling anyone before then."

"Two weeks later, early July, we take Grandma and her best friend crazy Mary to the airport. Grandma's never flown on an airplane before. But she isn't afraid and crazy Mary was going with her. It was her destiny to be on 'Queen for a Day.'" She'll be gone for three days and I was already missing her. She was my Rockstar," I say, as a tear makes its way out of my right eye and begins rolling down my cheek.

"Why do you call your grandma's friend crazy Mary?" Christina interrupts.

I chuckle, not surprised it's Christina asking.

"Mary wasn't actually crazy, but she had this uncanny thing she did with her tongue that we all disliked."

"Grandma would tell her, 'Mary, put your tongue back in your mouth.'"

"What did she do with her tongue?"

I did a quick imitation of Mary. I stuck my tongue out and curled it up over my lip. "Mary had a permanent red ring on her upper lip from all the saliva from her tongue. Because of that, everyone called her 'Crazy Mary.'"

As I get back into the story, I notice Christina trying to curl her tongue over her upper lip. I don't say a word. I'm chuckling inside.

"At the airport waiting for Grandma to board the plane, she bends down to kiss me. She whispers in my ear, 'Cross your fingers, both hands Yianni, to bring Grandma good luck to be 'Queen for a Day,' okay?'"

"'I will Grandma, I'll even cross my legs.' Seconds later she's walking to the airplane. I stand at the window, throwing her kisses and waving goodbye. In those days, you boarded the airplane outside of the airport. You walked on the runway to a portable stairway to the plane. Things were very different then, not sophisticated like today."

"I was so excited the next two days. I wish my mom was around to share in the excitement."

"Me too, Mr. Yianni, me too, I wish she was there with you, too."

I can't help but think that this precious angel has a kind and caring heart. I hope she grows up with this heart and nobody ever takes it away.

"Finally, the day comes for Grandma to be on TV. Papa's sitting in his favorite arm chair, made of overstuffed brown corduroy and wide enough to fit Papa's big frame. The chair's sitting in line with the TV. It's back far enough for me and Victor to lie on the floor in front of him, with my arms, legs and fingers crossed for good luck."

"Uncle Victor's messing with the rabbit-ear antenna. He's trying to bring the picture in clear enough so we could see. The TV's a black-

and-white Philco, with a bubble picture tube. It's considered an antique today."

Bobby says, "What's a black-and-white TV?"

Laughing, I say, "Everything on TV was black and white. Color TV wasn't invented yet, not until 1959, as I remember it. We got our first color TV in 1960. I remember Mom bought a console color TV with a record player inside, and two portable color TV's, all made by Sony. She bought them with her lawsuit settlement from the car accident. We got them after we moved from San Francisco to San Diego."

Charlie says, "What's a record player?"

I forget these kids were never exposed to the same things as I was. I explain what a record player is in the simplest of terms.

"It's a device that plays round, flat plastic things, called records. They have music recorded on them. You can do a Google search on the computer to see one."

Charlie agrees. Then I return to the story.

"Uncle Victor gets the lines out of the TV. His timing's perfect, as I yell, 'There she is, there's Grandma on TV,' while I wiggle on the floor with excitement. Uncle Victor comes from behind the TV, as we hear Jack Bailey introduced to the audience."

"All the way from the Moulon Rouge Resort Hotel in Hollywood California. Meet our host, Jack Bailey."

"Jack Bailey tells the television audience and those at the show, 'Today we have four special guests. Each of them has a special story and each of them has a very special wish.'"

"He turns to the audience. He throws his right arm while pointing his finger toward the crowd, kicks his left leg forward, and says, 'Would you like to be 'Queen for a Day?'"

"Let's introduce our first guest, 'Mrs. Christina Meta.'"

"There she is, there's Grandma."

"Jack Bailey says, 'Tell us about yourself, where are you from and are you married with children?'"

"'I'm here from San Francisco myth my friend Mary and some of my friends from the Daughters of Penelope. I'm married to my Lambro since 1924. I have two beautiful daughters still alive and three sons. My daughter Barbara's in the hospital myth a broken back and a broken neck. She was in car accident and I want to send her love and kisses.' Grandma throws a big kiss to Mom."

"My daughter Genevieve and sons, Odysseus, Alexander and Victor are at home. I want to say hello to my grandchildren, especially my Yianni who's also watching. I lost my Margarite in 1937 when she died from a burst appendix. I lost my other son Spiro, who died six months after he was born."

"The camera pans the audience and captures many of them wiping tears from their eyes. You can see the sadness, seconds after Grandma tells about Margarite and Spiro."

"Jack says, 'I detect you have an accent.'"

"Yes, that's because I'm Greek and I come from Greek lands in the country now called Albania."

"Albania, oh my, is that where you married your husband?"

"Yes, Mr. Bailey, when I married my Lambro in 1924 we lived in a village called Narta. It was a different village than the one he was born in. It's forty kilometers away from his village. Lambro bought some land to build us a home before we could be married."

"This is fascinating, if you don't mind me asking, how did you meet?"

"Mr. Bailey, it's the custom in our country to marry someone from our own village. Lambro was from Zverness, a small peninsula on the west side of Albania, next to the Adriatic and Baltic seas. He came to America as an illegal alien. He was in the Army in World War I. (The audience clapping)."

"He became a citizen, so granted by the President of the United States. In 1924, he went back to the Old Country to find a wife in his village. The custom is to bring all the single girls or women, age fifteen to fifty, who have never married. The man chooses a bride. My Lambro didn't like his choices, so he broke custom. He came to Narta to visit his cousin Zoe. She was ex-communicated from the village because she divorced her husband. When he got to her home, she tells him, 'I have someone I want you to meet,' and that was me."

"How old were you?"

"'I was eighteen and my Lambro was thirty-seven.' The audience gasps as they hear the age difference. Grandma goes on to say, 'My

Lambro's much taller than I am.' The audience responds with a laugh, they can see Grandma's quite short."

"'Oh my, that's a significant difference in age.' To Grandma and Papa, age didn't matter; they loved each other very much. 'I wasn't going to comment about your height, but since you brought it up, how tall are you?'"

"'I'm four feet nine inches and my Lambro is over six feet, about like you Mr. Bailey.' The audience laughs. 'Things were not good in Albania late in 1924, so Papa made the decision we should come to America. We lived in Philadelphia. After the loss of our son Spiro and the birth of our second son Odysseus, we decided to move to San Francisco.'"

"Christina, may I call you Christina?"

"Yes."

"Christina, I know you have a very special wish if you could be 'Queen for a Day.' Would you like to share that wish with these fine people and our television audience?"

"'Yes,' she says. With tears rolling down her cheeks, she holds up a picture of her mother. 'I haven't seen my mother since we left in 1924. She's 89 years old. I would like to see her before she dies. If I'm 'Queen for a Day,' my wish would be to go to the Old Country.'"

"The camera pans the audience. Many of them have their hankies, wiping tears from their cheeks and eyes."

I'm crying as I'm telling the story, just like I did then.

"Then it's time for commercial break."

I take a quick glance towards Christina and Barbara. I notice they're wiping tears from their eyes. Christina lays her head on Barbara's lap and continues to lie there while I continue with the story.

"During commercial break, within seconds, the telephone rings. It's on the table next to Papa's chair. He's talking Greek, then he calls out, 'Yianni, telephone.'"

"I turn to see he's holding the phone, waiting for me to answer. I take one look at the TV to see if Grandma's there and then I answer the phone."

"Hi Yianni, did you see Grandma on TV, doesn't she look beautiful?"

19

"Oh Mommy, I wish you were here. Grandma looks so beautiful, but she looks scared too. I wish I was there with her."

"Before Mom can say another word, I glance back at the TV and I yell out, 'Look, there she is.' I put down the phone, without even saying goodbye. I knew she'd understand. Oh, Grandma looked so beautiful and I don't think I ever saw her smile as big as she did that day. I knew she was happy and I knew she just had to win."

"The camera moves to Jack Bailey as he introduces the next contestant."

"She's a younger woman who said if she could be 'Queen for a Day' her wish was to receive a washer and dryer. She told Mr. Bailey she has four children, two of whom were twins. Keeping up with the laundry was an all-day chore because she was washing everything by hand. Everyone in the audience could relate. Dryers were a new invention and very expensive to own. A few seconds later they go to commercial break."

"Uncle Vic's messing with the rabbit-ears again, trying to bring the TV in clearer. Papa yells him 'Enough, leave it alone.' He comes back to lay on the floor with me. I remember him putting his arm over my back. We're very close. He's more like a brother to me than an uncle. I know sometimes I'm a real pain in the butt for him and his best friend Jim. They're always stuck taking me with them everywhere they go. I guess it was all good, because we're still close today."

"After commercial break, the camera turns back to the other woman. She talks about her husband and her four boys. She says it is difficult keeping up with twins. Having two children the same age demands a great deal of work and creates lots of dirty diapers."

I interrupt the story to say, "We have twins in the family. Auntie Joann and Uncle Alex had twins, Denise and Diane. They aren't identical, but very cute in their own way."

"The woman completes her story. Then she says, 'Mr. Bailey that's what I would want if I could be 'Queen for a Day.' All I ask for is a new washer and dryer.'"

"Then he goes on to the third and fourth contestants. I don't remember their wishes anymore. After the last commercial break, Jack Bailey turns to the audience, 'So who will it be? Will it be Christina

Meta who hasn't seen her mother since 1924? Will it be Mrs. Valsvig, who needs a washer and dryer to keep up with the laundry needs of her twins? Will it be the third contestant and then finally the fourth contestant?'"

"The audience applauds, and the applause meter goes wild. 'Who will it be, we'll find out when we return in a few minutes after the last commercial break.'"

"I was so excited I almost peed my pants. I ran to the bathroom and got back in the nick of time to see Grandma on TV, one last time."

"'Who will it be ladies and gentlemen,' Jack Bailey says one more time? 'Will it be Mrs. Christina Meta?' The audience claps loudly and yells her name. 'Will it be Mrs. Valsvig with the twins?' Again the audience claps loudly and yells her name. 'Will it be contestant number three or contestant number four?' as he says each of their names."

"The camera pans the audience. It moves to Grandma, Mrs. Valsvig, and the other two contestants each a couple of more times."

"For the last time, Jack Bailey turns to the audience. 'Ladies and gentlemen, it is my honor to announce today's 'Queen for a Day.' There's a few moments of delay as we can hear the audience screaming out the different names. The winner and 'Queen for a Day,' (after a long pause,) Mrs. Valsvig. The mother of twins, granting her wish to have a brand-new washer and dryer.'"

"Thank God, they didn't show Grandma's reaction. I know she's crying, because I was too. Papa's angry. He gets up from his chair, snaps back at Victor, 'Turn that damn thing off,' with deep authority in his words. Papa never cusses. We know he's mad as he walks away, turning back toward the TV, waving his arm in disbelief and saying, 'A pasha.'"

Telling this story is excruciating for me. Once again, I can feel Grandma's pain, and my own, for that matter, as if it's 1956 all over again. As I shared every detail of the show, I couldn't stop the tears flowing. I wiped them away, hoping that Christina and the rest of her family didn't notice. Glancing over at them I find they're crying too. I see Barbara wiping away tears. All except Ray, he's still stoic and stone-faced, like my dad always was.

Christina sees me wiping the tears. She says, "Oh Mr. Yianni, that was a sad story, but it's okay to cry because we're crying too."

She makes me smile, then I say, "Do you want to hear the rest of the story?"

"Is it going to make me cry some more?"

"No, the rest of the story will make you smile."

"Okay, I want to hear more."

With Christina's approval, I tell the rest of the story.

"The next day, after 'Queen for a Day,' Grandma's scheduled to arrive at San Francisco airport. We get there in time to see the plane land. I see Grandma walking from the airplane to the inside of the airport with crazy Mary by her side. By the time Grandma reaches us, most everyone is crying and consoling Grandma. They're bawling like babies."

"Papa's standing by Grandma's side, but he's not crying. He's holding Grandma's hand. At some point, I walk up to Grandma and tug on her dress. She turns in my direction and bends down to hug and kiss me, then she says, 'What Yianni? Mhat do you want to tell Grandma?'"

"While giving her a kiss and a giant hug, I say 'Grandma, someday I'm going to the Old Country.'"

"Grandma's tears disappear. She turns to Papa and says, 'Did you hear that Papa, did you hear mhat our little Yianni said?'"

"Papa responds with a shake of his head signifying 'No.'"

"Grandma says, 'Our little Yianni, Yianni Capedoni says that someday he's going to the Old Country.'"

"The tears stop. Only smiles of admiration from everyone, as if they knew it would be me who makes them all stop crying. Papa and Grandma reached out with their hands to grab mine and then we walk out of the airport together."

"When we get home, Grandma takes off her dress and tucks it away in her suitcase. She calls it her 'pain box.' She never wears that dress again. And no one ever mentions the 'Queen for a Day,' except for me, because no matter what, Grandma has been my Queen for every day."

"There you have it Christina and family, that is the end of the story."

Christina doesn't say a word, but comes over to me. Unexpectedly, she jumps into my lap and throws her arms around my neck. She stays there for a few seconds. I'm breathless. Then she looks up at me and says, "Mr. Yianni, did you ever go to the Old Country like you promised your Grandma?"

Before I have a chance to answer, her father interrupts. He announces in a deep tone to his voice, a voice of authority and a tone I didn't care to hear, "It's time to go."

Before Christina leaves my lap, she says, "Will you tell me another story Mr. Yianni? I liked that one."

"Of course, Christina, it would be my honor."

Barbara leans over to give me a kiss on the cheek. She says in a low tone that only I can hear, "Thank you for sharing that story with us. It touched my heart. We can't wait to hear the next one. How about this same time tomorrow?"

"Tomorrow at two works for me. I'd like that, and thank you for letting me tell you my story."

The boys shake my hand, but their father's half way across the park. He walks away without even saying goodbye. Something my father would do, I'm thinking.

Then Barbara takes Christina by the hand. Before they get too far away, I hear Christina ask, "Can we go see Grandma tonight?"

Chapter Three

Grandfathers are for loving and
fixing things.

~ Author Unknown

It's a beautiful day. It's two o'clock. The birds are singing beautiful songs and there's a bit of a breeze, but no chill. I'm here a few minutes before they arrive, sitting on the same bench as before. For a few seconds, I close my eyes long enough to ask for guidance in my choice of words. I'll show my truth as I see it, through the filter of my own eyes.

Within seconds, I see the whole family heading my way. Charlie, Bobby and Christina are running ahead to reach me, while Mom and Dad are walking slowly behind. I notice they're not talking, not even saying a word, and they aren't holding hands, barely even walking side by side.

Christina's excited. She can't wait. "What story are you going to tell, what story are you going to tell?"

"I need to spend a couple of minutes with your mom and dad to get their permission. Why don't you and the boys go over to the swings while I give them a synopsis."

"Okay, but what's a syn... synopsis?" she asks, with a pause between words.

"A synopsis is a brief description of the story. It's just a little longer than the title."

"Oh, okay," she says, and runs with her brothers to the swings.

I'm about to give the synopsis, when Barbara says, "You can tell any story you want. For some reason, we believe your stories are something we need to hear and that they won't hurt our kids to hear them."

Ray takes a moment to tell me, "Christina and Barbara were so excited after hearing the story about your Grandma being on 'Queen for a Day,' that we made the decision that you can tell any story you want, even if some of them might be sad, ugly, or even painful."

"Okay, that's how it will be. Why don't we sit on the grass over by the tree?"

They call over the three kids. Ray tells them to sit and be very still while I tell the story. He speaks to them quite sternly, in a strong, demanding voice. Once again, I'm thinking of my dad. Always so demanding and demeaning when he spoke, everybody had better be listening or there will be hell to pay.

I sit in front of the tree, so I have something to lean against. It's hard for me to get up or down, because I'm such a big man, close to 330 pounds. Once down, I tell Ray, "After we're done today, I'm going to need a hand to get back up."

"No problem, it'll be my pleasure."

"Mr. Yianni, Mr. Yianni, what story are you going to tell?"

Although there's some reluctance and fear in telling them this story, in my heart I know it's the right story to tell.

"I traveled to the deepest part of my soul to find you a story today. This story's a very hard and painful story for me. But if I don't tell you this story, the later stories won't make sense."

This is a pivotal story about my life. I can feel the presence of spirits surrounding us, as if they're waiting to hear the story too. For a brief second, it feels as though Mom, my aunt and Grandma are sitting there in front of me.

"Once upon a time in place far, far away, hidden in a town close to San Francisco, is a little boy named Yianni. The year is 1953 and at this stage of my life, I'm three years old."

"We're living in the house in San Mateo, south of San Francisco. I can still see that house in my mind today, just as it was back then. It's a small neighborhood. The school my brother went to for kindergarten is just behind our backyard fence. The house is mostly white, but the windows, doors and the eaves have royal blue trim. There are three concrete steps, sideways to the house, a small stoop at the top, just left of the door. A stoop is similar to a porch. To the left of the front door there's a large single-pane glass window. The window's a foot shorter than the top of the door and about a foot up from the bottom. It's about five-feet tall. The driveway is on the left side of the house, and there's a gate on the side that leads to the backyard."

"The backyard is grass and weeds. There's a swing set in the middle. Around the perimeter of the fence and on the side of the driveway are small hedges with thorns, about three feet tall. There are three bedrooms and one bathroom on the right side of the house. The living room and the dining room are on the left side. There's a doorway that leads to the garage between them. Just to the right of the dining room is the kitchen, with a small pantry in the back corner, just before the door that opens to the backyard."

"I wish we had a house like that. We live in an apartment and we have to come to the park to swing."

I give Christina a wink, seconds before her dad tells her, "Christina, hush your mouth, let him tell the story."

Which she does, without any smart talk back.

"At this time in my life I only have one friend. His name is Tommy and he lives directly across the street. Tommy's the same age and he's deaf. Back then, everyone said Tommy was 'deaf and dumb.' He is deaf, but he's not dumb. I could understand him, sometimes even more than his mom. We have a special connection that no one can explain. He didn't speak words, only grunt sounds. He's learning how to sign, which is in the early stage of development, so Tommy was in a test group learning to sign."

Christina interrupts, "What's 'sign' Mr. Yianni?"

"Sign is where you learn to speak and see with your hands, not with your voice and ears."

Her dad throws his right hand up in the air as if he was going to slap her. Then puts his left finger over his mouth and says to her, "I'll show you what sign is. Stop interrupting."

This guy is my dad. He sounds, looks and acts just like him. These poor kids.

The stage is set and I move on.

"It's a warm summer day and Mom's cleaning house. She decides it's time to clean the window next to the front door. My brother, Donald, and I are playing tag. Mom tells us to take the game outside. Donald chases me out the front door trying to catch me. Even though he's older, I'm faster than he is, and I have tricks up my sleeve. When we're out front, I decide to run to the backyard. The gate's partly open, just enough for me fit through. Donald almost caught up with me and reaches out to touch me, but I trick him and run up the back stairs into the kitchen. From the kitchen. I run through the dining room, then the living room and back out the front door."

"I'm ahead of him, but he decides to jump the three steps. He's gaining on me. As we go around the corner of the house a second time, I close the gate behind me to slow him down. Donald's tall enough to reach the latch and open it. I run back into the house and back toward the front door. By this time, Mom has taken the glass window out to clean it. I take a short cut and jump through the open window instead of going through the door. Donald can't believe I jumped through the window opening. He sees me do a tuck and roll. When I hit the ground and I get back to my feet, I pull away from him. He stops to catch his breath and finds it hard because he can't stop laughing."

"We're having a blast chasing each other. He continues to chase me around two more times. On the last time, little do I know, Mom has put the window back in. It's so clean, I can't tell the difference."

"Oh no, what happened?" asks Bobby.

"Well as you might have guessed, I jump through one more time, but this time the glass is back in. I leave an imprint of the outline of my body on the glass, just like in the cartoons. I get up from the ground and I keep running. I don't stop to see if I'm hurt or anything. I just know I'm in for a beating when my dad gets home. So I hide."

All three kids look at each other, and not their mom or dad. They drop their heads, afraid to look up. They don't want to catch a glimpse of their father's eyes. I spot what's going on, so I continue with the story.

"I find a place to hide in the neighbor's hedge. A couple of minutes after I hide, Dad pulls into the driveway. Mom runs to the door and starts yelling my name. She calls me John Earl whenever I'm in trouble. If she calls me Johnny or Yianni, I know she's protecting me. Now that Dad's home, she's yelling 'John Earl.' I know I'm in trouble. I stay in the bushes a long time, staying super quiet so no one finds me."

"When Dad gets out of the car, he sees the glass on the ground near the steps by the front door. He turns to my mom and says, 'Where is he?' He always assumes whenever anything gets broken or damaged it's me who did it. Nobody else in the family can do any wrong. If my brother breaks anything, it's me who pays the price. For some reason, a reason I never find the answer to, my father hates me."

I notice the kids squirming and moving close together. A part of me thinks I should stop telling the story, but another part tells me to keep going. So I do.

"By now, everyone in the neighborhood is looking for me. First in the backyard, then the front and in the neighbor's yard. At some point, Donald spots me hiding behind the hedge. I hold my finger to my mouth. I tell him, 'Shush, don't tell him where I am. He's going to beat me if he finds out.' My brother honors my demand."

"Mom's yelling. 'Johnny, where are you? Come home so I can take care of you. I know you must be bleeding, tired and cold.'"

"At the moment she says that, I notice I have a few cuts on my arms. I can feel the cuts on my face. But there's not much blood. I'm too afraid to feel any pain. I see my friend Tommy and his mom walk by. It's starting to get dark. I'm afraid and it's beginning to get cold. I want to call out to them, but I'm not ready for the consequences so I remain silent."

"Everyone has gone farther down the street or in the schoolyard behind our house. I notice Mom in front of the neighbor's house where I'm hiding. She calls out my name. I know Dad's a few houses away, so I come out of the bushes. I call out to Mom with a soft voice, 'Mommy, mommy, I'm right here.'"

"She runs over to grab me into her arms. 'Come on. Let's get you cleaned up before he gets back. We both know what's going to happen when he does.' Just inside the door off to the right is the hallway that leads to the bathroom. Mommy takes me there."

At that point in the story, I'm doing my best to bring the story line down to their level. I see them squirming and fidgeting, giving me the impression they might be getting nervous or scared. They're still not looking at their dad, but every now and then they glance at their mom. She scoots a few feet away from her husband to get closer to her kids.

"Mommy's sitting on the toilet lid, holding me in her lap. She's washing my face, my hands, and putting Band-Aids on my cuts. Within seconds Dad walks in. He reaches through the door to grab me. Mommy does her best to hold me tight by wrapping her arms around me. Dad tells her to let go, but Mommy tells him, 'Let me finish cleaning his cuts.'"

"Dad lets go of my arm. He's reaching for his belt, the wide one. He snaps it loud enough to let me know he's about to give me a beating. He usually threatens, but never hits."

"I know by the tone of his voice that it's not a threat this time. I begin to shiver and beg Mommy not to let me go. But she reminds me that he might turn on her too. I'm not sure how he can call me a young man at three years of age. I barely understand what it means when he says he's going to beat me."

"A few seconds pass, just after he tells the neighbors they've found me. He reaches through the door a second time. He grabs me from Mommy's lap. Hauls me into his bedroom. He closes the door behind him. Then he starts pounding me with his belt. He's a mad man."

"Mom opens the door and begins clawing at him, trying to make him stop. He turns around and attempts to belt her, but misses and then continues hitting me. She runs to the living room to call her dad. Papa answers the phone. She says, 'He's beating him, he's beating our Yianni.'"

"Papa knew Dad had a mean streak in him. He gets my Aunt Genevieve to drive him to San Mateo. Our house is about twenty-five minutes away. Dad continues to whale on me and he's not using his belt, he's using his fist. He doesn't seem to care how much he's hurting me. I'm screaming for Mommy and crying at the same time. Donald's standing in the doorway yelling at him to let me go. Dad turns to him and says, 'Do you want to be next young man, if not, go to your room.' Donald knows what that means, so he backs away and goes into our room."

"Seconds later, Mom comes in and starts swinging at him, telling him, 'Enough is enough. Stop hurting him. Papa's on his way, so you better stop. You're next up for a beating.' That gets his attention, because he finally stops."

"He goes into the kitchen to grab a beer, while Mom takes me into her arms. She says, 'Papa's on his way, he won't let Daddy hurt you anymore.'"

"Dad steps into the garage just before they drive up. He knows Papa will be looking for him. While Papa's looking for Dad, Grandma comes into the room to see how bad he hurt me. She turns to my aunt and says, 'We need to take Yianni to the hospital, he's hurt really bad.'"

"Grandma starts looking for him too. She's little, but she's a feisty pistol when she's mad. She finds him first. 'Mhat's the matter myth you? He's only a little boy, you crazy man!'"

"Papa hears Grandma yelling at him. He finds Dad in the backyard drinking his beer. I don't know what he said. I know he told him he was taking us away. Mom gathers up some clothes for each of us. She has Auntie Genie open the trunk of her car. We pile in. She's driving a 1951 Desoto. Mom's holding Chrissy, who's barely one, sitting in the back next to my brother and Grandma. Papa's cradling me in his arms. We're sitting in the front. My aunt takes me to the nearest hospital, which happens to be the same hospital where I was born, Mary's Help."

"When we get to the hospital, Grandma stays in the car to watch over Donald and Chrissy. Mom and my aunt follow Papa into the emergency room. A nurse sees him carrying me in his arms. He says, 'Take care of my grandson, he's been beaten and he might be broken.' Papa didn't have good control of the English language and sometimes his Greek accent made him hard to understand. But the nurse understood, grabbing a bed on wheels as Papa lay me down."

About this time in the story, Christina's crying and she blurts, "Did your daddy go to jail?"

I tell them, "No, in those days people turned a blind eye when things like this happened." I put my left hand up to the right side of my face to demonstrate and turn away from their dad as I say in a whisper, "Of course in today's world, he would go to jail."

Seconds later, Ray stands up and moves away. He's an earshot away from the story. He's turned his back to us, so we can't see his reaction. Barbara gathers the kids in close. She's holding Christina tightly in her lap.

"The doctor comes into the room to check me out. When he's done, he takes Papa, Mom and my aunt into the hall. With the curtain closed, I hear him say, 'He's really bruised and will be sore for some time. I don't think he has any internal bleeding or broken bones. I think it would be best if we keep him here overnight to make sure he has no concussion.'"

"Papa says, 'I'll stay with him. You need to take Donald and Chrissy to my house.'"

"Mommy comes in to see me. She gives me a hug and a kiss. She tells me, 'The doctor thinks it will be best if you stay overnight. Papa will be with you and we'll be back tomorrow to pick you up.'"

"Okay. I feel safe when I'm with Papa."

"'I know,' she says as she waves goodbye and walks away."

I notice Christina clenching her mother's arms.

"The next day, the doctor checks me out one more time. He shines a flashlight into my eyes. Then he turns to Papa and says, 'I think it's safe to take him home. He'll be quite sore for about a week or two. He'll continue to be black and blue from the bruising for some time, but that too will eventually go away.'"

"'Yes, but the scars will take a very long time to go away,' Papa replies. Then he calls Mom to pick us up."

"Mom shows up alone, driving my aunt's car. She talks to the doctor, then comes into the room to get us. Papa cradles me in his arms as we find our way to the car."

"He and Mom talk all the way home, but I have no idea what they're saying. It's all Greek to me. Papa's voice is decisive, loud and agitated. What I do remember, is that one week later my dad came to the house, thinking he could take us all home. But he had to beg Papa and apologize to him for what he'd done to me."

"I was standing at the door and I could hear Papa say, 'You can take Barbara, Donald and Chrissy, but Yianni's staying here with us. You don't deserve to be his father. You wait here and I'll get them. You're not welcome in my home. I'm very angry with you.' Whenever Papa said he was angry, everyone knew it was true. He usually had this look of disgust and disappointment. There's no denying that he's angry. He meant it when he told him to stay right there."

"A few minutes later, Mom, my brother and my sister left. I stayed with Papa and Grandma, and that was just fine with me."

Christina says, "Is that the end of the story?"

"Not quite yet. Just a little more to go."

"Another week goes by. The following Sunday, after Grandma and I walk home from the Greek Church, my dad shows up alone."

"He's speaking with Papa. I can hear them talking. Dad's begging him to let me come home. He promises Papa he won't ever hurt me again."

"You better never lay a hand on him as long as I'm alive. If you ever hurt him again, it will be the last time you'll lay a hand on anyone."

"Papa turns away and walks back into the house. He tells me, 'Yianni, get your stuff together, you're going home. You'll be safe now and your dad won't ever hurt you again.'"

"I plead with him not to let me go. 'I want to stay here with you papa. I don't believe him, and you shouldn't believe him either. He's a liar and he's mean to me.'"

"Papa takes me into his arms, 'You'll be safe Yianni. Your father knows there will be a price to pay if he hurts you ever again. Give Grandma a kiss and say goodbye.'"

"I give Grandma a kiss and I beg her not to let me go. But Papa insists it's time for me to go. I reluctantly say goodbye. When I get to the car, Dad insists that I sit in the front seat next to him."

"'No, I'll sit in the back.' I climb into the seat directly behind him. It's safe there because I know he can't reach me while he's driving."

"On the way home, he says something to me that he's said many times over the years. He says, 'You need to forgive and forget.'"

At this point, I stop telling the story.

"Is that the end of the story? Did your daddy ever hurt you again?"

"Not with his hands Christina. Not for a very long time, but verbally, he abuses me or tries his best to harm me with his words most of the rest of my life. You'll hear more about my relationship with him as I continue the stories."

Ray comes closer, then says, "Let's get going, it's time to go." He says it with such forcefulness they know they'd better get going. Without saying another word, he starts walking across the lawn. Not even a goodbye, and he didn't stay long enough to help me up.

Barbara comes over to help me up. She gestures to the kids to get up and scoots them toward their dad. As they walk away, each of them turns to me and says goodbye. Barbara whispers in my ear, "Thank you for sharing that story. I know it was painful, but it was a very important story for us to hear. I'm sure you noticed my kids squirming when you were telling about the beating. They're afraid of their father, just like you were afraid of yours."

"Will I see you again tomorrow?"

"Absolutely, yes, we'll see you tomorrow." She turns and walks away.

They're halfway across the grass, when Christina turns and runs back. She jumps into my arms, gives me a kiss on the cheek, a bear hug and then whispers in my ear, "Your daddy is mean, just like mine." Then she jumps down and runs toward her mom.

Tears stream down my cheeks as I watch her run to catch up.

Chapter Four

How could a father wish his son
had died, when he himself was
already dead?

- John Egreek

Tuesday, I wake up expecting a good day, but I have a knot in my gut. This is usually an indicator something's about to go wrong. Since my expectations are high, I focus on the positive thoughts instead. I believe we control most of what happens on a daily basis, even though sometimes things don't work out the way we want them to.

I hear Grandma saying, *"Yianni, don't sweat the small stuff. Usually if it's something small, it's not important enough to remember."*

That lesson took me a very long time to learn, fifty-two years to be exact. I do my best to avoid negativity. It is my way of coping. Each day we're subject to the high road or the low road. Life is not perfect.

I get to the park with Rascal, my dog, and am surprised to find they're already here waiting. I see Christina, Charlie, Bobby and Barbara, but no sign of Ray. Each of them takes a moment to hug me. First Christina, then the boys, and then last but not least, Barbara. Oh my, the love from this family overwhelms me. There's no greater feeling than the love of another human being. I wish this was my son and his family, but I'm happy to settle for them. It's important to hug from the deepest part of your soul. Grandma used to say, *"Yianni, if you don't hug from you heart, then you shouldn't hug at all."*

I turn to Barbara, "No Ray?"

"No Ray. He doesn't want to hear your stories. He says they mean nothing to him. I tried to tell him that in every story there's something for everyone. When you open your mind, then you open your heart. He's not ready to open his heart and that makes me sad."

"Those were wise words Barbara. At the very least, you gave him something to think about."

"Tell the story, tell the story, Mr. Yianni."

With a chuckle, "Okay Christina, I'll tell you another grizzly story about my crazy life. But first I want to know if any of you know how to swim?"

Surprised, they all tell me they know how.

Wow, "I'm impressed."

"When I was your age, I didn't know how to swim. I was around lakes and rivers, but never learned how to swim until a few years later, when I was nine. There weren't many swimming pools in San Francisco. I can remember the one at Playland by the Sea, 'The Plunge.' We could only go in the pool accompanied by an adult. If you were a teenager, you had to prove you knew how to swim."

Charlie says, "What's Playland by the Sea?"

"It was an amusement park with rides, a slide, games and a roller coaster that actually went over the ocean. I was too small to ride, and too scared. The rides were similar to the ones at the Fair Del Mar, have you been?"

They confirm, by saying, "Yes."

"I have fond memories of Playland by the Sea. I remember the Fortune Teller in a glass booth, then there was the laughing lady, she never stopped laughing. You could hear her laughter everywhere in the park. It was magical, because she made everyone laugh. Grandma used to say, *'Laughter is the best medicine.'*

"There was the hardwood slide. It was a very high, at least so it seemed to me. We had to sit on a gunny sack and if we got sideways or off the sack, wearing shorts, I remember it would burn my legs. I liked the slide, but I didn't like the burn. My favorite memory was the pink candied popcorn. It was really good."

Charlie, looking for a chance to have some fun says, "What's a gunny sack?"

"A gunny sack is a cloth sack that is often used for animal feed or flour. They're loosely woven threads so the air can get inside, but the feed or flour can't get out through the threads."

"Oh, I've seen one before," says Charlie.

Then I start with the story.

"Today's story is about a weekend trip to Clearlake California. We drive north from San Francisco to Santa Rosa, then go northeast to the south end of the Mendocino National Forest. It's about ninety miles away, but it seems like twice that much. The highway in the 50's was single lane. We drove most of the way on Old California highway 101."

"When we get to the state park, Dad puts the tent up. My brother and I are expected to get him the tools. We spent most of our youth getting tools for our dad, without him ever explaining to us what they were or how to use them. We learned that on our own. If we didn't get him the right tool, there was hell to pay. He'd hold the tool over his head and motion as if he was going to strike us with it and then say, 'Dammit, next time I send you after a tool you better move your little butt faster.'"

"I swore that when I was a dad, there was no way I would make my kids pay the price for not getting my tools fast enough or for getting the wrong tool. That was easy to say, but when my oldest son Brock, whose name is now Roc, was six, I sent him to the barn to get a crescent wrench. He ran as fast as he could. He had no idea what a crescent wrench was. He had to ask his stepmom to show him."

"As he runs back with it, I'm at the top of the ladder fuming about how long it's taking. When he gets there, as he hands me the wrench, I hold it over my head and start to say, 'Dammit, next time I send you after a tool...'"

"Without saying another word, I climb down from the ladder, embarrassed and ashamed of myself. I look my little boy straight in the eyes, and tell him, 'I'm so sorry. I swore to myself years ago, that when I become a dad I won't do to you, what my dad did to me. He humiliated me, and I won't do that to you. I'm so sorry. I'll do my best not to do it ever again.'"

Charlie looks up at me, with sadness in his eyes as he says, "My daddy does that to me. He never says he's sorry."

I really didn't know what to say, but hopefully one day Charlie will remember this story and not repeat the same mistake with his children. But then it struck me to tell him, "You know Charlie the one thing it takes to fix a problem is to recognize there is a problem. Hopefully, when you get older, you'll be watching for them and recognize these bad traits that your father is instilling in you. You'll have the power to stop it for the next generation."

Then Bobby stops us cold, "Can we get back to the story. I want to know about your camping trip at the lake."

"I'm sorry, I digress. It seems these stories just keep pouring out of me as I relive them. Forgive the intrusion," I say with a laugh.

Before I get a chance to get back to the story, Christina asks, "What is digress?"

I let out a belly laugh, then I think, *"I better choose words these kids know and understand."* I tell Christina what digress means and go back to telling the story.

"After pitching the tent, we jump into the car to go to see friend's, George and Ruby. They own a cabin in the pines just to the west of the lake. George finished building his boat a couple of weeks earlier and tomorrow they were going waterskiing. I loved his boat and for many years I dreamed about building my own boat someday. I never built one from scratch like George, but I did own a '57 Chris Craft in my thirties. That's a story for another time."

"When we get to the cabin, their German Shepherd, named Tinker, was not too happy we were there. George warns us not to play with Tinker."

"I ask why. He tells me this dog is special, he's a guard dog and he's true to me above anyone else. Then he shows us. He tells his wife Ruby to act like she's going to attack him. Ruby does, and Tinker goes into attack mode. Thankfully George is holding him back or he would have torn Ruby apart. Then he tells his son Danny to act like he's going to attack Ruby, again Tinker goes into attack mode. I know he would have torn Danny apart. Then he tells my brother to go after Danny as if he was going to hurt him."

"Donald did as he asked, once again Tinker would have torn my brother apart. George goes on to tell us that tomorrow when we're at the lake, if anyone goes under water, Tinker will go after them to make sure they are all right, all of us, he said. He's also a lifesaving dog."

"After a nice visit with them, Mom decides it's time to go back to the campsite to get some sleep. I remember she was really excited about waterskiing the next day. Mom was pretty good. I remember seeing old movies with her skiing."

"The next morning we woke up to the smell of bacon, eggs, toast and hash. I can smell that food today, as I stick my nose in the air and take a good whiff."

The kids look at Barbara, then Charlie says, "Mommy, can we go camping someday and will you cook us breakfast like that? It sounds so yummy."

Barbara looks at me, gives me a wink and says, "Oh sure kids, someday we can all go on a camping trip."

Christina blurts out, "Can Mr. Yianni come?"

"We'll see when the time comes."

"The lake's calm and it's almost ten in the morning when we hear the sound of George's boat approaching the shore. We finish breakfast just in time. But Dad tells Donald and I to wash the dishes while he and Mom go waterskiing. He asks his friend John Earl, my namesake, to watch over us. They take my sister Chrissy with them because Mom didn't feel comfortable leaving her behind with John Earl."

"Donald says, 'Why can't we go in the boat?'"

"Dad throws his hand in the air, makes a fist and says, 'Because I said so.' His favorite words. Everything was 'Because I said so.'"

"They're gone for a couple of hours. Every now and then, they'd fly by the shore so we could see them skiing. They'd just wave and then the boat would disappear. Morning disappeared and it was a few minutes past noon. It was really hot. John Earl, standing by the shore with his feet in the water, tells me to stick my feet in. 'You'll feel cooler.'"

"I walk up next to him. A few minutes later, he walks into the water to get his whole body wet. Another friend of the family, Tinny, is downstream fishing. I was hot, so I followed in behind John Earl. He didn't know I was there."

"The water got deep fast. I begin thrashing about because I can't swim and I'm going under. My lungs were filling up with water and I'm gasping for air. I didn't know how to stay afloat. John Earl still has no idea that I'm in trouble. I can still remember how helpless I felt. I was drowning and was about to go under for the last time."

"Tinny thinks he sees a fish jumping out of the water. He throws a glance in my direction. He watched for a couple of seconds and then saw it wasn't a fish. It was one of my arms popping out of the water. There was no time to waste. He has no idea this would be the last time I'd come back up."

"I was drowning. I stopped breathing and my life was disappearing. Tinny throws down his fishing pole and dives into the water to search for me. John Earl still has no clue that anything's going on. A few seconds pass, feels like an eternity to me, when Tinny grabs me by the arm and pulls me up out of the water. He swims to the shore on his back, holding my head above the water. By the time we reach the shore, I'm gone, I'm not breathing, I'm dead."

"In the 50's, nobody knew CPR and very few knew mouth-to-mouth resuscitation. They're future concepts. John Earl, who had finished his swim, notices something happening on shore. I'm surrounded by people I don't even know. I see them, but I'm not in my body. They're yelling, crying, it's utter chaos. My brother's scared, he's shaking. Mom and Dad are nowhere around."

"One woman suggests they attempt to make me vomit. Look, there's the boat making another pass. Mom's waterskiing and she sees the crowd. She figures there's something wrong with one of us, so she crosses the wake and nearly skies on to shore. The minute she lets go of the ropes she runs in my direction. I see her, but nobody can see me."

I notice Charlie, Bobby and Christina gasping for air. They're holding their breath wondering if I'm back to life. It's funny how people react when they hear someone's not breathing. Their breath becomes shallow and withdrawn.

"A few seconds later, Mom is there. George stops the boat at the shoreline, jumps out and runs to catch up. Ruby has my sister Chrissy and my Dad's drifting slowly up the shore. When George gets there, he knows exactly what to do. He starts to give me mouth-to-mouth. When he stops to take a breath, he pushes on my stomach. After a second try, he clears my throat one more time. Just before he goes back to mouth-to-mouth, I begin to vomit. Water's shooting out my mouth, I'm gasping for air. I'm back in my body. I vomit a few more times."

"Ruby had gotten her car. She says, 'Come on, Barb, there's a medical infirmary down the road. We can take him there.'"

"When we got to the infirmary, Mom's slapping the window with her hands. A nurse opens it and says, 'What's wrong?'"

"My son nearly drowned, he needs to see a doctor."

"The nurse tells her, 'I'll call the doctor. He's at home and it will take twenty minutes for him to get here.'"

"Just tell him to hurry."

"Mom's doing her best to console me. I realize there might be a price to pay with my dad because I spoiled his day. Before the doctor gets there, Dad and George come walking in. I hear George ask how I was. Dad never says a word. He didn't even come in to see me. The doctor arrives. He checks me out and doesn't find anything wrong. Then he goes out to talk to Mom, Dad, Ruby and George."

"While the doctor was checking me out, John Earl had come into the infirmary. He's upset and concerned. He knew he blew it."

"Mom walks up to him and starts pounding on his chest. 'I thought you were going to watch my boys. You promised you'd keep an eye on them. What happened, where were you?'"

"John Earl just hung his head. He says nothing as she beats on him. I couldn't see because the doctor closed the door when he walked out. I could only see the outline of their bodies through the frosted glass."

"Mom notices the doctor standing there. She stops whaling on John Earl. She turns her attention to the doctor, who says, 'He checks out okay. I'd suggest taking him home and putting him into a warm bed.'"

"Mom thanks him and then Dad shocks them all when he says, 'Dammit, this kid is always ruining things for us. I wish he would've died.'"

"George, Ruby, Tinny, John Earl and Mom can't believe what came out of his mouth. George turns to him and says, 'That's your son in there, you asshole. If that was my son, I'd be in there with him and nothing would stop me from caring for him.'"

"My brother froze. They're all yelling and screaming at Dad, telling him he was crazy, and he should be glad that I'm still alive."

"It was the last time we went camping as a family. George and Ruby no longer wanted to be their friends. No one knows what ever happened to John Earl, it was the last time we ever saw him. We see Tinny one year later, but that would be the last time we ever see him, because during that trip he has an accident with his Jeep and one of his daughters is killed."

"Dad has no idea I heard him. I remember saying, 'God, why did you let me live?' It's then that I realize my dad really does hate me. I kept it a secret for years. On the way back to the city, he says, 'You better not tell your grandparents, because if any of you do, there will be hell to pay.'"

"I remember thinking to myself, if only Papa knew, Dad would be the one who'd pay the price. I was scared either way. Because he was my dad, I didn't want anything to happen to him, and because he was my dad, I didn't want anything to happen to me. Nearly drowning left a scar in my psyche for many years."

Christina asks, "What's a psyche?" She had a tough time saying it.

I did my best to tell her it was a hidden part of our soul, deep inside of our subconscious mind. "It's the place where we bury things that we don't want to remember. We bury them, hoping they never come back. But they're always there, deep inside our DNA."

Bobby asks, "When did you learn how to swim?"

"Four years later when I was nine. I went to a Coast Guard approved swim class at Playland by the Sea. But even then, I was still afraid of the deep water. The last day of lessons, they required us to jump from the high dive. It was our final test. As I climb up the ladder, halfway up I start to cry. I couldn't jump. I was just too afraid I might drown."

"Mom explains to them afterwards that I nearly drowned. So, they passed me."

"Two years later, when I was eleven, I finally gave up my fear of the deep end. It took a girl, a neighbor girl from across the street. I was chasing her when she jumped into the deep end of her pool and I followed in behind her without realizing what I'd done. My fear of deep water was gone forever. Later in life, while working construction at a power plant, I find that my fear of heights was gone too. That day on the high dive was not about being up high, it was about going under water."

The kids realize the story's over. They're not asking for another one. I surmise they didn't care for this story, but Charlie puts it into perspective when he says, "Your daddy was a mean and terrible man. I bet you hate him!"

"You know Charlie, hate is a powerful word. But how could my father hate me, when he himself was already dead. He had no love for me, but he also didn't love himself. No, I don't hate my dad."

Christina sums it up best, "Well he's a really, really mean man."

"You're right, he is. He'll most likely die angry and all alone without any of his kids by his side. Grandma used to say, *'Anger is a disease and if you carry it around long enough, it will kill you.'*"

Barbara turns to the kids and suggests it's time to go.

They hug me goodbye.

Barbara hugs me last, then kisses me on the cheek as she says, "Can we see you again on Friday?"

"Of course, sounds fine by me, providing it's fine by them?"

"Yes, yes, we want to hear more."

"Okay, Friday it is."

Barbara asks the kids to start walking toward the car, then turns to me and says, "Yianni, I'm so sorry you had to grow up without a real dad. I don't know how you've been able to move past the pain. I'm starting to see my childhood and the effect of my father's drinking as it relates to me today as an adult. I think it's a shame that any child has to live through what you've had to live through."

"You know Barbara, life has been very lonely for me. The damage that he did was far beyond anyone's comprehension, but even though he hates me, I don't hate him, I don't even pity him. In fact, if you've ever watched the TV show 'Shark Tank,' one of my favorite Sharks, Mr. Wonderful, says it best how I feel about my dad, 'You're dead to me.' He's not speaking of death, he's speaking of forgetting. I think about my father every time I hear him say it. My father's dead to me. I forget I even had a father, because I really never did. I don't need him to keep on going. Now I understand what he meant when he said, I need to forgive and forget."

"Wow, that's powerful."

"The pain never leaves, it just numbs you. The same's happening with my relationship issues with my son. I'm becoming numb to the loss, but the pain never leaves. I think about him and his family every day. But now, I think about you and your family too."

With a big smile, a bit of a blush on her face, Barbara asks for my phone number. "Just in case anything comes up and we can't make it, I'll call you."

We exchange numbers and she runs to catch up with the kids. I watch them disappear and then decide to sit there a bit before heading for home.

I take a moment to think back to the day Christina came into my life. I'm so thankful to the universe for sending me this angel and her family. They embrace my storytelling muse.

Chapter Five

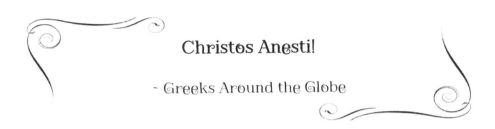

Christos Anesti!

~ Greeks Around the Globe

I wake up Friday morning excited to see Christina and her family, even Ray if he decides to show.

Rascal and I get to the park before two. I spot Barbara and the kids heading across the grass. I see there's someone with them and it's not Ray. They draw close, I see a resemblance and I suspect this must be her mom.

I stand to greet them. Barbara introduces her mother. "This is my mother, Vasiliki."

I'm tongue tied, I can't speak to address her as tears roll down my cheeks.

"You have the same name as my great-grandmother. I never met her, only saw pictures of her. Grandma talked with high reverence about her. Barbara knew her name from an earlier story, but she never told me her mother's name."

I glance at Barbara and say with a hint of sarcasm, "How dare you, keeping your mother's name a secret from me."

Barbara laughs, I turn back to her mom and say, "It's an honor and a pleasure to meet you."

"The pleasure's all mine. Barbara's spoken highly of you."

"What part of Greece are you from?"

"I'm from Ioannina."

"Wow, I had a real-life déjà vu when I was there. It felt like I was home. It was the strangest feeling I've ever had. I even look like the people that live there. I stayed for an extra day because of it. People were always talking to me in Greek as if I was one of them. I told them I was from the states and I don't speak Greek, they shook their heads in disbelief. One man, the owner of a restaurant, could've been my Uncle Victor's twin. They say we have a twin somewhere in this world. I saw his in Ioannina," I tell her with deep fondness in my voice.

"You don't speak Greek, Yianni?"

"I wish I did Vasiliki, but my dad was adamant that my grandparents couldn't teach me. He was afraid Mom and I would talk behind his back, which we would have."

"What a shame, Yianni."

As soon as I finish talking about Ioannina, Christina asks, "What is a déjà vu?"

I do my best to tell her. "A déjà vu is a strange feeling we get as if we've been somewhere before. I had the feeling that I'd lived in the same place where your Grandma's from."

"You lived there a previous lifetime," says Vasiliki.

"You're probably right. Or, it was a synchronistic event leading up to meeting you today."

Seeing Christina always makes my heart sing. I have a gut feeling she and my granddaughter are much alike. I hope she's as curious as Christina is.

After the greetings are complete, I ask them if they're ready to hear some more stories. Of course, I already knew their answer would be a resounding yes.

I then set the scene. "Today's story happened in 1956, the year Grandma was on 'Queen for a Day.' No, I'm not going to tell you that story again."

Charlie says, "But I liked that story. Grandma hasn't heard it. Even though it was sad, it was a remarkable story. Your grandma was a Queen."

"Thank you, Charlie, today's story is about Greek Easter, April 1, 1956. Greek Easter is a very special day for Greeks around the globe.

That Greek Easter was a very special day, because it was also Grandma's birthday. She was born on April Fool's Day. I used to tease Grandma on her birthday. I would call her on the phone and say, 'Happy Birthday Grandma.'"

"Then she would say, 'Oh, thank you Yianni.'"

"Then the devil in me says, 'April Fools.'"

"It made Grandma laugh. She would say, 'Damn you Yianni, you tricked Grandma again.'"

Then I ask, "Do you celebrate Greek Easter?"

The kids look at their mom and Grandma as they shake their heads to signify "no." I glance at Barbara and Vasiliki, who have bowed their heads to hide their embarrassment as they say, "no."

Barbara says, "I do have some fond memories, when my grandparents were alive. But, those memories disappeared when they died."

I begin my story. "While living in San Francisco, the time for Greek Easter was a very festive occasion. My grandparents were the hosts of the city after the Easter Service at the Greek Church."

"Papa never attends, he stays behind to finish cooking the lamb. I can only remember one time seeing him in church with Grandma. It was Sunday, a few weeks earlier, when my brother Don, Uncle Victor and I were baptized. The whole family was there with our godparents and most of our Greek friends. My dad wasn't, he had no desire to be there. No telling where he was."

"I remember it as if it were yesterday. The three of us were in a pool of water. None of us knew how to swim, but it was only waist high for Donald and Victor. The water touched my chin. The Priest held Victor and Donald under for a few seconds while he pronounced them baptized. Holding me with both arms, he dunks me under for only a few seconds. Mom told me later that she was gasping the whole time. She knew I was afraid of going under. But the Priest knew about my near-drowning. He cradled me in his arms, comforting me, and telling me I was safe. I remember coming up and seeing Papa and Grandma sitting there in the front row of the church next to Mom. Their smiles lit up the church. I knew they were very proud of all three of us."

"Back to Greek Easter. Greek Easter is by far the most popular of Greek holidays, even more than Christmas. The Greeks believe in life after death and so the death of Christ is a huge time for celebration. The same holds true for a Greek family member when they die. Death is a celebration of life."

"More than Christmas?" Christina asks.

"More than Christmas."

"How can that be? Nothing's more important than Christmas!" says Charlie in a tone of disbelief.

"It is to the Greeks. Don't get me wrong, we celebrate Christmas too, but not like we celebrate Greek Easter."

"Saturdays before Greek Easter were fun. While downstairs at Grandma's, you could find my mom, my aunts and a few of Grandma's friends busy preparing the food. In early 1956, we lived in the same house upstairs. They cooked moussaka, spanakopita, tiropita, dolmades, Fasolaia, (Greek style string beans). The avgolemono soup was the best in the world. Grandma's dolmades and avgolemono soup were my favorites."

"Her avgolemono was not made with rice. Most people take a shortcut and use rice; she made hers with spaghetti that she cut short. Today, in the supermarket, it's called Orzo. In those days, Orzo and grape leaves were homemade."

"Grandma grew her own grapes. She would take the leaves, wash them and prepare them for cooking one year before. The grape leaves were tasty. Grandma soaked them in olive oil after she cured them. She would add rice, lamb and beef mixed together. Then add basil, oregano and garlic to her special recipe domatoe sauce. Grandma calls it domatoe sauce, because she has a tough time pronouncing it with a 't'."

Christina yells, "My grandma calls it domatoe sauce too."

We all laugh. I throw a wink to Vasiliki, then continue, "Possibly they're correct and the rest of the world is wrong. Mom made dolmades as good as Grandma. She passed the recipe to my first wife. She makes them as good as Mom, if not better. I hope she passes the recipe to my daughter. By far, dolmades are my favorite dish, with moussaka a close second."

"I will tell you, the Greek desserts are the best. I mean, who doesn't like sweets? Grandma made the best baklava. Auntie Genie made the best Kourambiedes. They're powder sugar coated butter cookies that melt in your mouth. I can taste them now. They learned from Grandma's dear friend Joann, a Greek from Constantinople. She and her husband Yianni were my sister's Godparents, who I wished were mine. They lived in San Diego near the tennis courts where I used to play tournaments. I'd walk to their house from the courts and Mom would pick me up there after she closed the bookstore. She always had Greek food on the stove and desserts on the table."

"I know, I digress. The kids and Barbara know that word very well by now."

"While the cooking's going on inside, Papa's outside turning the spit, cooking the lamb. It took him three days and three nights to cook it. He turned the spit one turn at a time. Papa would only leave the spit for a couple of hours at a time to take a short nap or to go to the bathroom. One of my uncles would spell him when he did. I was too small to turn it. It was his job and he was always proud of the outcome."

I interrupt the story again. "I have an everyday reminder of Papa hanging on my wall. He's sitting like an Indian. He's wearing his favorite shirt and hat, while turning the spit, with a lamb cooking away."

"I want to see it," yells Christina.

"Someday I'll show you."

"The Saturday night before Easter, Grandma boils the eggs and everyone helps to color them red. Red is significant to the blood of Christ. The egg itself is representative of the sealed tomb."

"The next day we play 'Tsougrisma.' Cracking the egg represents the opening of the tomb. The object of the game is to determine whose egg is the strongest. You have to wait until the end of the game before you can eat your egg."

Christina says, "Can we play sometime, Mommy?"

Barbara tells her, "We can play sometime, but we better let Mr. Yianni explain how to play, don't you think?"

"Oh yeah, I guess we should," she snicker's out loud.

"Here's how you play."

"Papa starts it off by holding his egg steady in his right hand. Grandma's next, so she raises her egg above his, then taps the top of his egg. As they tap, everyone says, 'Christos Anesti' which means, 'Christ has risen.'"

"If Grandma's egg breaks, she's out of the game. If Papa's breaks, he's out. The winner takes the lead. They go to everyone in the room. Grandparents first, then their oldest child. Then the game moves to friends and family, starting from the oldest to the youngest. This continues until someone's declared the winner. Sometimes they play it where you have to break both sides of the egg."

"The contest determines who has the strength of Christ. The winner will have good luck during the coming year. We Greeks are very superstitious."

"The kids play a separate game. Kids have a bad habit of striking the eggs too hard. The winner strikes the adult winner's egg. They do this out of fun, to determine who the real champion is. I have fond memories of this game."

I notice Barbara wiping tears from her cheeks. I say nothing.

"What about the Easter Bunny?" asks Charlie. "Does the Easter Bunny come for Greek Easter?"

"No, the Easter Bunny only comes for a traditional American Christian Easter, as far as I know, Charlie."

He asks, "Is it the same day as Greek Easter?"

"Sometimes it is, and sometimes it isn't. The Greek Easter follows the Greek calendar, which is different than our calendar."

"What was it like when they both were on the same date?" asks Bobby.

"I only remember it happening once, when we celebrated both. We had our own custom for traditional Easter. I would join my brother and sister by hiding a carrot somewhere in the house. The Easter Bunny would find it, eat some of it, and then leave a basket full of goodies wherever we left our carrot."

Then Bobby says, "Mommy, we should do that. We should hide a carrot for the Easter Bunny next Easter!"

"That sounds like fun. We'll do that next year. We can start a new family tradition," Barbara tells them.

"The next morning," I continued, "we go to Church for Easter Mass. Right after, we head home to make last minute preparations for the arrival of the Greeks in San Francisco. In 1956, the voters elected a new Mayor of San Francisco, George Christopher. The Greeks helped him to get elected, so he came too. Greek himself, many of the people coming provided financial support for his election. It would be a slap in the face if he didn't show. I remember him arriving in a white stretch limousine. Everyone came with their favorite dish. There's so much food that we ate leftovers for a week afterwards."

"Papa's proud being Greek, along with cooking the best lamb. It's an honor for him to host the celebration. They called him 'The Big Greek from San Francisco.' Not only because of his lamb, but also for his homemade red wine and his hospitality. Papa took immense pride in all three."

"Is that the only reason they call him the Big Greek from San Francisco?" Charlie asks.

"Not the only one. He used to carry large loads of lumber and big beams over his shoulders everywhere in the city. Because he didn't drive, he carried lumber given to him by contractors to build his homes. He was as strong as an ox."

"After Papa died, Greek Easter died too. We never celebrated it as a family again. But I've never forgotten the fond memories of our Greek Easter."

Then I turn to Barbara and Vasiliki to ask them to tell their version of Greek Easter.

"Yeah Mommy, tell us about your Greek Easters," her three kids say.

"Our Greek Easter wasn't as elaborate and as special as Yianni's. I remember, now and then, we held Greek Easter at our house, but most of the years we went to our relative's. But your Yiayia, our grandmother, is a good cook. She makes everything that Yianni mentioned," as she throws a look at Vasiliki. "Like a typical young girl, second-generation Greek, I didn't want to learn how to cook, so I only know how to cook a few dishes. And sad to say, your dad doesn't care for Greek food. The only thing different in our Greek Easter is that we didn't cook a whole lamb on a spit. We bought a leg of lamb from the grocery store and cooked it in the oven. We colored the eggs red and played the same game. That's why tears came to my eyes when Yianni told the story. I will always remember how special Greek Easter was," as she wipes away her tears.

Christina moves close to her mommy to console her. Then she says, "Oh, Mr. Yianni, that was a delightful story. I want to celebrate Greek Easter someday."

I nod with approval. Then I add, "Christina, you better ask your Grandma to teach you how to cook everything." I throw another wink at Vasiliki.

Young Bobby says, "Mr. Yianni, are you going to tell us another story today?"

"Not today, Bobby, today's story is one of those special stories you want to always remember. Telling you another story might make it too easy for you to forget."

He accepts my explanation. Then Barbara turns to me and says, "When can you tell us the next story, this one's definitely for my memory book."

"Well let's see, today is Friday and this weekend is Memorial Day weekend. How about we plan on meeting next Wednesday?"

"Next Wednesday it is," she says.

Then we share cheek kisses and hugs. I reach out to shake Vasiliki's hand and kiss her on the cheek. As I do, she says, "I guess I better start teaching my daughter and my granddaughter how to cook Greek food. Your story has inspired me."

I throw her a big smile and a wink of approval. I hope my ex-wife teaches my daughter and my granddaughters how to cook dolmades. It would be nice to know she passed my mom's recipe to them. I should have learned too.

Chapter Six

Wednesday rolls around and there's plenty of chores to keep me busy for the morning. Around ten, my phone rings. I look at the screen to see who it is. I see that it's Barbara calling.

I say bright and cheery, "Good morning."

Barbara says in a muffled voice. "Hello, Yianni, I'm calling to tell you we won't be meeting you at the park. Can we meet for lunch at the Lakeside Café around one?"

"Of course, lunch works for me." I sense a break in the tone of her voice. "Is everything okay?"

"I'll tell you over lunch. I need to go for now," she says without saying another word.

After the phone call, I go to my chair, bow my head to my chest and close my eyes. I stay completely silent. I ask for spiritual guidance. A few seconds later, I experience a rush of inspiration and comfort.

At 12:45 I drive to the Café. I'm a stickler about punctuality. On the way, the song "Johnny Angel" by Shelley Fabares comes on the radio. I go back many years as this song paints a picture in my mind. From the very first time I heard "Johnny Angel," I've been searching and hoping that one day I'll become someone's Johnny Angel. Together we'll see how sweet heaven will be. What a dream.

My mind comes back to focus as I pull into the café parking lot. I notice Barbara sitting on a bench in front. She has her feet up, her knees to her chin and her head buried in her arms. When I arrive, she stands up and runs to me with her arms outstretched. I wrap my arms around her, holding her tight until she's ready to let go. I know that's what she needs.

When her grip loosens, I take a short step backward and let go. From the corner of my eye, I notice she's sporting a black eye. There are bruises on her face. I give her another embrace, holding her tight enough that I can feel her heart beating. I loosen my grip and step away, then I say, "Come on, let's go inside."

Once inside, I ask the hostess to give us a booth toward the back. I know Barbara will feel more comfortable sitting away from the crowd. As we sit down, the waitress hands us the menu and I notice her glancing at Barbara's black eye. I throw up one finger to my mouth, asking her not to say anything.

For the next few minutes, we look over the menu. We don't say a word. A few seconds later, the waitress returns to take our order.

Barbara says she's not hungry and that she'd settle for a glass of water. I insist that she needs to eat something, so she agrees to order a hamburger plate.

We sit in silence before I say, "Do you want to tell me what happened, or would you rather not?"

Barbara tells me she met up with her husband last night. He'd been drinking, and he was insistent that she return home with the kids. He insists that she stop bringing them to see me. "When I defy him, he smacks me in the face a couple of times. He grabs me by the arms and tells me one more time. I bruise very easy. It doesn't take much. I hate it when he does this."

"He's done this before? Once is too much as far as I'm concerned. It might be best that we stop meeting?" I say, with sorrow in my voice. My heart's surging with anger. What I want to do, is go over to her house and rip him a new one, but I do my best not to let her know.

"No. We're not going to stop seeing you. You've brought too much joy into our lives. You mean a lot to my kids. Since my father passed, learning about their heritage is important. You're giving us a new perspective on life. They're learning a lot. We're not going to stop, I will divorce him before we ever do that."

"Okay, we'll continue."

"Let's not talk about me anymore. I've said enough. I want to forget it for a bit. Today I'd like to know more about you. Tell me about Yianni."

"What would you like to know?"

"Let's start with your family, your home and your job."

"I got married two times. I have three beautiful adult children from the first marriage. Marriage for me has not been good. Both marriages. Never because of my kids. I wasn't cut out to be a husband or a father at that time in my life. I made a ton of mistakes and it seems some of them kept repeating. I never seem to get the lesson."

"What do you mean, you never get the lesson?"

"It's my belief that everything that happens to us is for a reason. There's a lesson in every good thing we do and in every bad choice that we make."

"The first mistake I made, was quitting tennis and college. I was on a half scholarship at the University of Nevada, Reno, playing tennis. It was my junior year of college, but my first year there. I wasn't eligible to play because I had gone to another University that same year."

"What happened?"

"All thanks to tennis. It was in Reno that I met Mia, a young girl who had the uncanny ability to love without conditions. Young and dumb, I had no idea what that kind of love was. How can you, when you live with parents who fight and bicker all the time? They never display affection; how could anyone ever understand what love is? My parents were in a love/hate relationship. There was more hate than there was love. I know my mom hated my dad at the end. She told me many times. She could never come to grips to do anything about it. They were not role models for any of us. Long story short, I push Mia aside, quit college, stop playing tennis and marry the mother of my children."

"I can't even remember the date of our marriage. What I do remember, on our wedding day, as she's walking down the aisle, my eyes fill with tears. And they're not tears of joy. They're frightful tears. I knew that I was making the biggest mistake of my life. I didn't love her and she didn't love me. I didn't have the guts to walk away, even though my gut said, run, go out the side door and run for your life. I knew the relationship was wrong. The marriage started with a 'divorce mentality.'"

"What do you mean by a divorce mentality?"

"From the first day we're married, all I can think about is how to end it and I'm sure that's what she was thinking too. I didn't think about ways to keep the relationship alive. Neither of us did. That's my opinion of a divorce mentality. But don't get me wrong, she played a significant role in making me feel this way. We didn't make love until three months after we married. She was a virgin. Every man's dream is to marry a virgin and to be the one to pop her cherry. But I didn't even get to do that. She went to the doctor and complained that she was too small. The doctor gave her these devices to insert inside her to expand her opening. It took three months."

"You didn't make love for three months?"

"That's right. Three months."

"That's crazy. You mean you didn't explore at all when you were dating?"

"It depends on how you define explore. We had some great make-out sessions. The only exploration was touching her breasts and she kept her hands to herself. She never touched me."

"No wonder you had a divorce mentality."

"Seven years later, two divorces and three children, our relationship comes to an ugly end. I came home from work one night two weeks before Christmas. It was eight months after the birth of our youngest son. She tells me, 'I've got my three kids, all from the same father, so now I want you out of the house this weekend.'"

"You mean you divorced her twice?"

"Yes, two times. Before our first divorce, I met an awesome woman. Her name was Terry and I met her at a night club. We were the same age, she was gorgeous, with blonde hair, blue eyes, my height and she was fun and exciting to be with. She reminded me of Mia. She was my affair. Terry was married too, but separated from her husband and living with her mom and dad. We spent time together whenever I could find time to break away from my wife. We knew what we were doing was wrong, but we enjoyed each other, and we made each other feel special. My wife never made me feel special. She hated making love, so like most men in that situation, I went somewhere else to find intimacy. Terry provided what I was missing. At that time, I was ready to leave my wife and spend the rest of my life with her."

"Then one-night Terry tells me she's going to make a go of her marriage and that we couldn't see each other anymore."

"Oh, my gosh! You guys were both miserable, in love, having fun, why go back for more hate and discontent?"

"My sentiments exactly. But during that stage of my life, I wasn't emotionally aware enough to recognize what love was. I don't think Terry could either."

"It wasn't long after that short affair that my wife and I divorced for the first time. We owned a condo in Oceanside, so she and the kids stayed there, and I moved away. I moved in with a friend from high school, Jay. He had a two-story, A-frame style home in El Cajon that he co-owned with his ex-wife, Holly."

"Jay let me live in one of the rooms in his house for fifty bucks a month while I was going through my divorce. One Saturday morning I woke up to find that Jay had gone surfing, but someone was in the house. I could hear her singing. When I go to the laundry room to check the noise, around turns beautiful and gorgeous Holly, Jay's ex-wife. Holly, a brunette with beautiful deep brown eyes, like yours. I fell for her in seconds. I've always had a thing for brunettes, especially brunettes with brown eyes. I'm sure it's because most Greeks have black or mahogany brown hair. Plus, a high percentage of them have brown eyes. Anyhow, Holly was there doing her laundry. She tells me she's Jay's ex-wife."

"We spend the next couple of hours talking. It feels like we've known each other for years. We click. Before I know it, we're dating. We had some awesome times together. One of our dates was a very special one that to this day, I have never forgotten. Holly enjoyed tennis, which made her a perfect match for me."

"One Saturday night I took Holly and my daughter Natalie to the World Team Tennis Match in San Diego. We see some of the greats play. There's Billie Jean King, Arthur Ashe, Rosie Casals, Rod Laver and more. It's a great night. Even the KGB Chicken was there. He's a comedian dressed in a chicken suit, which overnight became the joy of San Diego sport fans."

"Natalie's enamored by the Chicken. At one point, the Chicken was in our section. He was down about seven rows in the same aisle from where we were sitting. Without saying a word to me, Holly takes Natalie by the hand and they go down for a closer look at the Chicken. They're standing right in front of him and he grabs Natalie by her hand and displays her to the crowd. She's having so much fun. It's a magical moment in Natalie's life, Holly's and in mine. Holly turns to come back to her seat. Natalie, not quite ready to go, stays there with the Chicken, who's sitting down holding Natalie on his lap."

"I'm watching them the whole time. We have no idea what's going on with the tennis match. Too bad cell phones weren't invented yet. It would have been an entertaining video. Finally, the Chicken had to get back to his voodoo comedy. He has a knack for doing voodoo with his hands. It gets the crowd hooting and hollering."

"I go to get Natalie and bring her back to her seat. She was so excited, soon after she climbs into my lap, she falls asleep. I have my arms wrapped around her. The excitement gets the best of her. While she's sleeping, she pees her pants. I'm soaking wet, but I didn't care because my precious daughter is one happy little girl that night. It's a memory of a lifetime."

"Holly and I continue dating for a couple of months. A couple of weeks after watching the team tennis, Holly shows up one night with a surprise for Natalie. It's a replica stuffed animal of the KGB Chicken. She loved that stuffed animal. I mean, what six-year-old wouldn't love a toy that reminds her of a magical time in her life? I was in love with Holly."

"Oh no, I get the feeling there's a 'but' coming?"

"Yes, there's a but coming. I missed my kids. My divorce is final, but I had never signed the final papers. One day, after bringing the kids home from my weekend visitation, my ex shocks me. She comes on to me and takes me into her bedroom to make love. I didn't resist. What can I say? When it comes to sex, I'm weak and can't ever say no. In the act of making love, our youngest son Ryan's conceived. Sad but true, it's also the last time we ever make love. Once she finds out she's pregnant, that's it. In seven years of marriage, we made love no more than twelve times, three of which brought about our children. She hated it from the start. I should have annulled the marriage before the kids ever came about," I say with a laugh and a shrug of the shoulder.

"Only twelve times? My gosh, when you were that age that should never have happened. The most vital and exciting time for a man is when he's in his twenties. You poor guy Yianni, no wonder your marriage didn't work. Were you still living in the condo when you divorced the second time?"

"No, soon after we got back together, we sold our condo in Oceanside and bought the house here in Lakeside. The property was large enough for me to put in a tennis court. One of my dreams. Mom helped us with the down payment. Married a little over seven years, we had moved thirteen times. I was not moving again. I swore that would be the last time. That was in October 1977."

"Our son Ryan, the one who's not talking to me, was born in April. Then December of that year, my wife informs me she wants a second divorce. Two weeks before Christmas, she says to me, 'I have my three kids, all from the same father, I want you to leave this weekend. It's over and I want a divorce.'"

"To which I respond, 'If you want a divorce that bad, there's the door and you're taking it. I've moved you thirteen times in less than seven years. You can load up the truck and move yourself this time. My mom was the one who helped us get into this house, I'm keeping it and you need to be the one to leave.'"

"Then she repeats, 'I want you out of this house this weekend.'"

"My response is simple and direct, 'If I leave, the bank is going to own this house. I'll stop paying for it.' She knew I was serious, so that weekend she packs up the truck and drives away with the kids. At that point, I didn't care about her anymore. I'm finished with her, but there's a huge price to pay."

"What do you mean there's a huge price to pay, Yianni?"

"She is the most vindictive person I've ever known. She stabbed me in the back and helped to destroy my relationship with the kids. That knife's still in my back, deeper now, thirty-eight years since our divorce. She's the monster behind the problem with my son."

"Doesn't she know that it might be important for your kids to have their father in their life? What kind of mother is she?"

"A vindictive one, that's all I can say. Don't get me wrong, I wasn't the greatest of husbands. I was a great provider. I went to work every day, paid the bills, didn't drink, never did drugs and I don't smoke. What more could a woman ask for? She played a role in me becoming unfaithful. I had a lot of sleepless nights, staring at the ceiling every time she turned me away. Infidelity caused me to become withdrawn from the relationship. I had become argumentative like my parents. But it had nothing to do with our break-up. She'd planned that from the start the second time around. No one will convince me otherwise. Our relationship was dead before it ever started. From the beginning of our marriage, it was always what I could do for her and never what she could do for me."

"I know my husband would have looked elsewhere too if he was in your shoes, Yianni. But that's one thing that's not lacking in our relationship. We both enjoy intimacy. His only problem is the alcohol."

"Looking backward, I'm not proud of the person that I was. But today, I'm a completely different person. I know it's easy to look backward and point the finger. I understand now, when you point the finger, there are four other fingers pointing back. To this day, my kids have never heard me say an unkind word about their mom. But I don't care anymore if they see how I feel. I've kept it pent up inside for too long. If only they see things from my side, just once. Of course, I understand, no one can understand your situation because they don't wear the same shoes that you do."

"The season between us had come to an end. I've paid a huge price for thirty-eight years. She continues to harm my relationship with the kids. We may never recover, and I blame her for her role in it. Nobody will ever convince me otherwise. At this stage in life, I don't care if my kids know how I feel about their mother. I despise her. She's horrible and she's vindictive. She has caused me nothing but pain and discontent."

"Well, don't give up Yianni. There's such a thing as karma. Who knows, your kids might one day be in your shoes. Life has a funny way of putting us in front of a mirror and the image that we see, fits the shoes of our parents."

"My, aren't you the Greek philosopher Barbara, wise beyond your years. But if life has its way, I hope my kids never have to live in my shoes. My shoes have worn out and my feet hurt. They've been stepped on enough this lifetime."

Barbara laughs, "Well what about Mia? Tell me about her."

"Oh no, that's a long story for another time. There is one more story to tell that happens the day after my wife leaves, though!"

"More? I can't wait to hear."

"Yes more, but let's finish our food?"

"The day after my wife and kids left, something strange yet magical happens. I'm at work at the Nuclear Power Plant. Construction noise is very loud, making it impossible to hear PA announcements. Late in the afternoon, one of my co-workers asks me if I ever called the operator. 'She's been announcing your name all day,' he says."

"When I call the operator, she says, 'Your wife Terry is looking for you, it's a family emergency. There's something going on with the kids.' Then she gives me the number."

"As I walk to the pay phone, I'm thinking, who the heck is Terry? My wife's name isn't Terry. Then it hits me—it's Terry, who I had the affair with during divorce number one."

"That's spooky," Barbara says with a chuckle.

"I call her. First thing she says, 'I woke up this morning with the urge to talk to you. I wasn't sure how to find you, but I remembered you work at the plant, so I figured, nothing ventured, nothing gained. Why not give it a try? How are you?'"

"For a second, I'm in shock, the excitement sends me reeling. I'm standing there with the phone in my hand shaking my head. I can't believe the timing. Then I tell her, 'I'm fine and I can't believe your timing because my wife and I split up for the last time yesterday.'"

"She tells me she's divorced. Then she says, 'I'd sure like to see you sometime.'"

"'Is tonight too soon?' I couldn't say it fast enough."

"She gives me her address and that night after work, instead of going home, I go to Terry's. We talk and get re-acquainted with each other. When I stand up to leave, she wraps her arms around and whips a big kiss on me. Then she says, 'You're not planning to go home, are you?'"

"We kiss again, this time when we stop, she grabs me by the hand, and without another word, leads me upstairs to her bedroom. Before I know it, four months have gone by and we're having the time of our life. She treats me better than my wife ever treated me. She's all I can think about. Every night there's a warm meal waiting and the night ends with fun in the bed. What more could any man ask for?"

"We talk about everything and enjoy being with each other. For the second time in my life, I'm getting a taste of unconditional love. Yet I don't recognize it, and something happens that scares me away."

"Oh no, not again?"

"Yep, again. She has two adorable sons. One night she tells the boys to go upstairs and give Dad a kiss goodnight. I hear her and start thinking, *I'm not their dad. I'm not divorced yet and we aren't even married. I've been a failure with kids, how could I be a father to hers?*"

"The boys come into her room. I'm lying on their mother's bed. They have snot hanging from their nose. This scares me, my kids never have snot noses. I grab a tissue to wipe their noses. Then I give them each a kiss on the cheek."

"The next morning, I'm thinking, *'run get the hell out here.'* I walk out her door and never look back. Years later, I realize I let the love of my life get away. I often wonder what my life would have been like with either Mia, Holly or Terry. If I only I'd known then what I know now."

"Years later, after my second marriage, I recognize there's a pattern related to my choice in women."

"The second marriage was worse than the first. She helped my first wife put the dagger in deeper. My boys hated her, and I stuck up for my wife and not my kids. One day while I'm away at work she cleans out my house and my bank account. It appears she had this planned for some time. The day before, I received a vacation and holiday check from the Pipefitters Union. It was a little over nine thousand dollars. The largest one I' ever gotten. I sat at the desk writing checks. One to pay off the car, one to pay off a MasterCard account and others to reduce accounts. It's the first time I had a glance at financial independence."

Barbara gasps.

I continue to tell her what happened next. "After writing checks we go to the post office to mail the bills. When we get home, I fill out a deposit slip for her to put the check in the bank. Then we go to bed. We have the best time ever. She hasn't made me feel this good in a very long time. I should've recognized the clues."

"Clue number one; The following morning, she gets up with me."

"Clue number two; She makes me lunch, then walks me to the door as I'm leaving for work."

"Clue number three; Her youngest daughter, the one I taught how to play tennis, comes to the door. She gives me a huge hug and a kiss, then says goodbye."

"I still can't believe I didn't see the clues."

Barbara gasps again and then says, "Oh my gosh, you poor man."

"There's more to this story. My daughter Natalie was living with me at the time. When she came home from school, the house was empty. Furniture, everything, was gone, even a brand spanking new console TV. I bought it only a week earlier. The only things left behind were the furniture in Natalie's room, and not even a bed for me to sleep in."

"Natalie was standing at the door when I got home from work, crying. To this day, I have never forgotten the look on her face. The tears rolling from her eyes. As I walked up to the porch to greet her, she says, 'They're gone Dad, they took everything, they're gone.'"

"She's devastated, and I don't know why. They weren't nice to her. All I could do was give Natalie a big hug and say, 'That's okay honey, we're better off without them.' I was in a bit of shock, but my daughter needed consoling and that was more important at the time. She takes me into her room to show me the mess they left behind. They went through every piece of the house searching for anything of value.

Besides my clothes, the only thing they left alone was my tools, but they did steal my high school class ring. I figure they sold it for the gold."

"At some point during the confusion, it strikes me to think about the vacation and holiday check. I'd given it to her to deposit. I called my boss to tell him I needed to take the day off. I explained what was going on. I needed to sort things out."

"The next day I went to the bank. The bank, as it turns out, had a policy about cashing checks that were in someone else's name. But there's a flaw in their policy. There's a crook in the bank and it was one of their employees."

"My ex went to a teller who she knew, they were friends in high school. She somehow forgot that I knew her. We had been introduced once, at a nightclub. I spotted her when I was talking to the bank president. I asked him who the teller was who cashed the check. When he told me, I said, she is a friend of my ex-wife's."

"The president called her over. She had allowed my ex to change the deposit slip, allowing her to withdraw half of the funds. Then she let her write a check to her sister from the account for the rest of the funds. The deposit slip didn't have my initials for the change. She had violated policy and he fired her right in front of me."

"Please tell me they gave you the money back."

"I should've insisted that the bank return my funds. But at the time, I wasn't thinking straight enough to make that happen."

Barbara gasps again and says, "And what about those checks that you sent out the night before?"

"The checks that I sent paying off my car, credit card and the rest of the household bills, they were all bad checks. Today I would be in a lot trouble for writing those checks. After leaving the bank, the first thing I did when I got home was to call the creditors to let them know the checks were bad, and tell them what had happened. I told them the same story I told you. Lucky me, they made no attempt to cash them and sent them all back to me at no charge."

"Yet, that's not the end to this story. For the past three months, I had been working seven days a week. The hours varied between ten and seventeen hours a day. I was a foreman at the Nuclear Plant. I supervised a crew of twenty-three craft persons. Because I was working so many long hours, I had turned the bill paying over to my wife. I had no idea what she was doing. But she had written the check amounts in the checkbook, and then gone to the bank to withdraw the funds. The stealing started three months before they left."

"She had this whole theft planned out. She knew exactly when it was time to leave. Right before the shit hit the fan. Two days later, I woke up to find my car was gone, repossessed. Two days after that, I receive a hand-delivered letter from the bank telling me that my house was in foreclosure."

Barbara gasps as I continue...

"There's more unwelcome news. I began receiving letters from the IRS and the California State Franchise Board, billing me for taxes owed. During the three plus years we were married, she refused to sign tax returns. They were never filed for tax years 1983-1986. The IRS was demanding $22,000.00 from me and the State was asking for close to $15,000.00. The tax situation is a story for another time. I get too darn disturbed even thinking about that one because the IRS made me pay them twice," I tell her.

"It's a good thing I was working long hours. Within three months I'm able to bail my house from foreclosure. The repossessed car was sold by the lender at a higher price than I owed. The slate is clean on that one. No hits to my credit. My divorce lawyer, the same one from my first marriage, tells me I should file bankruptcy. But I couldn't do that."

"I tell him, 'No Ted, I have to take responsibility for the bad choice and the mistake that I made by marrying her. It may take me a long time to pay the debts, but they are my responsibility. It's my lesson to learn and I'm not going take the easy way out and file bankruptcy.'"

"He looks at me and says, 'I've never in all my years as a lawyer had a client take responsibility for his mistakes.' Because of it he didn't charge me a penny for my divorce. It took me close to fifteen years to clear the debts."

Barbara's gasping again.

"It's obvious to me now, that my marriages lacked the keys to success: love, commitment, and trust. In no way am I putting complete failure on my wives. I'm responsible for choosing them. The failure was mine, in the choices that I had made."

"It took many years for me to figure it all out. My norm was to go after women who I needed to win over. Always trying to gain their love."

"What do you mean by it being your norm?"

"I figured you might ask that. Those choices were in direct relationship to the relationship I had with my dad. I'd spent the majority of my life trying to win his love. I gravitated toward women who challenged me most to win their love. Those who loved me unconditionally, I pushed away."

"I am okay with not having a relationship with my father today. Even though he's still alive, we've only spoken three or four times since my mom died in 1981. When Mom was dying, she did her best to make me promise to keep the relationship alive. But I told her, 'Mom, it takes two people to make a relationship work, not one.'"

"I have finally come to a place in my life where I made peace with the contract my father."

Barbara interjects, "What do you mean by the contract that you had?"

"It's my belief that we choose our parents, they don't choose us. They're chosen before we come to the physical plane. They're chosen because they accept the responsibility to set us up with our lessons. They help us refine our soul and expand our life purpose."

"Then you know what your life purpose is? I've always wondered what's mine?"

"I don't know completely, and I'm not sure any of us ever do. But most of us seem to keep on looking. What I do know now is that I believe I'm on the right path. My heart's open. I have love and compassion for everyone in the universe. Even for those who have harmed me and never loved me."

"Wow, you are an amazing man. I don't know how you can do it. I'm having a tough time loving my husband right now."

I thought for a moment before replying.

"A few years ago, I sat down and wrote a letter to my father, informing him that our contract was over. I told him that I no longer looked at him as my worst enemy, but as my greatest teacher. Now, whatever you do, don't even think that means I agreed with his methods. For all the bad he did to me, both the verbal and the physical abuse, none of it was ever acceptable in my eyes. And I know it's hard to fathom, but without his hatred and abandoned love, I never would have found my heart. I used to blame my father for my failures and my bad choices. But one day I woke up and realized that I made my choices."

"So how about your relationship with your kids today?"

I hang my head ashamed to tell her, "Not very good."

"Okay, so how about Mia?"

"First we eat. Your burger's getting cold, and don't you need to get home?" I ask, concerned for her welfare.

"I'm in no hurry to get home. The kids are with my mom and my husband is at work, so I would like to hear the story about Mia."

"Okay, I give in. But I'm going to leave some things out because they're longer and not as important. This story is a completely different chapter in my life. I'm not sure where to begin."

She darts back with a quick comment, "From the beginning."

I chuckle and say, "Actually, I'm going to skip towards the end."

"Mia was the first love of my life. She loved me unconditionally. I could do no wrong. Unfortunately, I wasn't ready for that kind of love, so I pushed her away. I found out later, that when Mom was dying, she remained in contact with Mia. Mia had said she was pregnant and for years I thought I might be the father of her child."

"However, since the advent of the computer and the internet, you can find out a great deal about someone, even someone who has died. The other day I put Mia's name in the Google search engine."

"What came up?"

"A family tree, recently updated by her son, Richard Edward. The date of her death is the same day as my mom's, exactly two years later, November 10th, 1983."

"Oh, my gosh, Yianni, that's strange don't you think?"

"Yes, it's spooky strange. Even worse is what I'm about to tell you. When I was with her in '71 she said she was eighteen. I never doubted her because she looked to be that age. I mean, how could she join the Peace Corp for heaven's sake? Guess what?"

"What? Stop holding me in suspense."

67

"Embarrassed to say, she was born March 23, 1956. She wasn't eighteen, she was fourteen. I committed statutory rape and didn't even know it."

Barbara gasps, "Time to let her go?"

"You're right. That's why I skipped to the end. Even though I have fond memories of her, most of them washed away when I read this. Even worse, the little boy I met the first night we went out wasn't her brother. He was her son, born in 1968, conceived when Mia was eleven years old. All of those years thinking I made a mistake casting her aside just washed away. I'm finally over her."

"Yianni, before we go, I have a quick question for you. Do you still think about Terry and Holly? Do you wonder about them?"

"I wonder about Holly. I sure hope she's had a beautiful life since I left. Terry on the other hand, she's happily married. We say hello now and then on the computer. But I've learned so much about life, there's no way I would want to destroy her marriage. Okay, Barbara, that's enough about me," as I glance at the lunch ticket and pull out my wallet to pay the bill. I give the waitress a handsome tip because she kept our water glasses full.

Barbara asks, "Have there been any other women in your life since you divorced your second wife?"

I tell her, "Yes, but I'll tell you bits and pieces of that story as time goes on."

"Okay, I am going to hold you to that. When do we meet again?"

"How about next Wednesday?"

"Perfect."

As we walk outside, I tell Barbara another one of Grandma's secret blessings.

"Yianni, no matter mhat happens myth you in life, you have to regain your power and face life head on every time. If your dad or the world knocks you down, you get back up, regain your power and look them straight in the eye and smile. If you do this, you leave them myth an impression of you that says, 'They can't hurt you.' Remember this, 'Nobody's drama ever has to become yours unless you let it.'"

I wait a few moments in the parking lot and watch Barbara drive away.

Chapter Seven

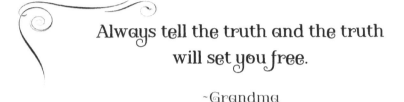

Always tell the truth and the truth
will set you free.

~Grandma

Time drags by for the next few days. Wednesday finally comes. I'm excited to see Barbara and her kids. I recognize they've taken the place of my son and his family. For now, I find it refreshing to have someone in my life, even if they aren't my family.

I arrive at two o'clock sharp. They're sitting on the bench waiting for me. As I approach, Christina jumps into my arms. Charlie and Bobby are no longer shaking my hand, they're taking part in the hugs. Then a nice greeting from Barbara and Vasiliki caps it off.

After the hug-fest is over, the kids are giggling and asking me to start telling a story. Their excitement and enthusiasm have me reeling with joy.

"The next few stories are sad ones, full of sorrow, full of pain. They are a part of this experience that I call life." I encourage them to stop me if they have any questions.

"As you remember, the last story was about Grandma's birthday and Greek Easter. Today I'm going to tell you about the first real tragedy in my life."

Christina jumps in with a question, "What is a tragedy?"

"It is something awful that happens to someone we are very close to."

Charlie, always the comedian, has something to say. "Getting beaten by your father, almost drowning and your grandma not winning 'Queen for a Day,' isn't that a tragedy?"

I sit for a moment, interested that he sees those events as tragedies. Deep down, I know his perception is correct.

I respond, "You know what Charlie, you're right, they were tragic. So listen to this. A few weeks after Greek Easter, Dad convinces Mom that we need to buy a house of our own and move away. They talk about it in detail. Dad suggests they ask Papa for the money. But they weren't going to tell Papa it was to buy a house. They concoct a story that they need money to buy food and clothes for us kids."

Bobby stops me to say, "But that was a lie?"

"You're right Bobby, they were going to lie. This story is about the family lie."

"That evening, Mom and Dad go downstairs to talk to Papa and Grandma. They ask if they could borrow a considerable sum of money. Just enough for a down payment on a house, but they never tell them that's the reason. They tell them it's to buy food and clothes for us kids."

"Papa's first response was, 'Ah Pasha. You're lying to me.'"

Christina asks, "What is Pasha?"

"Pasha is a word that describes disbelief." What it really means is they're full of it, but I don't tell Christina.

"Papa pushes them to tell the truth."

"They stick to the lie."

"Papa, disgusted and angry, says, 'I know you're lying. My answer is NO.'"

"Dad lashes out. He shocks them, and he shocks my mom. 'Then we're moving to my sister's house.' He figured Papa would buckle under. But he's steadfast in his decision. Papa turns his back and walks away."

"Mom and Dad then come back upstairs. I was listening to everything from the top of the stairs. I ran back to my room before they got back."

"Mom and Dad get into a huge fight. Dad tells us kids to go to our rooms. The fight continues, but a few seconds later, I hear a door slam shut. I look out the window and I see Papa heading down the street. Where's he going? Usually where he goes, I go with him."

"An hour goes by, Mom and Dad aren't talking to each other and Dad's drinking a beer. Mom's in her room crying. She knew she'd been deceitful to her father."

"I hear footsteps coming up the back steps. I look out my window and see that it's Papa, with two bags full of groceries. He knocks on the door, but no one answers. I run toward the door and my dad grabs me by the arm. He yells, 'Get back into your room and stay there. Do not open that door unless you want a beating!'"

"It's the first time he's threatened me in years. I run into Mom's room to tell her Papa brought us some groceries. 'Dad won't let us answer the door.'"

"By now Dad is standing in the doorway. He says, 'I thought I told you to go to your room and stay there.'"

"I figured another beating was about to come my way, so I latch on to Mom and she tells my dad to leave us alone. He walks away and goes back to drinking his beer."

"The groceries sat there all night. Early in the morning Dad left for work, so I went to the door to get the groceries. It was cold that night, so nothing spoiled because the night-time air was as cold as the refrigerator."

"That night, when my dad gets home from work, he tells us that at the end of the week we're moving to Art and Clara's. Clara's his older sister, the middle child of twelve."

"Your dad had eleven brothers and sisters?" says Bobby.

"Yes, there were twelve of them. Actually, there could have been thirteen, but one died at birth."

"Wow, that's a big family."

"Yes, but they were many years apart. Dad's oldest sister and oldest brother were gone from home before he was even born. He was the second youngest in the family."

"A few days later, we're saying goodbye to Papa and Grandma. I'm sad. I loved being close to them. They made me feel protected. Going to Art and Clara's was going to be no fun at all. Uncle Art was a drunk too, and was always picking on me. They didn't like me."

"Papa said nothing to my dad. But he spoke to my mom in their language. I don't know what he said, but whatever it was, it made my Mom cry. The trip across the city was very quiet except for Mom, who cried all the way there."

"Art and Clara have one daughter, my cousin Charlene, who was born with cerebral palsy."

"What's that?" asks Christina.

Hmm, how do I explain this one in simple terms? I take a stab at it.

"Cerebral, which means our head that houses our brain, and palsy is a problem or weakness in moving our body."

Charlie says, "So it's a problem with our brain and our body?"

"Yes, that's it. Any more questions?"

They all shake their heads, "no."

"The house is two-stories, with two bedrooms and one bathroom upstairs. A garage and laundry room downstairs. The garage is single car wide, but deep enough for two. To the left under the stairwell, they put a double-wide roll-away. That's where my brother and I sleep. I was very cold in there and they never gave us enough blankets to keep warm. My sister slept with my Mom and Dad in one room. Art, Clara and Charlene slept in the other bedroom. The kitchen's big enough to hold a small table for us kids."

"A few weeks after we start living with Art and Clara, Mom is in a bad car accident. It happens at the intersection of San Jose Avenue and Balboa Avenue. I remember those streets because years later my mom would never drive on them. She would always tell me that we had to drive around them, but never on them."

"What happened to her?" asks young Bobby.

"She's driving down the road toward the intersection. The lady driving in front of her stops at the light, even though it was green. She wasn't moving, so Mom slams on her brakes. Behind her a truck from a company called Montgomery Wards, a well-known company for a very long time, slams on his brakes too, but it's too late. He smacks Mom from behind and shoves her into the lady in front. Mom breaks her back and her neck."

"Did she die?" asks Christina.

"No, she didn't die, but she was in bad shape. She was in the hospital for a very long time after that. We never got to go see her because back in those days, kids weren't allowed to visit. My life became very lonely, except for the next few months."

"Why, what happens for the next few months?" asks Charlie.

"Since school was out for the summer and Mom was in the hospital, I stayed with my grandparents. That's why I was there when Grandma was on 'Queen for a Day.' I hated living with Art and Clara."

"That fall, back at Art and Clara's, we start at a new school, Cleveland Elementary. The only thing I like about my new school is my teacher. I've never forgotten her name, Mrs. Almanor. She was tall with long brown hair, very beautiful in my eyes. I had a crush on her."

Not surprised, Christina asks, "What's a crush?"

I laugh, then say, "A crush is when you think you love someone. You get goosebumps when you think of her." I stick out my arm to show her, even now I get goosebumps thinking of her.

"One of the scariest times in my life happens when I'm in school. I remember that day well. It was March 22, 1957 and there's an earthquake. It wasn't a small earthquake, it was the biggest one since the earthquake of 1906. It was Friday morning just before lunch time."

"My classroom, located on the fourth floor of the five-story school house, shook hard. We were told to duck and cover. Duck and cover was routine at that time. We used to practice once a week. We're under our desks, hands over our heads. The quake is strong enough to cause the blackboards to crash to the floor."

"There's pieces flying everywhere. They evacuated the school, one floor at a time. We stay under our desks until they tell us it's time for us to leave. My brother's class was last out, he was on the fifth floor."

"Once we're in the far corner of the playground, my brother comes running to my side. Everyone had to wait until someone from home came to pick them up. We had to wait for Aunt Clara, who had to walk about four blocks to our school. This was my first earthquake. I was scared for two weeks after. The only time I wasn't scared was when I was either in the bathtub or in a car. You can't feel an earthquake there."

"Living with Art and Clara was horrible. They made us eat everything on our plate before we could leave the dinner table. Aunt

Clara usually cooked my three most hated vegetables. Brussel sprouts, beets and lima beans, they were the worst. Most of the time they would make me throw up, so I used to stick them in my pockets. Once they let me up from the table, I flushed them down the toilet or stuffed them under my bed."

"A few weeks after that, Dad breaks his back in an accident at work. He was working for Borden's Milk Company as a mechanic. He and three other guys were carrying an engine block from one of the trucks. They lost their grip and Dad carried the bulk of the weight and broke his back when they let go. Now both parents are in the hospital."

"I remember hearing Aunt Clara talking to him on the telephone. She says, 'Don't worry about Donald and Chrissy, they can stay with me. Johnny will have go live with Barbara's side of the family. He's too much for me to handle.'"

"Mom called Uncle Alex and made arrangements with him to take care of me. I remember Uncle Alex picking me up. He said, 'Don't worry Johnny, you're better off with us.'"

"For the next year and a half, I was away from my family. The good thing was, I saw Papa and Grandma every day. And I'm back in school with my friends."

"My Uncle Alex and my Aunt Joann treated me as one of their own. I was in second grade. My life was upside down without Mom. While living with Art and Clara, my school work was a struggle. Uncle Alex went to the school to get my transfer papers and my grades. He finds I got F's in arithmetic and spelling."

"Uncle Alex takes the bull by the horn. He tells me he's going to help me fix that. The next night when he comes from work, he brings in a school size blackboard on wheels. On one side, he draws the times tables, on the other side he teaches me spelling. Every night after we finish dinner, we would spend time at the blackboard. He drilled the time's tables into me. He did this until I could answer his problems without writing them down. I became what is now called a calculator. I have never needed to use one because I could do it all in my head. I still do it today. My spelling got better, too."

"He taught me tricks in both spelling and arithmetic. I can't even teach those tricks to you because they're memorized. Spelling is easy when you learn to separate the word into syllables. The next report card, my grades went from F's to A's. It was a fast jump. I never needed Uncle Alex's help again. But he became my hero because of it. I remember telling Mom on the telephone what I had done. She was so proud."

"Uncle Alex was a genius. He did some secret work for the government. Years later, he was responsible for the design to cut and rebuild the carrier, the Midway. It's named the Midway because of the cut at mid-ship. It's here in San Diego, now a museum."

"Have you kids ever been there?"

They shake their head, "no."

"Then one day I will take you there. That's a promise and I always keep my promises." Just another one of Grandma's secret blessing. ***"When you make someone a promise, you always keep it."***

I hear the boys saying, "I can't wait. That will be really neat going there."

"I spend lots of time with my grandparents. When I wasn't in school I was usually up the street with Grandma and Papa. I often stayed with them on the weekends. Papa was always doing wood work projects outside. I'd either help him or I'd collect salamanders."

"What's a salamander?" asks Charlie.

"A salamander is like a lizard, but it has a round head. They don't move as fast as a lizard and they are a bit slimy. I haven't seen one in years. They usually live close to water. They can't live without it."

"There is one downfall living with Uncle Alex and Aunt Joann. He liked going to bars and he was a womanizer. They fought because of it."

"What's a womanizer?" asks Charlie.

"A womanizer is a husband who flirts with other women and cheats on their wife," I say reluctantly, eager to get back to my story.

"Uncle Alex would cheat on Aunt Joann. I was with him one time in a bar when he was with another woman. Kids weren't allowed, but he knew the owner and in those days the police weren't strict about it. He used to tell me to keep it a secret."

"Of course, I did. But one night he and Aunt Joann got into a bad fight. I ran up the street to get Papa. By the time we got back, Auntie

Joann was beat up pretty bad and Uncle Alex was in the backseat of a police car."

"Papa was very mad at him. He held up his fist and waved it at him. As if to say, 'I'm going to beat the hell out of you for this.' He tells the cops to take him away."

"But Auntie Joann would never press charges. Usually she just let him spend the night in jail and the next day she'd bail him out."

"Many years later they divorced because of his womanizing and his drinking."

"Even so, he was very special to me. Thanks to him I can spell and do arithmetic. I've never forgotten him because of that. And that, my friends, is the end of today's story."

Before I can ask Barbara, the kids are asking me when I can take them to the Midway or tell them the next story.

I turn to Barbara, who says, "How about tomorrow, same time and same place?"

"How about tomorrow, ten in the morning and we go to the Midway and I can tell a story there?"

The kids go crazy, "Can we go Mommy, can we go?"

"Sure, that sounds great. We'll meet you here at ten. Can you drive us?"

"Yes, we can all fit in my Lexus SUV."

Then Barbara says, "I'll make sandwiches and bring plenty of water for lunch."

We agree and say goodbye, hugs and all.

Chapter Eight

*The real history of the world is not
in the wars that were won or lost,
but the real history of the world
is in the story of our lives.*

~ Grandma

The following morning at exactly ten o'clock I pull into the parking lot at the park. They're standing by the curb. Before I can get out of my car, the kids are piling in. They're more excited than I expect. I help Barbara unload the food and transfer it to my car. Then I open the passenger door to let her in. Before she gets in, she turns to give me a big hug.

"Thank you so much for taking us," she says, "the kids haven't gotten to do anything fun yet this summer. This will be a highlight for them."

"The pleasure's all mine."

As we drive to the Midway, the kids are super excited about going. I can tell by the way they're talking. As soon as we arrive, Barbara grabs the picnic basket and Christina grabs my hand. We walk to the ticket booth and drop hands just long enough for me to reach into my wallet to pay for the tickets.

I hand them each a ticket and Christina re-grabs my hand. We walk up the gangplank and hand our tickets to the officer at the entrance. Perfect timing, a new tour is about to begin. For the next two hours, we follow the tour guide. The kids are amazed at the jets and helicopters on display at the top deck. They climb into the cockpit. We're having an awesome day.

At some point, Charlie asks me if I was in the military.

"No. At that time in my life, we were at war with Viet Nam. I was in college on a draft deferment."

"What's a deferment?"

"A deferment is like a hall pass. You only keep it until you're done with it."

"Oh, I understand. It means that when you're out of college, you get drafted."

"Yes, that's correct. At the end of my first year of college, the government changes the draft to a lottery system. In the first year, anyone eighteen or older, was eligible for the draft."

Charlie asks, "Even the girls?"

"No, at that time girls weren't allowed in the military. The draft was only for the guys." I continue to tell them that they put 366 ping pong balls into a bingo basket. They start with January 1st. They pulled 366 numbers, because some people are born on a leap year, February 29th. When they get to my birthdate, June 18th they pull number 341."

"That first year, everyone from one to two hundred and twenty-six was drafted. Everyone else went into the mix for next year. At the end of the year, they drew new lottery numbers for kids who were eighteen and not in our draft lottery. We keep our same number."

"That year, the eighteen-year-olds were drafted first. Everyone eighteen years old was drafted, unless they had a medical or college deferment. They never got to 341, so I was never drafted."

"My best friend Charlie got the number six in the lottery, but he kept his college deferment. Three days after graduation, he was drafted. When he goes for his draft physical, they find that he has a double hernia. He was sent home to get it taken care of. His doctor told him, you've lived with it this long, we can leave it alone and you won't have to serve. So, that's what he did."

Charlie spoke up, "Our daddy was in the Army. He went to Iraq once, and the second time somewhere else in the Middle East, but we don't know where because he won't talk about it. It was after that trip that he started drinking, Mommy said."

Not in his father's defense, I tell him, "Charlie, people do strange things when they come back from the war." Then I tell him, "My grandpa served in World I as a machine gunner. I didn't know that for many years, long after he passed away. There's one picture of him that I have engraved in my mind. He's standing with another man in uniform, full dress, World War I style hat on, standing tall and proud to be an American. I wanted to know about the war, but the war had left him with some mental scars."

"Did he get shot?"

"No, but my grandma was always persistent in telling me not to ask him about the War. She told me something that has stuck with me about wars. She said, *'Yianni, the real history of the world is not in the wars that were won or lost, but the real history of the world is in the story of our lives. Those stories are our battlefield.'*"

"I believe that we come into this life with various lessons to learn. We either learn them or we don't, but when we do we should share them. They are our stories. I guess that's what has driven me to share them with you."

"Papa was in World War I. He held the rank of Private and was a machine gunner in the 151st machine gun battalion. They were attached to the 84th Infantry Brigade. They were one of many battalions in the US Army's 42nd Rainbow Division, under the command of Major General William A. Mann. Before MacArthur took over command, he once said this about the Rainbow, 'Such an organization would stretch over the whole country like a rainbow.' The division had soldiers from twenty-six states, including the District of Columbia."

"The division was activated in August 1917 and after training at Camp Mills in New York September 5th until October 18th, 1917. They boarded the Navy ship the SS Covington and landed in St. Nazaire, France November 1st while the rest of the 142 Division landed in Liverpool, England."

79

"From February 17th through June 21ˢᵗ, they trained with the French. In early August of 1918, the command of the Rainbow is turned over to Colonel Douglas A. MacArthur. The division marches into the Argonne battle on October 11ᵗʰ, and then the most notable battle fought by the Rainbow transpires October 16ᵗʰ, 1918 at a hill called Cote de Chatillon. They successfully assault the German defenses. Because of this battle, the United States establishes a place at the peace table."

"The Rainbow Division saw more days of combat than any other division in the war and they suffered 14,683 casualties. Thank God, Papa was not one of them. He did, however, receive an honorary medical discharge because he suffered five percent mental distress because of the war. For the rest of his life, he received close to fifty dollars per month for his injury. However, for many years the nightmares continued. Because of the nightmares, we were never allowed to ask him about the war. Grandma didn't want the nightmares to come back."

"Thanks to the internet and the National Archives, who sent me his pay records and excerpts from the archives, I could piece together this part of Papa's time while he was in the Army."

With nothing left to say about Papa, the kids scatter about the top deck of the carrier to check out the planes and helicopters some more.

Barbara and I sit and talk. I ask her how things are going with her husband Ray.

"Not very good. He's angry that I brought the kids with you today. He never wants to take us anywhere and I just don't know how much longer I can keep up the fight."

"I'm no marriage counselor that's for sure. I mean with two failed marriages and multiple failed relationships, I usually wait for the woman to give up on me."

"You mean, you've never broken off with someone?"

"No, I did it quite often. But I took the coward's way out. I disappeared and stopped talking. They usually got the message."

"Oh Yianni, I can't believe you did that to anyone. That's a horrible thing to do to do!"

"You're right, it's gutless. And now it's payback time for all those times that I disappeared since that's the path my son Ryan is taking. Karma, what can I say? Paybacks come when we least expect them."

"Do you really believe there's such a thing as Karma?"

"I do. I absolutely believe it, but sometimes we never know when Karma will rear its ugly head."

"Is there anyone you wish you had treated better?"

"Oh my God. The list is too long to tell, I've forgotten some of their names. Sure, there's Holly, Terry, Cherry, and the one I hurt the most is Janet, my high school sweetheart. We met up after my second divorce. We had a few awesome weeks together just before Christmas. One day she calls to leave a message on my phone asking what to buy my kids for Christmas. Things moved too fast for me. She scared me away. I never answered her calls. She finally gave up a few days before Christmas."

"Oh, Yianni, that's terrible."

"Yes, it's terrible, because I never told her why. I just wimped out and walked away. I regret never telling her the reason why."

"Maybe you should tell her now?"

"I tried finding her. This was the second time I crushed her. I don't think she'd forgive me again."

"Is that how you feel about your situation with your son?"

"No, I don't know what forgiveness is needed to make things right between us. I forgive him because he's my son and I love him. I have no idea what I've done, so I just keep loving him."

"I sure hope you find out one day and he's not too hurtful, or mean to you for whatever it is. He just needs to be an adult and step up to receive your love and kindness. I know you have a big heart and he, his wife and your granddaughter are missing out on the real you."

"Perhaps you're right. Now back to you. Quit changing the subject back to me," I say with a laugh. "What are you going to do about your situation with Ray, or am I prying too much?"

"Okay, I will tell you about how things are between Ray and me, but before I do, I have one more question to ask you about your son."

"And your question is?"

"What about inheritance? You do have an estate that your children will inherit when you're gone, don't you?"

I do, but I'm not sure how I'm going to distribute it yet. "Most people think inheritance is economic gain. Money in their pockets or in their bank account."

"However, my grandma's attitude about inheritance had nothing to do with money. I heard Grandma tell my mom, my aunts and my uncles just after Papa died, '*Inheritance is not something you earn from the privilege of being someone's child; inheritance is something you earn when you understand the person who provided for you had an open heart and that they loved you. The honor of being loved by them is your true inheritance. You get nothing more than their love and you get nothing less than their love.*'"

"That was my first lesson and blessing from Grandma related to unconditional love. You get just their love. That's why many years ago, I made the decision regarding all three of my kids, 'I'm just going to love them. Nothing more and nothing less. If they choose not to accept my love, that's their fault, not mine. That is their inheritance.'"

About then, Christina shows up to say, "Mommy, I'm hungry."

"Shall we take a break?"

"Sure. I'm hungry and thirsty too. If we can get the boys to break away from the airplanes and helicopters long enough, we can have lunch together."

Barbara hands me a bottle of water and then goes to gather the kids. I could see they were having a wonderful time. The boys more so than Christina, but she was having as much fun as a little girl her age could. I know she enjoyed today's story. She always enjoys my stories, I think to myself as I watch Barbara gathering the last stray.

As we're eating lunch, the boys are reeling with excitement. They ask, "Mr. Yianni, have you been on any other real Navy ships?"

"You know boys, it's interesting you ask that. I was just thinking back to a time when I was in my thirties. I was in San Francisco for a Pipefitter conference. At the time, I was the President of the Pipefitters and Plumbers Union here in San Diego."

Before I can say anything else, Christina pops into the conversation and says, "You were a President?"

I take a couple of seconds to explain to her that I wasn't President of the country, but I was the president of an organization.

"Oh," she says.

Then I continue telling them that the conference in San Francisco lasted five days and when the weekend came, my girlfriend at the time came to San Francisco to tour the city with me.

"On Saturday, we had lunch at my favorite restaurant on Fisherman's Wharf. After lunch, we walked all around Ghirardelli Square and the different piers. When we get near Pier 39 there's a Navy destroyer tied up alongside the dock with a sign saying, 'Open to the Public.'"

"I ask my date if she wants to go aboard. She says, 'Sure, I've never been on a ship before and my son's in the Navy. Why not?'"

"As we walk up the gangplank, we're greeted by some of the sailors dressed in their whites. I know you kids are going to ask me what whites are, so let me tell you, They're white uniforms. All white with a blue tie, white sailor caps, and any decorations they might have received. If they were officers, their uniform contained the proper number of bars based on their rank."

"Just as we reach the boarding deck of the ship, we are greeted by an officer who is welcoming us aboard. We gather with a group of people who were there a few minutes before us and wait about ten minutes for a few more to come aboard."

"Once the proper number of guests are on board, they announce the start of the tour. They ask us to stay very close and not to wander away from the group. Our first stop is at the bridge. We see the wheel and the various control systems, but those that don't reveal any top-secret stuff. Soon after we leave the bridge, we pass through a corridor and I hear sailors playing basketball. I turn away from the group to walk toward the basketball court, as I recognize the voice of one of the sailors. A sailor steps in front of me and says, 'Sorry sir, this area is off limits.'"

"I tell him, 'I recognize the voice of one of the guys playing as a guy I went to high school with. I actually played basketball with him in high school.'"

"What's his name, Sir?"

"His name is Bob Marlin."

"The sailor says to me, 'What's your name sir? I'll tell Captain Marlin you're here.'"

"I tell him my name and then my girlfriend says to me, 'I can't believe you recognized his voice.'"

"While we're waiting, I say to her, 'If he comes out, you'll understand why it was easy to recognize him. He has a very distinct voice.'"

"Sure enough, a few seconds later, the sailor comes back and announces, 'Captain Marlin will be right out, sir, as soon as he towels off.'"

"By now the group is long gone, out of our sight. A few minutes later, 'Captain Bob Marlin,' my friend from high school, comes out, puts his big right hand in mine and shakes my hand like an officer and a gentleman."

"I introduce him to my girlfriend and then he takes us on tour of the ship. Much different than the one the other folks were on. He showed us the engine room, the officer's quarters, the galley, and he even offered us some food."

"However, we had to explain that we just had lunch at the Fisherman's and our stomachs were full."

"He then asks about the restaurant. He says they are in port for the next three weeks and his wife was coming to visit. He wants to know if it's a good place to take her."

"I said, 'Bob, I was born here in San Francisco and that's the only restaurant I would ever take a date to. They have the best Crab Louie salad you will ever eat, plus they keep bringing sour dough bread and real butter, until you tell them to stop. The same goes for your drinks. I've never had one of their desserts. Sour dough bread from San Francisco with real butter is dessert to me.' 'That does it, I'm taking my wife there.' Then he asks how long I'll be around."

"I explain to him that we were leaving around noon tomorrow, Sunday. Captain Marlin takes us to the gangplank, shakes our hands and says to me, 'I'm really glad you recognized my voice. It was an honor and a privilege to show you my ship.'"

"I've never forgotten that day kids. For me, it was a bigger honor to see my friend, happy to serve our country with honor, respect, honour and Love of our Country."

Then Bobby says, "I'm going to join the Navy when I get bigger."

I tell him, "Well Bobby, you've got plenty of time ahead of you to make that decision. Just make sure you join for all the right reasons."

Christina's curled up in a ball in her mom's lap.

Before I suggest that we leave, I think about what a treat it's been finding this family. I hold them near and dear to my heart. No different than I would if it was my son's family. I have a great deal of compassion and love for them.

Compassion is one of those blessings from Grandma.

"Make no judgments about anyone or any circumstance that surrounds you. We all have our own path, our trials, tribulations, decisions and lessons. It's mhat we do myth them that make the journey of life all worthwhile or not."

I suggest that we head for home. I try to help Barbara by carrying the food, but Christina jumps into my arms and says, "Mr. Yianni, will you carry me to the car, I tired."

How could I say no to this precious gem? I held her in my arms, imagining how good it would feel if this was Aubrey Rose. But I'm honored that Christina felt comfortable enough to ask me to carry her to the car.

After loading everyone into the car, I open the front passenger door for Barbara, hand her Christina, and the two of them gift me with the memory of their smiles melting my heart.

On the drive home, I'm expecting the kids to be settled, tired and quiet. Not so. They were bursting with joy and laughter. They kept asking when we could do something like that again.

When I pull into the parking lot, they did get me to commit to our next story day. I'm seeing that these kids enjoy hearing my stories. Since today's Wednesday, I need at least one day for rest, so I ask how they feel about meeting Friday.

Everyone says, "Yes."

Once we're out of the car, I help Barbara transfer the picnic basket and the remaining water to her car. To my surprise, as I go to open the door, her older son, Charlie, reaches up to give me a giant hug. He says, "Mr. Yianni, today was one of the greatest days of my life. I have always wanted to see a real Navy ship and those airplanes and helicopters were awesome. I have some models just like them hanging from a string on my ceiling. My dad helped me build them, long before he started drinking."

For a second my heart sinks. My dad never helped me build anything. That moment with Charlie touched my heart. The good news is that his memory of his dad before he was drinking was a good memory, and I thought he should do his best to keep it.

I tell him, "You know Charlie, I spent most of my life harboring ill feelings toward my dad. You might do the same thing one day. But anytime you start thinking about the bad in your dad, take ten seconds and think about the time you were making models with him. Making models with him should be one of those good times that you remember."

I want to tell him another one of Grandma's secret blessings regarding memories. The timing isn't right because everyone's tired, so I thought it would be best to save it for another time. But I couldn't help but remember Grandma telling me to cherish the good memories and to forget the bad ones.

She blessed me by saying, *"Yianni, the good memories help to mold our happiness. Hold onto them. By holding on to the bad memories, at some point in our life they become the ones that destroy our soul."*

Chapter Nine

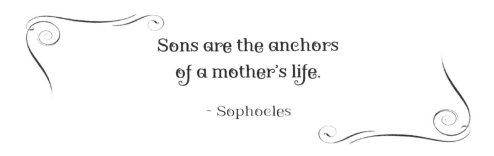

Sons are the anchors
of a mother's life.

~ Sophocles

Friday morning. I'm ready to see Barbara and the kids. I decide to go the park a few minutes earlier than usual, as I want to make sure I get that bench under the oak tree. I bring Rascal and a clean handkerchief today, because I'll probably shed some tears.

Within seconds, I see them coming. I notice Vasiliki's with them too. As they approach, I stand up to greet them. Before I get a chance to say anything, Christina hugs my right leg and says, "What story are you going to tell us today Mr. Yianni?"

"That's a secret. I don't want to give it away."

"Okay," she says with a slight sound of disappointment in her voice.

I finish greeting them and then Vasiliki asks me, "Are you telling these stories in chronological order to your life?"

"Not all of them," I tell her.

"I know your husband passed away a few years ago, but what was his name, out of curiosity. It seems we have many family names in common."

"His name was Spiro," says Vasiliki. "Do you have Spiro's in your family?" she asks.

"I do. My great-grandfather's name was Spiro. My grandfather's full name was Lambro Spiro Meta and his first-born child was Spiro Lambro Meta." I just shake my head in total disbelief. I can't believe how small this world is. Thank God I stopped believing in coincidences.

The kids are ready for the story. I set the stage. I ready my handkerchief and before I utter a word, Christina's waving her hand.

I turn to her as she asks, "Why do you have that white hanky?"

"I don't want to give away my story. You'll know soon enough," I say with a chuckle.

I gather my thoughts. This is a hard story for me to tell. It causes me a great deal of pain. I take a long deep breath, look to the sky and then say, "Shall we begin?"

There's a resounding "Yes!" loud enough to be a yell.

"In late 1957 Mom flew to the Mayo Clinic for her back and neck surgery. The plan was to pin her back and her neck, so she could retain some mobility. She makes medical history with this surgery. It's the first surgery of this type. No doctor has operated on a patient with both a broken back and a broken neck. Mayo Clinic's the most renown hospital in the world at that time, but there would be a long recovery after the surgery."

"Mom was gone close to seven months. She comes back in a full body cast, from her neck down to her knees. Her arms and hands are mobile. Her knees to her feet have movement. There's a small opening so she could go to the bathroom in a bed pan."

"I can remember seeing her in that body cast as if it were yesterday. Mom smile from ear-to-ear when she sees me. I reach up to kiss her, but she could hardly move. She is strapped to the bed, to protect her neck during the flight home."

Tears roll down my cheeks, so I take a moment to wipe my them, then continue. "Thinking back, my Mom was the bravest person I've ever known, plus she was my best friend."

As I wipe away the tears, Christina says, "Mr. Yianni, don't cry. Your Mommy was really brave, and you have to be brave, too."

This child is so in tune with me.

"The first day Mom came home, we were living in our new house, located in Daly City. It was a Bolger home, built by the Bolger

Construction Company. I have no idea how they got the money to buy that house, but I have a feeling that because of the accident, Papa gave it to them. He would do anything to make Mommy happy."

"That was the first day I'm back with the family. It had been close to two years since we were separated. It's probably what made me so distant from my brother and sister for most of my life."

Vasiliki stops me with a question, "How about today, are you close to your brother and sister today?"

"Today I'm somewhat close to my brother, however my sister still lives in Kansas and we don't communicate much at all. We might trade Christmas Cards or Birthday Cards now and then, but that's about it. My sister and I just never had much in common. We have different views about life, so I don't have much to say to her. I know that's not the way it was meant to be. We didn't bond as children, or as adults, for that matter."

Then I went back to the story.

"I know Mom's medical bills were being paid by Montgomery Wards. It was determined that their driver was at fault for the accident. The lady in front was guilty too. However, that wasn't determined until a couple of years after the accident."

"A hospital bed was brought to our house for Mom to lie on. It would be thirteen months before she could get the body cast off, sometime around the beginning of 1959."

"They hired a nanny to take care of her and us kids. Dad was recovering from his broken back and wasn't able to move her around. Grandma wanted to take care of Mom, but she was too small. She wasn't strong enough to turn her over or lift her to put the bed pan under. Grandma was the perfect choice to watch over us kids. But that wouldn't sit well with Dad."

"Kora was our nanny. She's a nice black lady, short and squatty, but very strong. Not as short as Grandma, but stronger. My brother teased me about my new school. He would say, 'It was a round school for square heads.'"

The kids start laughing.

"I have no trouble making new friends. I have one friend, Sammy, he's black like Kora. I believe it's these two-people who taught me not be prejudiced. They're people to me. Their skin color makes no difference. It's what's in a person's heart that matters most."

"Daly City is only a few miles away from San Francisco. On weekends, I would stay with Papa and Grandma. Usually Auntie Genie would come to visit Mom, then take me to the city with her whenever she left. If it wasn't for Mom, I would have rather stayed living with or near them."

"When I was with them, Grandma would send me to the Chinaman's store to get her beer and cigarettes. We called it that because the owner was Chinese. It was never said with disrespect. The owner's daughter was one of my Mom's good friends growing up and they went to the same high school after Mom left the Greek school."

"Grandma loved her beer and her cigarettes. Like Mom, she smoked too much. Grandma smoked Raleigh cigarettes. A coupon came with every pack. She could buy toasters or coffee machines with them."

"Grandma gave me the empty beer bottles. I would turn them in at the Chinaman's for a nickel each. With a nickel, I could buy my favorite Hershey candy bar and for a dime, I could add a soda pop. That's how I got hooked on soda."

Charlie jumps in, "You could buy a candy bar and a soda pop for nickel and a dime?"

"Yes. And, the candy bars were twice as big as they are today."

Vasiliki backs me up and tells them it was true.

"Papa on the other hand, was not much of a beer drinker and he didn't smoke cigarettes. He drank his wine. He made his own wine, which he made for many years. My Mom used to tell me the story about his wine-making days. When she was a teenager, she would come home from school and would have to spend a couple of hours crushing the grapes, sharing turns with her brothers and sister in the vat."

I notice Bobby waving his hand, "What is it, Bobby?"

"What is a vat?"

"Excellent question. That was the same question I had when Mom told me the story. A vat is a round shallow tank. Papa's vat was made of redwood. It was about three feet deep with a wine crusher on a spindle in the middle of the tank. As Mom explained it to me, she had to tie a rope connected to the spindle around her waist and walk in a circle, counter-clockwise around the vat. Between the crusher and her feet, the grapes were crushed until there was only liquid. Papa would make wine and Raki, a strong Greek alcohol. No one ever told me the rest of the process. But I remember seeing the vat in the basement of the middle house."

"Mom hated her turn in the vat. She hated it because it made her skin turn purple. She told me she used to beg Papa and Grandma not to send her to school during wine season. She was afraid her friends would see her purple feet and make fun of her. Her skin was permanently stained from crushing the grapes. No matter how much she scrubbed them, no matter what she tried, she just couldn't clean the stains. Papa made wine every year until he died. Greeks from all over the city enjoyed his wine, especially during the holidays."

"Even I liked his wine. To this day, I haven't found a wine that tastes as good as Papa's. It's a taste I've never forgotten."

"I was always finding ways to make money. In school, science was my favorite subject. We studied biology and I got to look through a microscope. I wanted one for myself, but there was no way I could ask for money we didn't have. One day I was at the dentist's office for a checkup. I spotted an advertisement in a magazine. By selling fruit and vegetable seeds, I could get could get a microscope if I sold enough."

"I asked the dentist if I can have the magazine. He told me yes. After the visit, when I get home I cut out the advertisement and filled out the application."

"Mom heard me rustling about looking for the scissors and asked me what I was doing. I didn't tell her, but I did ask her for a stamp so I could mail something. Without asking me any more questions, she told me to get her purse, so she could give me stamp. Once I got the stamp, I licked it and placed it on the envelope."

"Without saying a word, I ran out of the house, down the street corner to put the envelope in the mail slot on the corner post. But there was just one problem. I was too short and squatty to reach it. I kept jumping up, hoping to get high enough to throw it in the slot. But I couldn't jump high enough to make it."

"One of the neighborhood ladies was walking her dog. She noticed me jumping up in the air with this envelope dangling from my fingers.

She asked if I need help. I handed her the letter and she put it into the slot. Then she asked, 'So what was so important in that post?'"

"I'm sending off for some fruit and vegetable seeds for the garden, so I can sell them and make enough money to buy a microscope."

"'Oh, how sweet,' she said with a smile. 'Make sure you bring them to my house so I can buy some of them for my garden,' as she points to her house located right there on the corner."

"'I will,' I said, then I ran back home."

"A couple of weeks later, one day the mailman knocked on the door. In those days, the mailman came to your door. Usually he put the mail in the slot in the door. But he couldn't put packages in the slot, so he knocked. I answered the door and he's holding this package with my name on it. As he handed it to me, he says, 'So Johnny, what's in this package?'"

"I hold my fingers to my mouth to signal to him not to talk too loud, as Mom was sleeping and I didn't want her to hear me. Then I told him, 'It's vegetable and fruit seeds that I'm going to sell them so I can get a microscope.'"

"He says, 'Open it up so I can be the first one to buy a package from you. I'll give them to my Mom to plant.' They were twenty-five cents."

"When I close the door, Mom yells out from her room, 'Who was that at the door?'"

"It was the mailman, I'll bring you the mail."

"When I got to her room, Mom noticed the package under my arms. 'What's inside that package?'"

"It's a package full of fruit and vegetable seeds for the garden."

"What? Are you going to plant a garden?"

"No, I'm going to sell them so I can make enough money to get a microscope."

"You're going to do what?"

"I tell her again."

"Then she says, 'Who are you going to sell them to?'"

"'All of the ladies in the neighborhood.' I am confident that I will."

"Mom laughed and then wished me good luck."

"A few minutes later I went next door to sell a pack to Mrs. McCusker. She's glad to buy them. Then I went to the house on the corner and knocked on the door. The lady answered, and I said, 'Hi, I'm Johnny from down the street. I'm that little boy you put the envelope in the mail slot for. Would you like to buy some vegetable and fruit seeds?'"

"How much are they?"

"'Twenty-five cents per package,' I tell her."

"Then she asks, 'How many packages do you have?'"

"Thirty."

"She says, 'If you can tell me in three seconds how much that adds up to, I'll buy them all.'"

"In less than two seconds I blurted out the answer, 'Seven dollars and fifty cents.' She had no idea I could add faster than a calculator. All of that work with Uncle Alex paid off."

"She then said, 'You're absolutely correct, let me grab my purse to pay you.' As she handed me the money, I handed her the box full of seeds."

"I was gone for less than fifteen minutes. When I returned to the house, I told Mom that I sold all the seeds. She can't believe it. She called me her little 'entrepreneur.'"

"What's that?" asks Christina.

"An entrepreneur is someone in business for themselves," I told her, then continued.

"It's hard watching Mom suffer in the body cast. She's always yelling out with pain, especially when she has to go to the bathroom. Kora would turn her over on her belly so she could go, then turn her back to her stomach where she lay most of the time. She'd always be itching too. She'd ask me to squeeze my arm down through the cast to scratch her back."

"I never said no. I really loved my Mom and I would do anything for her. The only thing I hated more than her being in that cast was her smoking. My Mom smoked her whole life. She started when she was just eleven years old. I hated it. There she was, laying on her belly, body cast and all, and still smoking. It made me sick, because I knew she was killing herself."

"I told her all the time, 'Those things are going to kill you someday.'"

"Did they kill her?" asks Charlie.

"That's a story for another day."

As I continue, "One day I was hanging out with my Jewish friend, Georgie. He lived a couple of blocks away, across the main thoroughfare known as Westlake Blvd. Georgie's dad owned a small corner grocery store. We were goofing around in his garage, which was full of things for the store."

"Georgie told me, 'Whatever you do, don't touch anything in here. My dad knows exactly how many things there are. This is inventory for the store.'"

Before I can go on, Charlie's asking me what an inventory is. I explain to him that an inventory is the goods that a store owner buys with his money, so he can sell them to his customers to get their money. They turn into profit. And before he can ask the question, I explained what a profit is.

"Anyhow, as we we're messing around in the garage, I notice these small packages of Ludden wild cherry cough drops. There were two cough drops in the package and they sold for just two cents. I did something I knew I shouldn't do, I took one box and stuffed it in my pocket. A few minutes later I was telling my friend Georgie I needed to go home."

"On the way home, I popped both of those cough drops into my mouth. I remember, they tasted very good. When I got home, I went straight to my room, because I knew the cough drops had made my tongue turn cherry red. I didn't want Mom to catch me. I walked quietly past her room, but I wasn't quiet enough, because she heard me."

"Mom yelled out, 'What have you been up to young man?'"

"What I didn't know was that Georgie's dad had called her. She knew exactly what I had done, and by the tone of her voice, I knew I was in trouble."

"Knowing I was busted, I went into Mom's room crying because the guilt was too much for me. However, at that same moment just before I left my room, I remember one of Grandma's secret blessings regarding the 'truth.' I heard her saying it to me then, just as I am telling it to you now."

"Yianni, the most important thing we have in our life is our integrity, our honesty. Always tell the truth, because the truth will set you free."

"Seconds later, Mom is asking me again, 'What have you done, Young man?'"

"I tell her the whole truth and nothing but the truth. She tells me to get her purse and to bring it to her. Which I did."

"Mom opens up her purse and hands me a dime, then says, 'Take this to Georgie's dad and pay him for those cough drops. Then tell him he has my permission to punish you however he sees fit.'"

"Did he spank you?" asks Christina.

"No, it was something worse than that," I tell her.

"When I get to his house, I tell him everything that I did. I tell him Georgie warned me, but I didn't listen."

"Then he tells me, 'This Saturday, I want you to come here to my house and work for me. I will show you then, what it is I want you to do for your punishment. Now go home and don't come back her again, until next Saturday.'"

"When I get home, Mom asks me what he said."

"I tell her, 'He said I have to come back to his house next Saturday to do some work for him.' I tell her I will tell her more on Saturday. And then I went to my room, afraid of what might happen when my dad finds out. But Mom never tells my dad what I did. She knew that he might beat me if he knew. She kept this one a secret all the way to her grave."

"Saturday finally came. I was at Georgie's at the exact time his dad told me to be there. He took me to the garage and tells me he wants me to move the entire inventory from one side of the garage to the other. He tells me that there had better not be anything missing or there would be a higher price to pay. For most of that Saturday, close to seven hours, I work moving things from one side to the other. I'm only given a break whenever I need to go to the bathroom and about noon, when Georgie's mom brings me half a sandwich and a glass of milk."

"When I tell Georgie's dad I was done, he comes into the garage to inspect my work."

"'Excellent job,' he tells me. Then he says, 'Now go home and never come here again. You are no longer welcome in my home.'"

"He then turns to Georgie and says, 'Find yourself a new friend.'"

"That was a tough lesson for a boy my age. But it was an important lesson, one that I learned and remembered my whole life. It was the last time I ever stole anything, and it was the last time I ever lied, too."

"In January 1959, Mom finally got that awful body cast off. Instead of flying her back to Mayo Clinic, the doctors flew here to remove it at San Francisco University hospital. Because she was the first person to be pinned, they were very particular as to who should remove them."

"As Mom told the story, first they took off the body cast. Then they removed the pins. Mom was in a wheel chair at the hospital for a few weeks before they finally stood her up for the first time."

"Kora was no longer our nanny, because she didn't like being around my dad without my mom as a buffer. They got into an argument one day, so she quit. A few weeks later, Mom comes home and Grandma Lil comes to help. She's was Mom's best friend Ginny's mom."

Chapter Ten

"Every weekend they let me, I spent with Papa and Grandma. Papa was always teaching me about the world. He would say, 'Yianni, someday when you get older, make sure you get a good education so you can get the best job there is.' Papa always wants the best for me."

"When I stayed with them, I slept in his bedroom. Sometimes I'd sleep with him. He and Grandma slept in separate rooms. Her room was across the hall. They never slept together, and I never knew why. Every now and then he would sneak to be with her, but only when he thought I was asleep. Then he would sneak back into the room with me."

"Papa always made me feel safe and secure. In March of 1959, I spent my last night with Papa. It was Saturday morning March 23, 1959. I woke up and spotted blood on Papa's night shirt. He wore these night shirts that were sleeveless and were made of cotton. They had ridges, vertical from top to bottom. They were made for comfort, but they were not made for holding blood."

"I woke him up, 'Papa, Papa, you're bleeding!'"

"He responds, 'Shush, don't let Grandma hear you, I don't want her fussing about the blood.' As he climbs up from his bed, he pulls his shirt over his head. He says it again, 'Don't tell Grandma about the blood. Don't tell her about the blood,' he repeats a few more times, expecting me to promise."

"I knew it was a promise I would have a tough time keeping. Still in my pajamas, I walked through the carpet doorway to the kitchen and sit down. Grandma's busy cooking breakfast, so I sit at the table with my head buried in my arms. I didn't want her to see me, because I was sobbing, but I was being very, very quiet about it. At least, so I thought."

"Grandma says, 'Mhat's the matter myth you? Why are you hiding in your arms?' I'm doing my best to honor Papa's request and not say anything about the blood. I stay silent, with my head buried in my arms."

"She speaks to me again. This time she pulls my arms away from my head, 'Mhat's the matter myth you and mhat's taking Papa so long to come to breakfast?' When she pulls my arms apart, she sees my eyes are filled with tears. She knows something's wrong, so she heads toward the hallway."

"I jump from my chair and run past her. I spread my arms and legs across both sides of the hall to stop her. 'No, you can't go there. Papa's taking care of the blood.'"

"Whoops, I said it."

"Grandma yells, 'Mhat blood?' Then she pushes me aside and goes into his room. Seconds later, Grandma comes out. She yells, 'Yianni, run down the street and tell Alex to get here myth his car.'"

"On the way, I grab my coat. I run down the street as fast as my little squatty legs will go, putting my coat on as I run. The house is less than half a block away. Within seconds I'm running up the stairs. Before I get to the door, Uncle Alex is standing in the doorway. I shout, 'Papa's bleeding! Papa's bleeding!'"

"Without saying another word, I turn around and run back down the stairs. No sooner did I get into the house, then the telephone rings. Grandma tells me to answer it. It's Mom calling to tell me what time they're going to be there to pick me up. I begin crying and tell her Papa is bleeding."

"She says, 'Put Grandma on the phone.' I hear the echoing sounds of the ambulance heading this way. Sirens in San Francisco are heard for miles. The sound of the siren bounces off the hills. Uncle Alex called them, and he got to the house seconds before the ambulance arrived."

"Soon after that, Mom was there too. The ambulance guys came in to check Papa. They carried in a gurney. When they saw how big Papa was, they knew there was no way they could carry him out. In those days, they didn't have rollers on them."

"They tell Mom and Grandma he needs to get to the hospital right away. Papa's adamant he won't go in the ambulance. They agree he can ride with Alex, who would follow them. Everyone's helping Papa get into Alex's Cadillac. I want to go, but they tell me that kids aren't allowed in the hospital."

"Before they leave, Papa takes me into his arms. He hugs me tight and tells me how much he loves me. I was really scared. I have no idea this could be the last time I see him alive. I remember seeing them drive down the hill. Papa turns to wave at me one more time. He's looking over his right shoulder, he waves goodbye. I stand there in the middle of the road, waving my arms wildly and yelling my last goodbye."

Tears roll down my cheeks. I stop telling the story long enough to grab the handkerchief to wipe my tears. Before anyone could say a thing, I continue telling the rest of the story.

"Papa was in the Veteran's Hospital in Livermore. Livermore is about an hour away from San Francisco, located across the bay, southeast of San Francisco. Mom went every day with my aunt or my uncle to see him. My dad, being the ass that he is, has no desire to take her. That was his way of saying he didn't care if Papa lived or died."

"It had been less than one week since I saw Papa. On March 29th, just before midnight, the telephone rings, so loud it woke us up. I can hear Mom run to the phone, sore back, sore neck and all. She gets to the phone within seconds, and seconds later she screams out, 'Papa is dead, our Papa is dead!' I knew it before she even said it. No one ever calls our house this late at night. My heart sinks deep into my soul. I feel the pain as she yells it again, 'Our Papa is dead!'"

"I run to console her. Before I can get there, my dad grabs me by the arm and tells me to go back to my room. 'Just let her be alone. Leave your Mommy alone.'"

"When he lets go of my arm, I ignore him. I run to be with her. She grabs me into her arms and she hugs me. We rock back and forth as she says, 'What are we going to do now that our Papa is dead?'"

"Dad comes into the room and says, 'I thought I told you to leave your Mommy alone. Go back to your room.'"

"Mom yells at him, 'You go back to your room and leave us alone. He's not going anywhere.'"

"We sit together for a few more minutes, then Mommy tells me to go to my room. I crawled into my bed and continued to cry. I cried in silence, then I cried out loud. My brother Donald, not much of a crier himself, opens the covers on his bed and says, 'Come here, tonight you can sleep with me.' We hadn't slept in the same bed together since living with Art and Clara. This was the last night we ever slept together again. Donald just knew I was in pain."

I grab again for the handkerchief. I'm struggling to stop the tears. I'm sobbing almost as much as I did the night Papa died.

Done crying, the story continued.

"The next morning, I woke up feeling lost and all alone. I couldn't help but think what would happen to me now that Papa has died. Who will stop my dad from hitting me now?"

"There was a lot that had to be done that day. Mom was busy making the funeral arrangements and the rest of the family were notifying the Greek community and all of Papa's friends. By the afternoon, every Greek in the city knows that the Big Greek of San Francisco has died. He'd no longer be seen carrying large lumber loads or beams on his shoulders."

"It was time to go to the mortuary to view Papa's body. Once in the car, Dad announces he's taking us kids to Clara's house. He says, 'This is for grownups. Kids aren't supposed to go to funerals.'"

"No way, I am going to see Papa and you're not going to stop me. I'm not going to Clara's."

"Then my brother says it too."

"Mom takes control of the situation. She says to Dad, 'Chrissy is too young to know what's going on, but Johnny and Donald are old enough. They have the right to be there.'"

"Dad didn't like it and put up a good argument, but Mom had made the decision. She put him in the position where he has no choice except to agree with Mom. She knew Grandma would want me there, too."

"This was one of the most intense times in my life. I had never seen a dead person. His body lay still in the casket. I kept waiting and hoping he would open his eyes. I kept watching his chest, expecting him to start to breathe. He just lies there, lifeless, not even a breath, not even a whisper. Reality sets in that I am never going to see Papa's smile again."

"As I stand before his casket, I whisper, 'It is only you and me here Papa, but I need to know who's going to protect me now. Who will watch over me? Who will protect me from my evil father now that you are gone, who?'"

"He just lay there with his eyes closed and said nothing. It's then that I realize he is really gone. I start weeping, strong and loud. Grandma comes up and grabs me by the hand. I stand frozen, as she whispers in my ear, 'Come myth me Yianni. Come myth Grandma.'"

"At the same time Grandma is taking me by the hand, my dad comes and grabs me from behind, clutches his arms around the center of my body and says, 'I want you to go sit in the car young man. You're embarrassing the family.'"

"Grandma turns to him. She looks him in the eye, with her fist clenched, her arm up in the air ready to punch him, as she says, 'Mhat's the matter myth you, he's grieving like the rest of us. Leave him be.'"

"Mom walks up to my dad. She's had enough of him. Mom tells him, 'You need to go outside and leave my family alone.'"

"We spend a couple of hours in the mortuary. We greet the Greeks and friends who came to say goodbye. Most of them walked up to Grandma or to me, because they all knew how much he adored me. They knew he was my protector and my best friend."

"For two days, we went to the mortuary and just spent the day viewing his lifeless body. I remember the second day I began silently questioning where Papa had gone. I kept saying, 'God, where is Papa now? Please watch over my Papa, God.' There was a part of me that felt he was still there and there was a part of me that knew he was gone."

"On the third day, we arrived at the mortuary to watch my uncles and a few family friends carry Papa's casket to the limo. Uncle Deso was here from Philadelphia. He never shed a tear. He was quiet and humbled by the loss of his dad. They had gone sideways a few years before. I wonder how he felt now that Papa was gone. Grandma, Uncle Vic, Uncle Alex, Uncle Deso, Aunt Genevieve and my mom got into the limo. The rest of us went to our cars. I want to go with the family, but Dad insisted, 'No.'"

"They put signs on our car that said, 'Funeral Procession.' Everyone turned their headlights on, even though it was mid-afternoon. First in line was a cop on a motorcycle, then the hearse carrying Papa, then the family limo, and then one car after another fell into line. No one stops for a red light, the cop, each time he gets to an intersection, holds back the traffic. This was the way it was done in San Francisco in those days. It was a way to respect the dead and a day for the city of San Francisco to say goodbye."

"From the mortuary, we head west away from downtown San Francisco, past the avenues, then south to the Greek cemetery and mausoleum, in Colma, California. Colma's known as the 'city of the dead.' All the cemeteries are there."

"The Greek priest gave the last rites to Papa, as family and friends paid witness."

"After the last rites, we get back into our cars as Papa's casket is taken to the Golden Gate National Cemetery. He was buried there, instead of the Greek cemetery with the rest of the family, because he was a military veteran from World War I."

"When we get there, his casket is transferred to a horse-drawn hearse, covered by an American flag, just like the one the future President John F. Kennedy was taken in a few years later. Another story for another day."

"The casket is removed from the hearse near the grave site. This time, my uncles and Papa's friends watch, as members from the military carry his body to his grave. It's here that Papa is laid to his final place of rest. The bugler plays 'Taps,' the military officers give him a 21-gun salute, and then the flag is removed from his casket. They fold it without a wrinkle and present it to Grandma saying, 'Thank you for his service.' The Greek priest says a final prayer. The whole burial ceremony takes just a few minutes. But to me it's an eternity. My Papa is gone."

"When it's over, everyone walks to the casket for one last goodbye. Some place a flower on Papa's casket. Some bend down to kiss it. Soon, everyone has gone to their cars. No one sees me stay behind. I stand at Papa's casket. I'm having one last conversation with Papa. The burial guys are watching from the sideline. Everyone's driving away. I didn't want to leave. I couldn't say goodbye."

"As Grandma's climbing into the limo, she spots me standing there all alone. She rushes to my side."

"Yianni, my little Yianni, come myth me. It's time to leave Papa to rest in peace."

"By now Mom realizes that I'm gone. She's back in the car with my dad and brother. She spots Grandma taking me by the hand. Without a word, she knows I'd be going with her. The ride to Grandma's house is quiet. Grandma holds me close to her, holding me tighter than she ever held me before. She knew in her heart we were both filled with pain."

"Once we get to the house, the Greeks of the city and their friends begin showing up with food. It's like Greek Easter, but instead of us feeding them, they're feeding us. Everyone was laughing and telling stories about their favorite memories of Papa. I couldn't understand why everyone was so happy. I sure wasn't. I went to Papa's room. I could still smell his sweat as I lay on his bed."

"Grandma realizes I'm nowhere to be found and comes looking for me. She finds me lying on Papa's bed, crying."

"Grandma says, 'Mhat's the matter myth you?'"

"Now that Papa is dead, who will protect me Grandma? I know he'll start beating me again."

"Grandma says without hesitation, 'I will, I will always be here to protect you. I will watch over you now, and will watch over you after I die. You will never be alone, and he won't ever hurt you again.'"

"Yeah, right, how can you protect me? You're so little, you're less than five feet tall and he's over six feet tall. How are you going to protect me?"

"Yianni, I want to tell you a story about the women from my country. This is an old, old story, but the women of my country are very strong. My mother told me this story when I was young like you. Now is an appropriate time to share it myth you. After I tell you this story, you will know that your Grandma, no matter mhat, will be watching over you. This is the story of 'The Legend of the Castle.'"

"I'll do my best not to butcher it too much, but this is how I remember the story."

ৼৡৡ

The Legend of the Castle

A heavy fog, much like we have here in San Francisco, shrouded the valley for three days and three nights. It covered the river completely. After three days and three nights of this fog, a strong wind arrived to blow the fog away and the mountains could be seen again. Up on the mountain there were three brothers at work building a castle. For some reason, the foundations that they built during the daytime, collapsed at night-time. Because the foundations kept collapsing, they could never finish building the castle.

One day, an old man walked by as the men were working and he said to the three brothers, "I wish you success in building the castle."

The three brothers said to him, "We wish you success, too old man, but we aren't having much luck building the castle. Day after day, we work hard and build up the foundations, but at night the foundations collapse." Then they asked the old man, "Do you know what we can do to make the walls stay put?"

The old man puts his finger and the thumb from his right hand up to his chin and laughed as he said to the three men, "Yes, I do, but it would be a shame if I tell you."

One of the three brothers said to the old man, "Let the shame be ours, because we are the ones who want to build the castle."

The old man reflected a while, then he asked them, "Are you married? Do you each have a wife?"

"Yes, we are married," they replied, "each of us has a wife. But tell us what we must do to build the castle."

"If you really want to finish the castle, you must swear never to tell your wives what I am about to tell you. The wife who brings your food to you tomorrow must be buried alive in the wall of the castle. Only

then will the foundations stay put and last forever," the old man said to them, just before he walked away.

The oldest brother broke his promise and told his wife everything the old man had told them, then told her not to come to the castle with their food the next day.

The middle brother broke his promise too, and told his wife everything.

Only the youngest brother kept his word and said nothing to his wife at home. The next morning, the brothers rose early and went off to work. They cut lumber with their axes, they crushed rocks, and the walls rose as their hearts beat faster and faster.

The mother of the three brothers knew nothing of their plot. She said to the wife of her oldest son, "The men need bread and water and their flask of wine, daughter-in-law."

She replied, "I'm sorry, dear mother-in-law, but I really cannot go today. I am sick with flu."

The mother then asked the second wife, who answered, "My word, dear mother-in-law, I cannot go today either, I must visit my parents today."

The mother then turned to the youngest wife, saying, "My dear daughter-in-law, the men need bread and water and their flask of wine."

The third wife got up and said, "I would be happy to go today mother-in-law, but I have my young son to feed my milk to and I am afraid he will cry when I'm gone."

The mother-in-law told her, "You go ahead."

Then the other two daughters-in- law told her, "You go, we will look after your boy. He won't cry."

The youngest and best wife stood up, fetched the bread and water and the flask of wine, kissed her son goodbye on both cheeks, and set off to bring food to the three brothers. She climbed the mountain and approached the place where the three brothers were busy working.

When she reached the men, she said to them, "I wish you success in your work, gentlemen!"

But something was wrong. The force of their axes stopped making noise, their hearts were beating faster and faster, and their faces turned white as snow.

When the youngest brother saw that his wife was coming, he hurled his axe into the valley and cursed the rocks and walls.

"What is the matter, my husband, why are you cursing the rocks and walls?" she asked.

The older brother-in-law smiled at her grimly and the oldest one declared, "You were born under an unlucky star, sister-in-law, for we have sworn today we will bury whomever came to feed us alive in the wall of the castle."

Then she said, "Then let it be, brothers-in-law."

The brothers, amazed by her answer, as she then said, "I have one request to make to you. When you wall me in, leave a hole for my right eye, a hole for my right hand, a hole for my right foot and a hole for my right breast."

Then the brothers asked her, "Why?"

She said, "My small son, when he starts to cry, I will cheer him up with my right eye as I wink at him. I will comfort him with my right hand as I reach out to him. I will rock him with my right foot and I will feed him with my right breast. Let the milk from my other breast turn to stone, so the castle walls will be strengthened. With the milk from my breast my son will become strong, he will be a great hero, and he will even become the ruler of the world!"

They then seized the poor young woman and walled her into the foundation of the castle. This time the walls do not collapse. They stay put and rise higher and much stronger. Even today, at the foot of the castle, the stones are still damp and mildewed from the tears of the mother's one eye as she weeps for her son and the walls are streaked white from the milk still oozing from her one breast.

"Grandma then tells me the moral of the story."

"The women from my country are taught at a very youthful age that they are the foundation and the strength of the family. The woman is the one who holds the family together. She does mhatever it takes to protect those members of the family whom she loves, those members she holds near and dear to her heart. You are the most important member of the family that I hold dear to my heart Yianni. Always

remember this story, so that you will know that Grandma is always watching over you."

Before I have the chance to tell the rest of the story, Vasiliki turns to her daughter and her granddaughter and says to them, "My mother told me this same story when I was just a little girl. I had forgotten it until Yianni told it to us just now. Remember this story, because it is we, the Greek women of our family, who hold the foundation of our castle, our home as we call it, together. Our castle is only as strong as we are," she says, as she throws a wink in my direction.

I knew from that wink that she was telling her daughter, Barbara, that the strength of her family was all up to her.

At that same moment, I knew this was by far one of the most treasured of Grandma's Secret blessings, now at work, not just watching over me but also watching over them.

Then Christina says, "Mr. Yianni, tell the rest of the story about your Papa."

I continue...

"After finishing the story, Grandma says to me, 'Enough tears. It's been three days and now we celebrate that our Papa is gone.' She reaches out her hand and says, 'Go myth me upstairs and no more tears for Papa. I'm watching over you now.'"

"I didn't eat much food that day. Greek Easter was only two weeks away and I wondered if we would even celebrate it now that Papa was gone. As it turns out, we never celebrated Greek Easter ever again."

"As the day came to an end, I realized that Grandma was going to be all alone for the first time in her life since coming to America. But how silly was that? Uncle Victor is still living at home. But he was withdrawing too, now that Papa was gone."

"I convince Mom to let me stay with Grandma. I knew she would need me more than ever now. Mom agrees, especially since there's no school for a week. It was Easter vacation. I spent the next five days with Grandma. At the end of the week, Mom brought us both home for the weekend."

"It was a traditional Easter. It was a family tradition that Saturday night before we go to bed, we hide a carrot wherever we want the Easter bunny to leave us a surprise. I woke up Sunday morning to find a dump truck loaded with candy. Soon after breakfast, we walked to the Lutheran Church behind the house for Sunday Easter service."

"We sat there listening to Pastor Charlie tell us about the death of Christ and how he died for our sins. I had little comprehension as to what a sin was and only thought that what he really meant was that he died for our souls."

"After church, I took my dump truck and proceed to play alone in the backyard. I didn't want to be around anyone. There was nothing for me to celebrate."

"At some point Mom happened to look out the back window. She spotted me just sitting there, all alone. The back window was open, and I heard her say to Grandma, 'I don't know what to do with our Yianni, Yianni Capedoni. I'm worried about him. He's so withdrawn from the rest of the family. I know he's scared now that Papa is gone. He's afraid there is no one left to protect him from his dad. He's so afraid he might hurt him again and I'm afraid too, because this time I'm afraid he might kill him.'"

"Grandma tells her, 'Don't you worry myth that. ***Even though our Papa is gone, I will be watching over him, guiding him, comforting him and protecting him from now on, until the day that he dies.***'"

"Mom stared at her in disbelief, she said nothing, only thinking to herself that her mother is two inches shorter than herself and many years older, so how in the heck is she going to do that?"

"At the time, I had no idea that this was by far Grandma's number one Secret Blessing."

I wipe my face to clear the leftover tears, blow my nose and put my hanky away. "Enough sadness for one day," I declare.

I notice Barbara and Vasiliki wiping their eyes too. Vasiliki tells me, "I am so glad I came today. I can see your love for both your grandfather and your grandmother was deep and very special. From the sound of things, I believe their love for you was just as strong."

I nod in agreement. Not much else to add. This story took a lot out of me.

Barbara recognizes that I'm exhausted. She tells the kids it's time to go. However, before they do, they all come up to me and thank me for sharing today's story. I can tell it touched their hearts.

Charlie and Bobby say they wish they had a Papa like mine. And then Christina, bless her heart tells me, "I love your grandma, just as much as I love mine."

Vasiliki was just a few feet away when she said it. Out of the corner of my eye, I could see that she had tears of admiration in her eyes.

I see Grandma is still blessing us, because this child is one of her shining stars spreading joy and love in our direction.

Then Barbara asks, "When do we hear the next story?"

"How about we meet at the park next Tuesday at two?"

Before anyone can answer, Vasiliki says, "How about Sunday at my house and I'll prepare a Greek feast?"

"Can't say no that. Sounds great to me. How about the rest of you?"

"Yes, yes!" they all respond with a roar.

Then I ask Vasiliki if she has a fence around her backyard and if it would be okay for me to bring Rascal along?

"Yes, absolutely, it will be great for you to bring him. I know my grandkids are as fond of him as much as they are fond of you." Then she gives me her address and we say goodbye.

Chapter Eleven

When someone steals from us,
they take a piece of our soul.

~ Barbara Meta

I'm anxious for Sunday because it's been a long time since I had a home-cooked Greek meal. Vasiliki promised a Greek feast. I'm sure she's fixing all my favorites.

I stop at the local flower stand underneath the highway in town to pick up a bouquet for Vasiliki. I feel it'll be a nice gesture on my part to arrive with flowers. I decide to pick up a bottle of wine from the Von's grocery store, which I pass on the way.

As we pull up in front of Vasiliki's house, Christina comes running out to the car to greet us. She jumps into my arms, gives me a big kiss on the cheek, and then asks if she can take Rascal to the backyard. I hand her his leash and off they go.

Seconds later I'm greeted at the door by everyone except Vasiliki. She's standing at the kitchen stove, with her favorite Greek apron on that says, "Zorba the Greek." Definitely fitting. Zorba the Greek is one of my favorite movies from the sixties, starring Anthony Quinn, an all-time favorite actor. I think it's because he reminds me of Papa. I hand her the flowers and the wine. As expected, they're a big hit.

The aroma in the house takes me home to Grandma's. I'm able to piece together the different Greek foods that she's cooking, just by the aroma.

She and Barbara scoot me out into the backyard with the others, while they continue preparing the meal. When I get outside, I'm surprised to find Ray standing near the tables. Of course, he's smoking a cigarette and drinking a beer. We shake hands and before I get a chance to say much more than "hello," the boys and Rascal come running to my side.

The boys want a hug and Rascal decides he needs to get right in the middle of it all. Only away from me for less than five minutes, he acts like I've left him all alone.

"He's definitely spoiled don't you think?" I ask the kids, to which they agree.

Then they grab his leash and continue to run around the yard. I'm thinking to myself, "I hope they wear him completely out."

Ray heads toward the ice chest to get another beer and asks me on the way, "Would you like a can?"

"No, thanks, I don't drink."

"Not at all?"

"Not at all. I haven't had more than two six packs of beer in my lifetime and I only have a glass of red wine on special occasions, like today."

He shakes his head in disbelief, "Why is that?"

"Well, if you remember my story about my childhood beating, my dad was just a mean drunk. I decided I didn't want to be anything at all like my dad, so I just never drank. Plus, I never liked the taste of beer and how it made me feel. I feel bloated whenever I drink it."

"Oh," he says without saying another word.

A few seconds later Barbara comes outside to see if I would like anything to drink. I happily settle for a cold glass of water with a hint of lemon. Then I ask for a small bowl of water for Rascal.

As she turns to go back inside, Ray grabs her by the arm, jerking her half-way around as he says, "What, you're not going to ask me if I want anything to drink?"

Barbara looks at me as she says with confidence, "You know where your beer is, and you seem to find it just fine without help from me."

I throw her a big wink out of the corner of my left eye. I recognize her response has the strength of a woman who's in control. *Bravo to you Barbara,* I'm thinking.

For the next fifteen minutes, I watch the kids play with Rascal.

Barbara and Vasiliki emerge from the kitchen, their arms full as they carry out the food. I ask if I can help, to which Vasiliki replies, "That would be great," as I notice her throw a look toward her son-in-law who doesn't even open his mouth to offer a hand.

It only takes the three of us one extra trip to gather the food. It smells fantastic, and as I expected, she cooked all of my favorites, Dolmades, leg of lamb, spanakopita, string beans in domatoe sauce (thinking of Grandma saying it), and of course my favorite of all, Moussaka.

Barbara opens the bottle of wine and pours us each a glass. Her husband Ray waves her off when she goes to pour his, so she says, "No problem, more for us."

"The food is fit for a king, or at least for Zorba the Greek," I said.

Vasiliki says, "No, not Zorba the Greek, today it's Yianni the Greek." This brought a smile to everyone sitting at the table. Even Ray cracked a bit of a smile.

Rascal's a gentleman. He doesn't beg anyone for a taste. He just lies at my feet, waiting patiently until I finally slip him a morsel of lamb.

At one point in the meal, the kids get a little loud. Ray decides it's time to end the noise. He turns to them and says, "You know the rules at the dinner table. Kids are to be seen and not heard from. Put food in your mouth and you won't be able to talk."

I can't believe what I just heard. I thought I just heard my dad talking. That was his favorite saying. But I can't hold back. I say with kindness in my voice, "You know, when I was a kid, those were the exact same words my dad used to say." Before I continue my sentence, I notice Ray smiling and seeming to pat himself on the back.

I continued, "But as a kid, I hated him for that. My friends all grew up with parents who felt the dinner table was a place for the family to talk about their day. Not to be seen and not heard from. Not to put food in their mouth just so they couldn't speak."

Ray says nothing, but I could see, and I'm sure everyone else could, that he was no longer proud of himself and seems to be a bit embarrassed.

I change the subject and tell Vasiliki how much I'm enjoying the food.

"Are you ready for dessert?"

"Dessert? No way, not right now, I'm still enjoying the main course, plus I need to let this digest before I can even think about dessert."

"Okay, after you tell us another story."

The kids and Barbara all follow with encouragement and I notice Ray feeling a bit awkward and uneasy, but I say, "Okay, a story it is."

"Yippee, yippee!" says Christina. "What story are you going to tell?"

"Today I am going to tell you about the next ten years or so of my life."

"As you remember, the last story I told you was about my experience as an eight-year-old boy losing Papa. I'm sure you remember, I was afraid about what would happen to me after Papa died. Grandma assured me I never have to worry. because she'd always be watching over me."

"Christmas 1959 was special. Mom won her lawsuit, so she bought my brother and I our first bicycles. They were Western Flyer's, fire-engine-red with streamers hanging out of the handle grips. She also bought me a tether ball for the backyard."

"Unfortunately, Christmas 1959 ends up being not so merry. After the unwrapping was finished, we were told to gather up the wrapping paper and hand it to Dad to put in the fire place. Mom told him that it was Christmas and he needs to take care of the wrapping paper without us. Dad was pissed because he has to do it while my brother and I get to take our bikes out for a spin."

"When we get back from our ride, we put our bikes in the garage. Dad's there finishing the cleaning and he gives us the stink-eye and then tells us to make sure we park our bikes on the far side of the garage so he can still get the car in. My brother and I look at each other with funny looks, as if to say, "He never parks the car in the garage, why now?""

"He's still peeved because he was stuck cleaning up the Christmas mess, while we get to have fun. After we get into the house, I decide to check out my new tether ball. I already pulled it and the rope from the box earlier. When I go under the tree to get the ball and rope, all that's there is the ball and no rope. I start looking around for the rope, but find it's nowhere to be found. Even Mom tries to find it."

"When my dad comes in from the garage, Mom tells him that he must have picked the rope up when he was cleaning up the mess. He's perturbed with her insinuation that he lost the rope and immediately tells me that I lost the rope. He tells me to go in the garage and look through the trash. It takes me close to an hour digging through the two trash cans but I never find it."

"Dad blames me for losing the rope. Late in the afternoon, he tells me to go into the garage to get some firewood. When I get back inside the house, he gives me permission to put one of the logs on the fire. When I open the screen, as I'm putting the log on the fire, I notice part of the tether ball rope. Dad put it in the fireplace when he built the fire. Instead of accepting the blame for putting it there, he continues to blame me. Just another example of how I could never do anything right in his eyes. He spoiled my Christmas with his inability to accept responsibility for burning the rope."

"The day after Christmas was a Saturday and there's a track meet going on at the high school three blocks away. My friend Sammy and I meet up for a bike ride. I told my parents where I was going, and my dad warns me to keep an eye on my bike."

"When we get to the track meet, we decide to watch the races. We lay down our bicycles and walk a few feet closer to the track. We were only there about ten minutes, but at some point, I turn around to check on our bicycles and I notice that mine is gone. I go wild, looking everywhere for my bike. Everyone around me helps to look. I had it one day, and now it's gone. Not only am I heartbroken, but I know there's going to be hell to pay for losing it."

"It doesn't take long before I give up looking, so I go home. As I walk up to the house, my dad spots me without my bike. He's in the garage, doing what he does best, drinking a can of beer. As I walk in, he grabs me by the arm, swings his loose arm at my behind and he says,

'Dammit, I told you to keep an eye on that bicycle. We'll never buy you another one. You'll have to buy the next one with your own money.'"

"Mom's disappointed in me, too. She doesn't get mad, but she backs Dad when he tells me I'll have to buy the next one for by myself. 'This is a lesson that you'll have to learn from,' she said."

"Did you buy a new bicycle?" asks Christina.

"Yes, I did, about three years later when I earn enough money selling 'Green Sheets' on the street corner."

"What's a Green Sheet?"

"I guess Green Sheets were before your time. A green sheet was the evening San Diego Tribune newspaper. They were sold on street corners by us kids as the drivers were heading home from work. They cost a dime. I'm sure you remember them, Vasiliki?"

"Yes, I do. My husband bought one on his way home from work every night."

Then I continue with the story...

"Mom's still going to the San Francisco University Medical Center for therapy. One day after physical therapy she comes home and tells us that her doctor, Dr. Hanson, said we should move to southern California. He convinced her it would be a much warmer and dryer climate. He told her that if we continue living in the Bay Area, that year's later Mom will feel aches and pains in her bones that will become unbearable. All of this, because of the moist and foggy air that constantly surrounds the San Francisco Bay Area."

"Mom made arrangements for her and Dad to go to San Diego to check it out. They fly down for a weekend and find a house here in El Cajon. They paid cash and arranged for a swimming pool to be built too. Mom couldn't wait to tell us."

"While they were gone, I stayed with Grandma and my brother and sister stayed with Aunt Clara. When I was with Grandma, it was kind of a dismal time, now that Papa's gone. She used to cry out loud for the loss of Margarite, but now she cries out for Papa. I woke up one morning when she was moaning out loud, 'Oh my Lambro, my Lambro I miss you so much. I will be myth you in less than ten years. Wait for me Lambro, I will be there soon.'"

"I hated it when Grandma got like this. I went into the living room where she was sitting in Papa's chair. I jumped up on her lap, faced her, and gave her a big kiss and hug, as I told her, 'Grandma, you're not alone. I'm here with you and I love you more than anyone in the world. You're my Queen and you can't ever leave.'"

"I was so afraid about what was going to happen with Grandma if we moved to southern California. Then I said to her, 'Grandma you're not going to die in less than ten years. Stop that talk. I don't ever want you to go away.'"

"She responded, 'Oh my Yianni, Yianni Capedoni, your Grandma's not ever going to leave you.' We sat there a few more minutes in a deep embrace."

"Then Grandma gets up to fix breakfast. While she's in the kitchen, I look at the picture of Papa on the wall and the picture of Margarite. For a moment, I knew I was sharing Grandma's pain. When we sat down at the table to eat our breakfast, I asked Grandma if she knew anything about the afterlife."

"She shrugged her shoulders, and then said, 'That's where Papa and I will be after I die. Don't you worry, one day when you die, we'll be there waiting for you.'"

"It's likely this is another one of Grandma's secret blessings, but I won't really know until the day I die."

"In 1960, President John F. Kennedy was inaugurated. We're packing for the big move. For the fifth time, I'm going to a new school. I'm really sad about leaving Grandma behind. She'll be too far away to visit and too far away to call on the phone. But Mom tells Grandma anytime she's ready she can come and be with us."

"When we leave San Francisco, a big piece of my heart is left behind. Everyone who has ever loved me is in San Francisco. Tony Bennett's famous song, 'I left my heart in San Francisco,' makes me cry whenever I hear it."

"Grandma decides to go with us for a few weeks when we leave for San Diego. Our furniture and all of our belongings are transported by a moving van, owned by friends of my parents."

"Uncle Spiro, the son-in-law to my sister's godmother, drives the Oldsmobile to San Diego. We're flying to San Diego. I sit with

Grandma on the PSA Electra jet. Once we're on the plane, I ask Grandma if she's is scared."

"Grandma reminds me, 'Don't you be scared Yianni. Remember, Grandma will always be myth you. I am your protector now.'"

"However, while flying to San Diego something happens. Grandma looks out the window and spots one of the jet's engines is on fire. She says nothing to me, but she calls over the stewardess and points out the window towards the engine, without saying a word."

"I remember seeing the stewardess nod, but then she says to Grandma, 'Oh that's nothing to worry about. That's normal for the engine.' She gives Grandma reassurance everything is okay. There's no sign of fear in her voice. A few seconds later she's in the cockpit telling the pilot. They play it down and about fifteen minutes later we land in San Diego, safe and sound. We never do find out what was really happening with that engine."

"A few hours later we arrive at our new home. It's the beginning of September, 1960. The house has three bedrooms and two bathrooms. Mom and Dad have a large room, in the far side of the house, on the northwest side. My sister Chris has the room next to theirs, and Don and I have the one on the opposite side of the hall, next to the bathroom. The swimming pool construction has been started, but it would be about five weeks before it would be done."

"Unfortunately for us, it was an inconvenient time to move. We arrived during a Santa Ana condition. We've never been in temperatures this high. It's dry and our blood is thick from living in San Francisco. The temperature is above 100 degrees. Hot winds blow in from the Northeast, from Santa Ana, thus the locals call it a 'Santa Ana condition.' It was too hot to cover up at night. We were miserable. We didn't get much sleep the first two weeks. Grandma couldn't take it, so she had to go back to San Francisco the second week."

"Soon after we arrived in El Cajon, an interesting sequence of events transpired. I often question what happened. Three months after we moved in, Pastor Charlie becomes the pastor at College Lutheran Church, in La Mesa. One month later, Dr. Hanson, the doctor who cared for Mom, moves to La Mesa. He's a partner at La Mesa Internal Medicine, and becomes our family doctor for the next thirty-seven years."

"I often wonder if this was a coincidence that both Pastor Charlie and Dr. Hanson end up there, or was it all a friendly conspiracy?"

Laughing, Vasiliki says, "They were just your Mom's soulmates."

Without responding, I knew she was right.

"My new school is two blocks away. I have no trouble making friends. In the following spring I try out for Little League Baseball. I was considered an eleven-year-old only because I would turn eleven during the season. I made the major leagues. Hit two home runs in tryouts and never hit another one again. I came close a couple of times, but most of the time I ground out or I struck out. I love baseball, but it never was my game."

"I was doing good in school. I was a human calculator, thanks to Uncle Alex. The teachers are amazed at how fast I can finish a test and not miss one question. They're so amazed that after 5th grade they meet with my parents to suggest that I skip 6th grade. They want me to move directly into 7th grade at the Junior High School."

"Mom's really proud of me. She tells the teachers that the decision is up to me. I decide not to skip. I want to stay with my friends. The next year was going to be an exciting time in my life as an American. The first manned spaceship would take off for outer space. Eventually, we see the first astronaut walk on the moon."

"It was an exciting time. Since we only lived two blocks away, I convince my teacher to let me go home with one of portable TV's. It was an awesome moment in time."

"Soon after April 1961, there's an incident going on between the United States and Cuba, known as the 'Bay of Pigs.' Russian Premier Khrushchev is threatening to join Cuba and back what would have been World War III. My teacher, Mr. Rodley, is so concerned that he, along with a lot of other Americans, built an underground bomb shelter on his property. All of the talk about the Russians coming has people really scared. One weekend he gave us a tour of his bomb shelter."

"That same year, Mom opens the Lutheran bookstore with some help from Pastor Charlie. She's away from us for six days a week. The only day she isn't at the bookstore is on Sunday, and after Church she's usually too tired to do anything else. We never did things as a family. We weren't much of a family."

"Dad's drinking more now. He's getting meaner and his demeanor shifts to anger at the drop of a coin. Whenever friends come to visit, I would do my best to be invited back to their house every chance I can get. It's easy to convince Mom, who would always say 'okay.' Dad on the other hand, would always say 'no.'"

"Mom decides I don't have to ask him anymore. 'If it's okay by her, then he didn't get a vote,' she would say. She was taking a stand, doing her best to gain back her power. She's the breadwinner of the family and she makes the decisions as to what I can or can't do. Because of this we grow closer, but Dad and I continue to move further apart."

"By the following summer, we're acclimated to the warm temperatures. The pool takes care of those sizzling summer days. During the summer of 1962, I pick up a tennis racket for the first time. I play my first tennis tournament, in the El Cajon championships and I win the age twelve division. Mom is super proud of me. I used the tennis racket she got with Blue Chip Stamps she collected from the grocery store and the gas station. My picture was in the local newspaper, and she circles the picture and writes, 'Bought with Blue Chip stamps.'"

"At eleven-years old, I start working for Mom at the bookstore. She put me on the payroll and gave me a paycheck. I made $1.50 an hour. My brother, on the other hand, went to work for Tom, the owner of the local Speedee Mart two blocks from our house. Speedee Mart was the original name of the chain that we now call Seven Eleven. My brother's making $1.00 a day and only works on Saturdays."

"Two years later, now thirteen, I was in the Speedee Mart picking up some bread and milk. Tom, the owner asks me, 'Hey John, do you want to work for me this summer, like your brother did the last two summers?'"

"Immediately I say to him, 'It depends, how much you gonna pay me?'"

"I'll pay you the same thing I paid your brother, one dollar a day."

"I laugh, then say, 'No way. If you want me to work for you, you'll have to pay me two bucks an hour.'"

"He laughs, then says, 'Yeah right, minimum wage is only fifty cents, what makes you think I'd pay you more than that and what makes you think you're worth two bucks an hour?'"

"Work me for a day and find out for yourself."

"Okay," he says, "show up Saturday and we'll see how well you do."

"Sure, but you're still going to pay me two bucks an hour."

"Okay, but only if you're worth it."

"I show up that Saturday at eight. He lines me up with what he thought was a full day's worth of work. Then he returns to the cash register to take care of the morning customers. Five hours later I walk up to the cash register and say, 'Okay Tom, I'm done. That will be ten bucks for five hours of work.'"

"There's no way you could be done. I gave your brother less than that to do and he never got done in eight hours."

"Check it out for yourself."

"I remember seeing his eyes almost pop out of his head. He says to me, 'Okay, come on up to the register and I'll give you ten bucks.'"

"We get to the register, as he's reaching in for ten bucks he says to me, 'You can work for me anytime you want this summer and I'll pay you two bucks an hour.'"

"No thanks, I'm gonna work for my Mom for a buck fifty."

"So why did you come to work for me today, if you planned on working for your mom all along?"

"'Because you had to be taught a lesson,' I said, with no disrespect."

"He laughs and says, 'So what lesson is that?'"

"'When you pay a buck a day, you get a buck's worth of work. When you pay two bucks an hour, that's what you should get in return,' I said, while pointing at the backroom."

"He just shakes his head in total disbelief. Then he says, 'I can't believe I let a thirteen-year-old kid teach me such a valuable lesson about business.'"

"Unfortunately for him, he wasn't a very good businessman and not very smart at all. A few years later he lost his franchise for selling alcohol to a minor."

"No, that minor wasn't me."

"Later in the year, November 22, 1963, President Kennedy was assassinated. We were taking a spelling test when we heard the news. In the middle of the test, the Dean came to the classroom door to speak to our teacher. He gave us the word to spell and then he went to the door to find out what was going on. When he comes back to the front of the classroom, he announces in his normal stern voice, 'The President of the United States has been shot.'"

"We all thought he was giving us the sentence that preceded the word he asked us to spell, which was 'abroad.'"

"Someone yells out, 'What was the word you asked us to spell?' The word abroad wasn't in that sentence so we were all a bit confused."

"Then he says, 'No, you don't understand. The President, John F. Kennedy has been shot.'"

"Immediately kids began crying. Others sat in disbelief as he explains to us that they're sending us home from school early. Those who were within walking distance could go home and those who take the bus will be leaving as soon as they can get the buses back to school. I lived within walking distance, so I headed for home."

"It was an interesting parallel in life for me. For the next three days, the only thing on television was related to the death of President Kennedy. Having experienced the death of Papa a few years earlier, all of my emotions came flowing back. We watch with the rest of the world as they lay President Kennedy to rest."

"I can still picture the day the funeral procession began. There's a horse drawn hearse carrying the casket just like the one that carried Papa at Golden Gate cemetery. My thoughts were no longer about the President, my thoughts were about Papa. Tears streamed from my eyes. When the bugler sounds 'Taps,' I cry even more. Same with the twenty-one-gun salute, even though it was on TV. They then show the earlier shot of his son, little John-John, saluting his father as the hearse carrying his casket passes by. It's at that very moment, I realize I never said goodbye to Papa. I went to my room and bawled like a baby. Mom knew that I was having a tough time and came in to see how I was."

"She tells me she was re-living Papa's funeral too."

As I wipe the tears from my cheeks, I turn to Vasiliki and say, "How about we take a break and have some of those desserts you cooked up?"

"That sounds like a great idea."

She and Barbara go into the kitchen to get the desserts. When they come back they're carrying a pan full of Baklava and a basket full of Kourambiedes.

"I'm in seventh heaven," I say.

Christina asks, "What's that?"

"Seventh heaven means I am in a state of boundless joy. It's the place where we will meet again when I'm gone," I say with smile.

We finish our desserts and I continue with the story.

"Life for me was good. My dad on the other hand, still has a chip on his shoulder. He's still a mean drunk, and he is angry about the life that he's been dealt. He has however, begun to soften up a bit, at least with my brother and sister."

"I, on the other hand, no matter how much good I do, it makes no difference to him. Grandma and Aunt Genevieve came to visit most of the summers. My aunt was working for a company called Bethlehem Steel. They have great benefits. So every fourth year, my aunt got eight weeks off during the summer. The summer of my sixteenth birthday, she packs up Grandma and brings her and my cousin Becky for a visit."

"Dad hates it when my aunt and Grandma are here. They're always talking to Mom in the Greek/Albanian language and he feels left out. Plus, he believes they're always talking bad about him. Kind of paranoid about it, I always thought."

"They arrive just a couple days before my birthday. One month earlier, my dad tells me there's no way I am getting a driver's license on my sixteenth birthday. He tells me I'll have to wait until I turn eighteen."

"On my birthday, my aunt gives me a short parallel parking lesson and then takes me to the DMV for the driving test."

"'You're sixteen, you've earned the right to drive, just like your brother did,' she says. She didn't even tell Mom. We went to the DMV in La Mesa where I had gotten my driver's permit six months earlier."

"First, they gave me the written test and I score ninety-six percent. Then I take the driving test and I score ninety-six percent. They do an eye test and declare I have passed the requirements to drive. No one had to sign for me, because they already had my parents signature on record from when I got my learner's permit. My aunt paid the fees, handed me her keys and we drive home."

"My dad's across the street drinking beer with his drinking buddy, something he did all the time. He doesn't see us pull up. When we get inside the house, my aunt goes over to my mom, who's working at the dining table and tells her, 'Yianni got his driver's license.'"

"Immediately Mom blurts out, 'Don't you dare say anything to Ray. Let me tell him.'"

"Later in the afternoon, Dad comes home. He's had plenty to drink, but Mom tells him anyway, 'Johnny passed his driver's test today and now he has his license.'"

"Who the hell took him to get his license?"

"'Genevieve did. I asked her to take him,' she lies."

"Dad says, 'I don't give a damn if he got his license or not. He's not going to be driving any of my cars.'"

"Then Mom says, 'He'll drive my car, the Oldsmobile, whenever he wants to. I'm the one who makes the living in this household, so who the hell are you to tell me what he will do or what he won't do?' she says with full control of her words, and meaning every word she said."

"The next night was Saturday night dance night. Dad usually drove me to the dance. As Mom hands me her keys, he says 'Nothing had better happen tonight or you will never drive again. I'll beat you to a pulp and you'll never be able to drive. I'll make sure of that.'"

"I call my buddy Steve and tell him I'd pick him up at his house. Steve lives up the hill behind us, on a dirt road about four blocks away. I pick him up and on the way down the dirt road I run the car into a rut."

"'Oh, my God, my dad's going to kill me if he finds out,' I tell Steve."

"Steve, whose dad was a lot like mine, runs back up the hill to his house and brings back a couple of shovels. We dig for a little over an hour before I'm able to get the car to move. We get to the dance about 9:30 and the doors are closed. They aren't letting anyone else in. I begin knocking on the door to get the policeman's attention."

"This cop comes to the door and says, 'I can't let you in. We're not selling tickets anymore.'"

"I say, 'Hey, look officer, I just got my driver's license yesterday and I got my mom's car stuck in a rut on the side of the road. If I don't produce a ticket stub when I get home, my dad's going to beat the living daylights out of me. You don't want to answer that call, do you?'"

"He says, 'Remarkable story kid, okay, come on in.' He didn't even charge us, but he did muster up a couple of ticket stubs. Those dances were a good thing and it paid to be honest about what happened, even if he did think it was just a story."

"Dad never knew what happened that night until I told him and Mom ten years later."

"Life was good, I got my driver's license, I was playing tennis tournaments and getting better by the day. School was starting soon, it was my junior year, and 1967 was just around the corner. And that's enough of the story for today," as I announce that Rascal and I should be getting home.

Then Charlie asks, "When can you finish the story?"

"How about we meet Tuesday afternoon at the park, at two?"

And then to our surprise, their dad Ray says, "How about four o'clock? I should be home from work by then."

"Four o'clock works for me." We then say our goodbyes and Vasiliki insists that I take home a plate full of leftovers and some more of those fantastic Greek pastries. There was no way I could say no, nor did I want to.

"The food was fantastic," I assured her.

The kids all say goodbye to Rascal and off we go.

Chapter Twelve

Grandmas hold our tiny hands for just
a little while, but our hearts forever.

~ Author Unknown

When Tuesday rolls around, I take care of some chores and then pull out the leftovers from Sunday. Around three-thirty I gather up Rascal and head to the park.

Much to my surprise, they're already waiting. We sit at one of the picnic tables under the Gazebo, next to the lake. The kids are playing with Rascal, so we spend a few minutes chatting.

I'm not sure if they tire him out, or he tires them out, but ten minutes later they're at the table begging for the story to continue where we left off...

❧

"Grandma and my Aunt are back in San Francisco by the middle of August. They get home just in time to enroll my cousin, Becky, in her new school. Before they left, we agreed that I would go to San Francisco the next summer, instead of them coming back down here. That would be great because I could spend some quality time with Grandma."

"Quality time was usually playing blackjack and talking about life. We didn't do much else."

" We were just making memories, as Grandma would always say."

"Years later, I realize making memories is another one of Grandma's many blessings. Unfortunately for me, it takes a few more loved ones to die before I realize how important making memories is."

"The fall seems to fly by. Near the end of November, Thanksgiving weekend, I went to Seattle, Washington to attend a Lutheran Youth League Convention. It was my first time away from the family since Mom's accident. I was with many of my friends from church. Kids from all over the country were there. While there, I met a nice girl from Phoenix, Arizona. We hung out and walked the streets of Seattle in our free time."

"Seattle is an interesting place. There were drinking fountains at every crosswalk downtown. The water was so pure, cold and tasted fantastic. Each time we reached a crosswalk, we took a drink of water."

"On the way home from the convention, Sunday morning, our airplane had to make an emergency landing at San Francisco International Airport. We were going to be delayed for about eight hours, so I called Uncle Victor who came to pick me up. He's living in Pacifica, just up the hill from the airport. Then I called my Mom collect, to tell her we were delayed."

"What's collect?" asks Charlie.

"In those days, there were no cell phones, only push button or dial phones. I went to a phone booth in the airport, dialed 'O' which gets me to an operator. When the operator comes on the phone, I tell her I want to place a collect phone call to my mother."

"When Mom answers the phone, she tells the operator that she will accept the charges. Which means, she's paying for the call, not me."

"Does that explain it well enough?"

"Yes, now I understand."

"Soon after talking with Mom, Uncle Victor shows up at the airport. He's still driving his '63 Comet that Grandma bought him when he turned sixteen. We trade hugs and then he says, 'How much time do you have?'"

"I tell him, 'Eight hours, long enough to have lunch at your house and then go to see Grandma.' His wife, my Aunt Shirley, and my two cousins, Vicky and Michelle, were glad to see me. After lunch, Uncle

Vic and I head to the City to see Grandma. We don't tell her we're coming, as we wanted it to be a surprise."

"On the way, Uncle Vic's his goofy self. He sings the oldies to me, just like always. Our favorite song, *The Lion Sleeps Tonight*, sung by the Tokens, comes on the radio. For the whole of my life, whenever I hear that song, I think of Uncle Victor. Every time the songs gets to the words, 'Wimoweh,' he turns the volume up. When I started driving, I did the same thing whenever I heard that song."

Then Vasiliki says, "I love that song too. My husband used to do the same thing."

"When we get to Grandma's house, she's living downstairs at the Faith Street house, the one I lived in when I was living with Uncle Alex. Uncle Vic unlocks the door, and silly me, I was thinking, why does he have her locked in, without realizing she can unlock the door from the inside?"

"Grandma's smiling tells it all. She's so happy to see me. First thing out of her mouth, 'My Yianni, Yianni Capedoni.'"

"Uncle Vic tells me he's going to take care of some things while he's in the city and he'd be back in a couple of hours to take me to the airport."

"That was fine with me. Grandma and I got to make a few more memories as we played Blackjack sitting on her bed. We lost track of time. Grandma didn't even smoke while I was there. She knew how much I hated it. Plus, her arms were hurting her and she was having trouble lifting them up to her head."

"When she tells me that her arms are hurting, I ask her, 'Grandma, do you want me to ferqoi you?'"

Christina says, "What is ferqoi?"

Before I get a chance to tell her, her grandma Vasiliki says, "Ferqoi is the Greek word that means massage. My grandma used to ferqoi me all the time. Come over here and sit with me and I will ferqoi you while Yianni's talking."

Back to the story...

"I ferqoied Grandma. She loved every minute of it. The whole time I'm rubbing her arms, pinching them, slapping them, doing everything she taught me about ferqoi and Grandma's yelling out, 'Oh, nen o moi, oh nen o moi.' That was her way of telling me it was hurting, but it feels so good."

Vasiliki laughs out loud and says, "Yianni, you are bringing back some good memories of my childhood like you can't imagine. My grandma used to say the same thing."

We share a few more memories and I tell her, just to make them laugh, that when Grandma or Mom ferqoied me, I would joke and say, "Oh, nen o moi, oh nen o moi." I love making people laugh and smile.

We all laugh together. Just talking about laughing makes people laugh. Then Christina says to her grandma, "I like ferqoi Yiayia."

Vasiliki nods her head and says, "Yes, it's absolutely wonderful isn't it, but don't forget, when I ferqoi you, you have to ferqoi me."

"Usually whenever I ferqoi Grandma," I continue, "she reciprocates, but this time I tell her it's not necessary because her arms are too sore. I deal another hand of blackjack."

"While we're playing, Grandma asks how things are with my dad."

"He's still drinking, he's still mean, and I still hate him."

"Grandma tells me, 'Yianni, remember mhat Papa and I told you about hate. Hate will eat you alive. It will cause you to get cancer. Don't hate your father. You don't have to like him, but don't have to hate him either.'"

"Reluctantly, I say, 'Okay, Grandma, but only because you're asking me.'"

"Yianni, Grandma is going to die soon and you don't have to worry about anything. I am your fýlakas ángelos and I will always be watching you."

Vasiliki interrupts me and says, "She's telling you she is your guardian angel."

"Oh, so you know what that means, let's see if you know what the next one means, too."

"'Stop saying that Grandma, you're not going to die soon. Why do you always say that?' An immediate sad face comes over me."

"She looks up at me and says 'Mhat's the matter myth you. We're all going to die someday, even you.'"

"I know Grandma, but it's going to be a very lonely and miserable time for me the day that you die, so let's not be in a hurry to go so quick."

"As I deal the next hand of blackjack, she says to me, 'Yianni, Yianni Capedoni. You don't have to worry. Besides having fýlakas ángelos watching over you, you will have your pnevmatiko odigo to turn to for guidance.'"

"What's that?" asks Christina.

"Say that again," asks Vasiliki.

"Pnevmatiko odigo."

"Do you know what that means?"

"I do, because Grandma shared what it meant to me. Just in time too, because Uncle Vic showed up to take me to the airport. I guess you know that one too Vasiliki? Why don't you tell the family?"

She turns to her daughter, son-in-law and her grandchildren, "Pnevmatiko odigo means Spiritual Guide. We all have one and we either recognize they are with us or we don't. Various religions believe they are the devil. But a spiritual guide provides us knowledge and understanding when we are open to hear them. I've been interacting with my guide for a very long time."

Barbara says, "Momma, why haven't you ever told me about your pnevmatiko odigo?"

"Because I've never had an opportunity to mention it before. It's not a subject that many people care to talk about, for fear of hearing someone say it's the devil talking. Most people are too afraid to say anything because they will be judged, scrutinized or even ostracized. I've just kept it to myself. Greeks have been interacting with their guides for years."

Before I continue Vasiliki says, "What did she say to you?"

"Grandma tells me what she learned about guides in school from Plato. 'Plato's teachings show us that each human soul has three components, comprised of reason, appetite and spirit. It's a simple yet complex theory. Each of us has an appetite for physical pleasure. Reason is what we use to determine right from wrong. Spirit guides us through the emotional state of being. When we're aligned with these three states, we function in a healthy life. Yet any one of them can take us over and then our state of being will change.'"

"Grandma tells me that it's not a myth that we each have a pnevmatiko odigo. We come to the physical plane with one odigo and at various times we interact with other odigos. They enter our lives to test us, teach us and to guide us. Much like the three components of the human soul that Plato was talking about."

"She goes on to say, 'Be careful myth having an appetite for physical pleasure Yianni. It can consume you. For example, I have been drinking beer and smoking cigarettes my whole life. They give me physical pleasure and I didn't let reason determine mhat's right and wrong myth smoking and drinking. If I would have let spirit guide me through the emotional state of being, Grandma would have lived a long life and quit smoking and drinking a long time ago. But after Papa died, I have no reason to be living, so I smoke, and I drink, and soon I will die.'"

"Stop saying that Grandma. You have me to live for. I'm still here and I need you."

"She shares another example. 'Your Uncle Alex, the womanizer, he was consumed by physical pleasure. Joann wasn't enough for him, so he went elsewhere to take care of his appetite. That's mhat they fought over. His drinking and his womanizing, and whenever Joann argued back, he beat her. Don't let appetite consume you Yianni.'"

"Okay Grandma. I'll do my best not to follow in Uncle Alex's footsteps."

"Then Grandma says, 'Yianni, do you remember I always tell you, you're going to live a long life? It's because you've dealt myth more than most this lifetime. You've seen that human pleasures can harm you if you don't use good reasoning and let spirit guide you through the emotional state of being. Use the example of your father, your mother, your Uncle Alex and his relationship myth Joann, and Uncle Deso the gangster, and don't let your life be like theirs. Turn to your pnevmatiko odigo for guidance. And don't you worry about anything, because your fýlakas ángelos, Grandma, will be myth you when you need me most.'"

"About that time, Uncle Victor shows up and Grandma has to cut the story short. He brought her some groceries, so while he's putting things away, we finish our last game of blackjack and then Grandma walks us to the door."

"I give her a giant hug and I notice she's crying. 'Mhat's the matter myth you Grandma?'"

"Saying it the way Grandma says it, makes her smile and laugh. Her tears dry up and then she says, 'Yianni, Yianni Capedoni, you always know how to make Grandma smile. I love you very, very much.'"

"We embrace and I kiss her one more time, as she whispers in my ear, 'Yianni, Yianni, Capedoni, don't ever forget your Grandma when I die. And don't be afraid, I'll always be protecting you. I am after all, your fýlakas ángelos.'"

Before I have the opportunity to finish the story, Vasiliki turns to her grandchildren, "I hope you kids paid close attention to Yianni's story about fýlakas ángelos. We all have guardian angels who watch over us and when I die, I will be yours. I'll be watching over you. Everything he says is what my grandmother said to me just before she died. She's my fýlakas ángelos. It's what grandmother's do."

"Well you know, Vasiliki," I said, "looking back, whenever I listen to Grandma whispering in my ear, 'Yianni do this, trust me,' and I do follow Grandma's advice, it seems I always draw an Ace and King. Blackjack, I win."

Seconds after say saying it, I'm astonished as I think back. I can hear Grandma saying, ***"Live a good life, you'll get a Blackjack, you'll always draw an Ace and King."***

A few seconds pass, and I continue with the story...

"Uncle Vic had taken longer than expected to get back to Grandma's house. When we get into the car, he says to me, 'What time is your flight?'"

"I tell him, four-thirty."

"He looks at the clock on the dashboard. It says five after four. Then he says, 'I don't think we're going to make it to the airport in time. What do you want to do?'"

"Just take me to the airport, I'll have to take another flight."

"Since you're late, why don't we stop at Silver Crest and see if there's anyone there that we know?"

"What's Silver Crest?" asks Bobby.

"Silver Crest is the name of a business we hung out at as kids. It's the first place I learned to dunk donuts in coffee. Uncle Vic wouldn't let me drink coffee, but he'd let me dunk my donuts in his. I still like dunking donuts in coffee today. I waited until I was thirty-three years old before I ever drank coffee. Quit it about three times, but today I just enjoy a cup of San Francisco blend coffee and some Hazelnut crème. Dunking donuts in coffee is still a human pleasure I'm not willing to give up."

"Yum, that sounds good."

"Don't get any wild ideas little man. I'm not going to be guilty of causing you to be like me."

"When we walk into Silver Crest, Uncle Vic says to the guy behind the counter, 'Hey George, you remember this guy?'"

"Oh my God, is that little Johnny? It's been what, eight years since I've seen you, just after your grandfather died?"

"Yes, that was probably the last time." Then he and Uncle Vic catch up and I head for the pinball baseball machine.

"After playing a couple of games of pinball, we leave for the airport. On the way there, our song *A Lion Sleeps Tonight*, comes on the radio again. Just making memories I think to myself, as Uncle Vic plays with the dial turning it up and down at the right time."

"When we get to the airport, I ask the flight hostess if I can put my name on a standby list for another flight and she tells me I can get on the one that leaves at eight o'clock. I call Mom to tell her I'm going to be home about nine-thirty because I missed my flight. She asks why, but I tell her we'll talk it about it when I get home."

"When I land at the airport, Dad's furious because I missed my plane. I tell him, 'I was visiting Grandma while Uncle Victor did some grocery shopping for her. By the time he got back to Grandma's, it was too late to make my flight, so we stopped at Silver Crest to say hi to George.'"

"Dad says, 'Dammit, you should not have wasted your time visiting Grandma. You should have been at home when you were supposed to be.'"

"I don't argue with him, I just say, 'You're right, I should have, but it's too late to do anything different now and I'm really happy I got to see Grandma.'"

"Mom didn't say a word, she just looked back at me and smiles. She knows how much I love Grandma."

"Soon after, it's Christmas again. We call Grandma on the phone Christmas Day and I tell her how excited I am about seeing her next summer."

"However, after the New Year, around the middle of February, Mom gets a phone call from my aunt, letting her know that Grandma has slipped into a diabetic coma. I was really shaken with the news. I begged Mom to let me fly up to the city with her, but she decides it's best that I stay in school and flies to San Francisco alone."

"When she gets there, my Uncle Victor, twenty-three and married, picks her up at the airport and takes her to the hospital. As soon as Mom gets there, she asks both Uncle Vic and Aunt Genevieve if anyone has called the Greek priest."

"'Momma would want that,' she says."

"They look at each other and then tell Mom they hadn't. Mom calls the priest, who comes to the hospital as soon as he can."

"When he gets there, he stands over Grandma and prays for her. He gives her last rites, figuring she may never come out of the coma. He then says a few words to my mom, aunt and uncle. Then he leaves."

"An hour later, Grandma comes out of the coma. It's a miracle! Even though she didn't respond to a word he said when he was there, she told Mom the next day that she knew he was there."

"'It was a miracle,' Mom said when she called me on the phone later that night. She called every night just before leaving the hospital. The second night, I got to talk to Grandma."

"I tell her, 'What's the matter myth you Grandma? Mhat do you think you're doing slipping into a coma?'"

"She says, 'I was practicing how to watch over you, Yianni.'"

"I was stunned, I didn't know what else to say to her, so I just tell her to get better and I would see her next summer. But my gut was telling me otherwise. I've known ever since Papa died that Grandma really didn't want to be alive."

"Mom comes home at the end of the week. She figured Grandma was getting better and she needed to get home to the bookstore. When Mom gets home, she tells me that when Grandma opened her eyes as she came out of the coma, she said to them, 'I want to go back to the room with the light.'"

"Mom turns to my aunt and uncle and says, 'What is Momma talking about?'"

"They say, 'Just before momma fell into the coma she was in another room. Maybe she felt it's much brighter in the other room.' My uncle goes on to ask them if they can move her back to the other room. They have no idea what she's talking about."

"Then Grandma says, 'I want to go back to the room with the light.'"

"Years later I figure it out. The light she was talking about was the light she saw while she was in the coma. The same light that would lead her to seventh heaven."

Bobby interrupts, "What is seventh heaven?"

"Do you remember we talked about seventh heaven once before? You might hear someone say, 'I'm in seventh heaven.' And yes, you don't need drugs or alcohol to reach it. But we all reach that state of euphoria when we die. That's why death refers to seventh heaven."

"Three days after Mom returns home, my aunt calls to tell us that Grandma has passed away."

"We pack up the Chevy Station Wagon and head to San Francisco the next day. As we're driving on old highway 101, just before San Clemente, we pass this weird looking round ball building. It has a sign that reads, 'San Onofre Nuclear Station.'"

"I ask my dad, 'What is that place down there?'"

"He says, 'I don't know, nuclear whatever that is, maybe they make bombs or electricity.' He has no idea."

"At that time, I say to myself, 'I'm going to work there someday.' Even though I had no idea what they did, this turns out to be another one of Grandma's Secret Blessings."

"When we get to San Francisco, it's another funeral much like Papa's. Two days of viewing and then she's buried on the third day. Grandma's buried at the Golden Gate National Cemetery, right alongside Papa. *What a fitting end and a fond memory to their lives.*"

"The funeral isn't a military style funeral like Papa's. It lacks the horse drawn hearse, no taps were played, no twenty-one-gun salute and no flag on her casket. But it didn't matter. I know Grandma is at piece lying there next to Papa."

"Things were much easier for me with her passing, even though I cried like a baby. I've always had the feeling that Grandma has never left me. I believe she's here with us now."

"She is," says Christina. "She's right over there, can't you see her?"

So as not to discourage her, I say, "Thank you Christina, yes, I see her."

"Mom told me she had promised Grandma that she would make sure my dad never hurts me. Mom had become my protector now. My dad would pay the price if he did anything to hurt me. She would make that perfectly clear, many times over the years that follow. I, too, was getting bigger and much stronger. Not just strong physically, but strong mentally as well. The hatred has disappeared, but the anger, fear and sorrow still remain."

"After the funeral, I'm the last one to walk away. I stand before her grave and say 'Grandma, you will always be my Queen. Thank you for blessing me with your presence and thank you for watching over me.' I kiss her casket, turn and walk away."

"A few steps from her grave, I stop for a moment, and turn to take one last look. I see Papa's headstone and the mound of dirt being readied to put over Grandma's grave, and for a moment, I see them both standing there holding hands, smiling back at me as if to say, 'Yianni, Yianni Capedoni, everything is going to be okay.'"

"After the funeral, my dad takes my brother and sister to Aunt Clara's house and leaves me and Mom to stay with my aunt. Each of my uncles, beginning with Odysseus the oldest, Alex and Victor were there. My cousin Becky and I were the only kids. We're told to sit on the couch and watch TV while they talk about the estate."

"But things get heated. It's a Greek trait we inherit when we're born, to be loud. But the argument is getting just a little bit out of control. Becky's sitting on the couch shaking like a dog. They're ten feet away in the dining room arguing about who should get what and why. There are still two houses on Holladay Street and the house on Faith Street to deal with. Then there's the two, one acre lots on the top of the hill. Mom's doing her best to convince them that the best thing to do is to sell everything and split it evenly among them. But things continue to boil as they become more argumentative and loud."

"At one point, I've had enough. I stand up and walk into the living room and say to them, 'You guys should hear yourselves. Grandma's barely in her grave and you're fighting worse than cats and dogs. I'm embarrassed to call you my family.'"

"I shock them. A few minutes later they stop discussing. My aunt comes into the living room to thank me for waking them up. She tells me later after everyone's gone, 'Our Yianni, Yianni Capedoni, always taking charge.'"

"I swore to myself, right then and there, that I would never care if anyone ever left me anything when they died. I can't believe how death can tear families apart. Such greed, I won't let death tear my family apart. It's all about making choices and I choose not to get involved when it comes to death."

"Uncle Deso was hell bent that there had to be money hidden somewhere in one of those houses. He said, 'That's what Mom and Pop always used to do, hide their money in the walls.'"

"The next day, he starts tearing the walls apart in the Faith Street house, downstairs where Grandma was living. When his brothers get there, they stop him. They spend the rest of the day going through Grandma's things. They find her jewelry, fifty cent pieces from her many trips to the casinos in Reno, and two giant boxes of Raleigh coupons from her cigarettes. They share everything evenly. Uncle Deso leaves for Philadelphia the next day. Everything else was left behind for Victor and my aunt to get rid of. Mom rents the houses, until she can get them sold."

"Perhaps my grandparents did hide their money from Deso? But Grandma barely had enough money at the end to buy cigarettes and beer. Uncle Victor spent his money."

"Victor was fifteen when Papa died. Since he was the only one around, it was up to him to watch over Grandma the last eight years. He took care of her every day until she died. I always thought if anyone should get the most, it was Uncle Victor because he took care of Grandma more than anyone. However, as things turn out, Uncle Victor's the most successful of them all. Using his genius mechanical brain, he invents a faster, more efficient way to coat optical lenses. He made a good living from it."

"Mom handles the estate. Everything's split between the brothers and the sisters. It takes nine to ten years before everything is sold."

"I learned a great deal from these events. I swore if any of my family dies, whatever they have left doesn't matter to me. Only the memories matter the most and nobody can ever take them away."

Then I suggest, "Let's take a break."

Vasiliki and Barbara thought it was good timing. They had made some sandwiches with the leftovers from Sunday and said we should eat them.

After we finished eating and I drink a bottle of water, we decide it's getting cold and we should all head for home. After agreeing on our next meet time and saying our goodbyes, we head for our cars. I can't believe how cordial Ray is. Who knows, maybe he's seeing the light.

As Rascal gets situated in the car and I start the engine, the radio blasts out a song that causes me to just sit there for a moment to listen. I can't believe the timing, "My Special Angel," sung by Bobby Vinton in 1963. The timing or synchronicity in hearing it is beyond me. The whole time I'm sitting there, every time he says My Special Angel, I'm thinking of Grandma.

My angel sent from above with heaven in her eyes. My special angel through eternity, here to watch over me.

Chapter Thirteen

Experience is a great advantage.
The problem is that when you get
the experience, you're too damned old
to do anything about it.

~ Jimmy Connors

We agreed to meet again on Sunday afternoon at Vasiliki's house. The week seems to have flown by. Rascal and I jump in the car Sunday morning, just before noon so that we can stop at the local grocery store to pick some treats for everyone.

When we get to Vasiliki's house, I notice Ray's nowhere to be found, so I ask why.

They tell me he decided not to come to the party. He stayed home to watch football and drink his beer.

"So, this is a party?"

"Every time we see you Yianni, it's a party," Vasiliki responds, "we enjoy your stories. Even though life has been cruel to you, you're teaching us about life. Don't ever stop telling your stories."

"I'll keep that under advisement."

Christina starts yelling, "Tell us a story, tell us a story!"

We get situated in the living room, it's a bit cold to be outside. I set the scene by telling them about my high school and early college days.

"High school is by far the greatest time in my life. I hooked up with a couple of guys who are still my best friends today, Bob and Charlie, like you boys."

"We're on the tennis team. Bob ends up as my workout partner and Charlie becomes my mentor. My grades skyrocket to A's after I start hanging with Charlie. 'No goofing off,' he used to tell me, 'Keep your eyes in your book, not on the girls.' We spend most week nights in the downtown public library studying. He pushed me to study hard. 'There's time for the girls later,' he would say. Or sometimes he would say, 'We didn't come here to meet girls.'"

"Charlie is a bit of a tightwad. He made me pay for gas, every time we went somewhere in his car. When we went in mine, I never asked for a dime. But, I have to say this for Charlie, when I was down and out many years later, he and his wife Barbara were there for me. Asking him for help is one of the hardest things I ever had to do. But they helped me to save my house from foreclosure when my second wife ripped me off. We're still best friends today."

"We can count on one hand who our real friends are. Very few people have more than five. Most of the people who come along are acquaintances, but faithful friends are the ones who are with us at the end."

"When our junior year is over, I go to San Francisco to visit my aunt. While I'm there, my aunt has a guy painting her house, so I end up working for him for a couple of weeks. Painting houses in San Francisco was challenging work and sometimes very scary. The winds would make it hard to steady the ladder. Most of the houses in the city are two and three stories tall, so the only way to reach the top is on a ladder. The Bay area fog is tough on paint. Most of the homes are made of wood or stucco and the paint lasts two or three years."

"After painting my aunt's house, the painter and I move on to a few more houses down the block. I make some good spending money while I'm there. After going home, I spend the rest of that summer on the tennis court with Bob. We hit tennis balls for eight hours a day under the blistering sun and came back in the evening for two hours or more to play under the lights. We played against Bobby Riggs one night. He was a well-known player who promoted tennis by playing the top women's champion, Billy Jean King, a few years after we played him. We played at night-time until the timer on the lights turned them off at ten o'clock."

"Our senior year of high school was by far the best time of our school life. We were expected to win the tennis championship that year and be the first school in history to beat Grossmont High School. Nobody has ever beaten them. We played two close matches with them, but fell short both times, losing by one point. But both Bob and I did our part. He won in number one singles and I won in number one doubles. I played with another friend of mine, Steve. He was the one I was driving with when I got the car stuck in the rut. Remember that story?"

"Yes," they say.

"Steve was quite the character, always the jokester. But that day on the tennis court he was as serious as could be. As a double team, we won both sets."

"At graduation Steve set up a rebellion. The principal and our counselor told us we couldn't wear blue jeans under our gowns. Blue jeans were not in the dress code at that time. So Steve convinces all the guys to wear jeans. At the end of the ceremony, we opened our gowns to show them we had jeans on. Steve on the other hand, he was naked. When he opens his gown, he shocks them all."

"We didn't see Steve much after graduation. He took up with the wrong group while hanging out at the beach. He messed around with drugs and before summer ends, he dies from an overdose of heroin. His death has an enormous impact on both Charlie and me. Because of Steve, we stayed away from drugs our whole life. We still talk about Steve today. 'Ever the jokester.'"

"Bob and I and another buddy, George from high school, all go to Grossmont College. We're recruited by the coach to play for the tennis team. College is a major challenge to adulthood. I either have to get an education, become a great tennis player, enter the military or enter the workplace. Papa's words stuck in the back of my mind as I continued with my education."

"We carried a minimum of twelve units and had to maintain a 2.0 grade point average. I passed my classes and was eligible to play tennis.

That first year I have a fantastic season. We take second place in our conference, only losing twice to our nemesis, San Diego City College, which ends up being number one in the state. But we're right behind them at number two. I play singles in the number four, five and six spots and number two in doubles. I have an awesome season. I won twenty-four matches and lost only one match in singles. We are twenty-two and four in doubles, playing with my high school friend George most of the time.

George and Bob have good seasons too, but my season breaks a long-standing record. Bad luck for me, the record only stands for one year. Next year, a new number six player takes my spot. He goes undefeated, winning thirty matches. I move up to number two, until I tear the ligaments in my ankle. After that I play mostly three and four, until the very end of the season when I earn my way back to number two. Bob is chosen as the most valuable player and I'm given the title as the 'Most Inspired Tennis Player' for the second season in a row."

"What's most inspired?" Bobby asks.

"It means I was recognized for my arduous work on the court and that my efforts contribute to inspiring my teammates to work just as hard."

"During the summer of 1969 we get word that my Uncle Alex is missing. No one has any idea where he might be. Five days later, a jogger running along Skyline Drive in Pacifica spots a car down in a ravine below the road that has slammed into the only tree in the area. Because of the thick fog bank for the past week, no one had noticed the car. It was well below the level of the road. When the runner gets to the car, he finds Uncle Alex, who is barely breathing and can't move because he's broken his back. The runner leaves him to call for help."

"A few minutes later an ambulance arrives and they pull him out of his wrecked car. I was on my way to San Francisco the very next day, so when I get to San Francisco he is the person I go to see. Uncle Alex is lying in bed on his side when I walk up to him. He smiles from ear-to-ear and his deep blue eyes light up the room. He is black and blue all over his body and is slow to talk about what had happened. We spend a couple of hours visiting. He was going through some rough times then. He and my aunt had finally split up and were going through a divorce. There he is, lying in the hospital all alone. His kids are all too young to drive and have no way of getting there. Since I was going to be in the City for a about a month, I go to see him as much as I can. He really smiles whenever I am there. His smiles always made a big impression in my heart."

"Besides being very intelligent, my uncle was also very intuitive. He had a feeling that he was going to die soon. He calls his best friend Mando, Uncle Mando as we always call him, and asks him to open a couple of life insurance policies. Uncle Mando has lots of contacts, so he knows exactly who to call. He opens one account for seventy-five thousand dollars and the other one for two hundred and fifty thousand. Those were large accounts in 1969. Anyhow, he lists my Aunt Genevieve as the beneficiary and wrote a will, spelling out what she was supposed to do with the money."

"He wants his kids to have something to remember him by. My aunt was to collect the interest on the funds, but was to give each of his five kids, an even share, when she felt they had reached the appropriate age and maturity to handle the funds."

"Just before I leave San Francisco to head home to San Diego, I go to visit my uncle in the hospital one last time. I thank him for taking care of me years earlier and teaching me arithmetic and spelling. Just as I reach down to kiss him goodbye, I thank him for being my uncle."

"That was the last time I ever saw him alive. A few months later, as he suspected, he died alone in a motel from a massive heart attack. He was just thirty-four years old. I didn't make it to his funeral because my sophomore year of college had started and I couldn't spare the time away from my studies. But I'm glad that I got to see him before he died. His smile that first day in the hospital left an imprint on my mind. It spoke a thousand words. I always remember his smile and everything he taught me."

"Years later there is an interesting parallel between my uncle and me, and one of his daughters and my mother. That will come out in another story."

"Uncle Alex was laid to rest in the Greek cemetery with his sister Margarite. There's a price to pay for my uncle's death. When my mom came back home from San Francisco, she has four of his five children with her. Turns out it was payback time for taking care of me years earlier. My aunt, divorced from Uncle Alex at the time of his death, finds out that his life insurance policies are not going to her, but to my Aunt Genevieve. She tells my mom and my aunt that someone besides her must raise her kids or she will put them in a home. She walks away from them. Mom takes the oldest son Joey, Cindy and the twins, Denise and Diane. My Uncle Victor takes Dennis, the younger son."

"Our house is full. Since my brother is now in the Navy, Joey shares the room with me. The twins and Cindy share my sister's room. Joey is quite a handful. He lashes out at everybody. He is angry about being abandoned by his mom. I tell him one day when he lashes out at me, 'Hey, we didn't ask to take care of you. My mom opens up her house and her heart to you. There isn't anything she wouldn't do for you and the girls, but one thing is for sure, I won't let you disrespect her. She's your aunt and she loves you.'"

"But he continues to disrespect her and us, so my mom sends him to Philadelphia to live with Uncle Deso, who is more capable of handling him than we are. He takes crap from nobody and Joey knows it."

"Soon after Uncle Alex passes away, my dad and I have our final fight. The world was turning upside down. Black people are rioting in the streets in Compton and all around the country. They want equal rights and the whole country seems to be crumbling to pieces."

"College students are being shot and killed at different campuses around the country. They were exercising their right to freedom of speech, speaking out in protest, against the war in Viet Nam, while others were lashing out about the racial violence. But the police and National Guard made matters worse. The Viet Nam war has escalated to the point that some of my close friends from high school had already been killed. It was important for me to stay in school because it would keep me away from the draft and the new draft was on its way."

"My dad, who spent time in the Navy, was always pushing me to enlist. He told me it was the right thing to do. But I felt in my heart and knew in my mind I could never kill another human being. At the same time all of this was going on, drugs were becoming rampant. Kids my age, older and younger, were getting high. Then one day my dad accuses me of being under the influence of drugs. He grabs me by the hair and tosses me across the room."

"As I bounce off the hallway wall, I decide this is going to be last time he ever does this to me. It is time to take a stand. I'm old enough, and I was big enough, to stand on my own two feet. When I bounce off the wall, fire comes into my eyes. I was so angry with my dad. I look him straight in the eyes and say 'I'm done with the physical and mental abuse. I've had enough of it and of you. That's the last time you will ever hurt me. The violence is over, do you understand? Don't you ever touch me again or I will kill you.' It was the first time and the last time I ever had to fight back."

"He knew by the look in my eyes that I meant business. From that moment on, he knew his bullying days were over. He never badgered me again with his words or his fists. He also didn't talk to me much anymore either, but that was okay. And as far as drugs were concerned, I guess he just never realized the impact that Steve's death had on me, nor did he care."

"My dad never took the time to know me. If he had, he would have known that I never took drugs or pain killers my whole life. Nor did I drank alcohol or smoke tobacco. Not too many people in my generation can say that. I learned a long time ago, it's okay say 'No.' It may not be one of Grandma's secret blessings, but it's definitely one of mine."

One final short story.

"Bob's dad is pushing him to join the Navy. His dad, a Chief Petty Officer in the Navy and still enlisted at the time we were in college, keeps telling him to quit wasting his time in school and join the Navy. One day, Bob and I decide to go to the Navy Recruit office in El Cajon. The officer at the recruit depot finds out we are college students and does his best to get us to sign on the dotted line. But Bob insists he needs to discuss the paperwork with his dad first. We left, paperwork in hand and walked out."

"Bob, the character that he is, spots a trash can on the edge of the curb. He walks up to can, tilts his paperwork toward the opening and says, 'Not.' I followed suit."

"The funny thing is, that a couple of months later, on a new TV show called 'Laugh In,' one of the comedians was constantly using Bob's phrase 'Not.' Bob however, was the first person I heard to coin that phrase."

"What do you mean by coin, is it money?" asks Christina.

"It means he was the first person to ever say it," I tell her.

"There was one last price to pay from the death of Uncle Alex. This is an important one to tell you about, because it will surface again later in my stories. It was a major financial burden on my mom. She's struggling to keep the bookstore open. The Lutheran Churches, the Pastors, everyone wants a discount. Mom can't afford to give everything away. She asks her sister Genevieve to give her some of the money from Alex's life insurance to help pay for the support of his kids. She needs to buy food and clothes. This time it's not a lie. But her beloved sister, my aunt, says 'No.'"

"They didn't talk to each other for eight years, but that's a story for another day. So, that ladies and gentlemen is the end of today's story."

The ending was just in time too. Rascal was getting restless and so was Christina.

We decide the next story day would be on Friday at two o'clock, once again at Vasiliki's home. We say our goodbyes and head for home.

Chapter Fourteen

Whispering in my baby girl's ear I say,
thanks to you, I believe in Miracles.

~ John Egreek

When Friday rolls around, I begin to gather my thoughts about the next story. At two o'clock Rascal and I arrive at Vasiliki's. As I'm parking the car, the oldies song, *Angel Baby* by Rosie and the Originals starts playing on the radio. It paints a vivid picture in my mind. I remember driving home from a Padre's baseball game, singing *Angel Baby* to my daughter. I always think of her when I hear that song, because she is my *Angel Baby.*

Barbara, Vasiliki and the three kids are standing at the front door waiting for us. So, I cut the song short and in we go.

When we get in, they ask me why I was sitting there in the car?

"Just long enough to hear most of the song, *Angel Baby.*"

Barely inside, Christina says, "Will you tell us the story now?"

"Indeed, let us begin."

"Today's story is going to be about miracles. Everyone at some time or another will witness a miracle. I believe miracles happen every day."

"In January 1972, I marry my first wife. She's beautiful. She has long mahogany brown hair, a bit on the chunky side, with large breasts and a nice butt. As she walks down the aisle in her beautiful white gown, I feel a tap on my shoulder as tears begin to flow from my eyes. That day was supposed to be the happiest day of my life. But it wasn't. I want to run out the side door. I knew she was the wrong person for me, but I didn't have the guts to run. So, I marry her. It was probably Grandma tapping me on the shoulder, hoping to get my attention."

"It was three months before we consummated our marriage. I was a frustrated young man, but when we finally did it, she became pregnant with our first miracle."

"At the time, I was doing laborer work at the San Diego Gas and Electric power plant in Carlsbad. We were building a new power station. Most of the laborers that I work with are Latino's. When it came time for the first layoff, I was one of the first they let go. I was a white guy and experienced reverse discrimination. I didn't like it, but there was no one to complain to. I did receive unemployment benefits."

"Things are getting tough for my wife and me. We have no money and I wasn't about to ask anyone for help. My Uncle Alex's best friend, Uncle Mando as I used to call him, when he was in town visiting my mom last summer, told me if I ever need a job I should come to San Francisco. He has connections with the Teamsters Union. We were living in a house in San Diego that my wife's mom and dad owned. They owned three houses at the time. My wife felt comfortable there, so I went to San Francisco alone."

"I stayed with Uncle Mando and his wife Mo. They enjoyed my company. They were really close to my Greek family. They have memories of both Grandma, Papa and Uncle Alex. Mondo said I remind him of Alex."

"On the following Monday, Mando calls the president of the local Teamsters Union. He tells him, 'My nephew is on his way down to the hall, put him to work.' Without argument, that's what he does. The union bosses never argue with Mando. He was a head buster in the early days of unionization."

Bobby asks, "What's a head buster?"

Not sure how to answer, I say, "His job was to keep people in line," even though I know the truthful answer is beating people up.

Mando used to tell me stories about those days. He told me once that he never killed anyone, just busted a few heads. When Mando was around, the union guys stayed in line. He was one tough dude.

"When I got to the Union hall the next morning, I walk up to the counter and announce 'I'm Mando's nephew and I'm here to see Henry.' Henry's the president of the union. He takes me into his office and says, 'So you're Mando's nephew?'"

"Yes, I've known him all my life."

"Which side of the family do you come from?"

"'The Greek side,' I tell him. The Greeks in San Francisco were well respected, so there was no way he was going to question my response."

"He writes out a dispatch sending me to Planter's Peanuts to work the nightshift. He tells me, 'It's a one-night job. Come back tomorrow and I'll give you a dispatch for another job.'"

"That night, while working at Planter's they have me stacking boxes full of peanuts and cashews. This forklift driver pulls up to load a pallet full in the truck. As he pulls up he says, 'Is that pallet ready to go?'"

"I turn to tell him yes, and he says, 'Johnny? Barbara's Johnny? Is that you?'"

"The forklift driver is my Uncle Victor's best friend, Jim. He and Victor used to take care of me when I was just a little runt, living down the street with Alex. The last time I saw him was at Victor's wedding."

"He jumps off the forklift and comes over to give me a big hug. Jim is six-feet-five-inches tall, has dark curly hair, and treats me like a nephew."

"He tells the floor boss, 'This guy's working with me the rest of the night.'"

"When we have our first break, Jim grabs a bag full of cashews from the assembly line, something I was warned not to do when I got there. He hands half the bag to me and takes the other half for himself."

"Jim notices I was a bit uneasy and he says, 'Look around you, they're all eating them. They just tell you not to, to scare you the first time you work here.'"

"Because of Jim, I was told to come back the next night. I only work for Planter's two nights, but because of Jim I never have forgotten those two nights. Planter's Peanuts is an icon to San Francisco. While driving up the highway from the airport, you can't help but notice the lit-up figure of Mr. Peanuts, touching the brim of his hat with his right hand and his right eye monocle. It lights up the San Francisco skyline."

"Years later when the Seinfeld show came on TV, the first time I saw Kramer I thought of Jim. They could have been twins, he looks just like him. He was just as funny as Kramer, too. Always a jokester."

"The Tuesday nightshift was my last one at Planter's Peanuts. The next day when I go back to the Union hall, Henry sends me to 'Koret of California.' They make women's clothing for JC Penny's, Macy's and a few other stores. I was working in the trimmings department. It didn't take me long to learn my way around the warehouse."

"I become good friends with my co-worker, John Valles. Most everyone in the warehouse didn't talk to him, but I was different. He took a liking to me, and I took a liking to him. We just got along."

"After working two weeks I learn this job was going to last for as long as I want it to. I move my wife to the Bay Area. We get a two-bedroom apartment in Walnut Creek, about five miles from where my Uncle Victor and Aunt Shirley live in Danville. Both cities are east of San Francisco, so I have to commute across the Oakland Bay Bridge."

"Things were good between us, and then on February 21, 1973 our precious daughter Natalie Jean is born. I name her after Mom's favorite actress, Natalie Wood. Her mother chose her middle name. Same middle name as her mom."

"My Natalie is perfect. She's nine pounds six ounces, twenty-three inches long and has ten fingers and ten toes. She has brown hair and beautiful brown eyes. Her hair is thick, both on her head and on her back. She's definitely a Greek baby girl."

"The day after she's born, I go to work a very happy and proud dad. I break tradition and I passed out bubble gum cigars. The label states, 'It's a girl.' It didn't take long to pass them out. I couldn't wait to get off work to see her again. Unfortunately, the day is cut short by a unexpected telephone call."

"When the telephone rings, my co-worker John answers it in the same way we he taught me to, 'Trimmings, John speaking.'"

"I notice a weird look on his face. He listens to the caller on the other end. While he's listening, I can't help but notice him watching me, and then he drops the phone, and calls me over."

"When I get there, he tells me it is my wife. I can tell by the tone in his voice that something's wrong. I pick up the phone. It's my wife and she's crying. She says, 'Hurry, you need to come to the hospital as quick as you can. They're taking Natalie in for surgery. She has a bowel obstruction and they're going to operate.'"

"Without saying a word, I drop the phone and head for my car. It's parked down the street about three blocks away. I'm running as fast as I can. As soon as I jump into the car, I fire up the engine, put it in gear and head for the Oakland-Bay Bridge. My car is fast. It's a '69 Plymouth Roadrunner, with a 383-cubic inch engine, a three-quarter racing cam, and it's a stick, four on the floor. I'm not paying attention to the speed limit. I'm oblivious to what's going on around me. My mind isn't on the road. Tears are streaming down my cheeks, all I can think of is my little baby girl. I'm thinking I might lose her and it will be a shame if she dies without getting to experience life."

"Just before I reach the Caldecott tunnels which pass through the Berkley Hills between Oakland and Orinda, I begin to pray."

"Oh God, watch over my precious little girl. Protect her and save her. Don't let anything happen to her. It's just not fair if she doesn't get to experience this life. There's so much for her to see and to do. She's a precious child and it would be unfair to let her die. I'll never doubt you, God. I know you are there. Just don't take my daughter away... Amen."

"As I pray, the words just fly out of my mouth without any thought as to what I was saying. I keep saying the same prayer, over and over. I sit adjacent to the surgery doors for six hours, while my wife is in a hospital bed two floors up. She's waiting for some news. The surgeon finally comes through the door and tells me. 'She's in critical condition, but in recovery for now.' Then we go to my wife's room so the doctor only has to explain everything once."

He explains that her bowel is atrophied, meaning there is a section of her bowel that didn't receive enough blood while she was in the womb and that portion of her bowel has died. It was a small section about one quarter of the way from her stomach. He then explains that because of the obstruction, one quarter of her intestine is the diameter of a banana and the other section is the diameter of a pencil. The banana section is twenty-five percent of her intestine, while the other section, minus the atrophied section is just under three quarters of her intestine. 'I tied off the small diameter section and left it hanging and reconnected the larger diameter section to her stomach. I figure the banana size section has a better chance for nutrient absorption.'"

"This baby is amazing. She's so full of life. Even though these times are difficult, there's a spirit about her that has me convinced she is going to survive. Her will to live is seen in her smile, she's just really a happy baby."

"Three months go by. My wife is home, continuously pumping the milk from her breasts. She stores it in the freezer. We visit Natalie every day. Unfortunately, we watch her through a window outside the critical care ward. Neither of us has even gotten to hold her since the surgery. I'm so thankful I held her in my in my arms right after she was born."

"My wife was lucky enough to hold her right before surgery, for a brief few minutes. Thank goodness she was a big baby when she was born. She's losing weight now. Her body has dwindled down to less than seven pounds. There isn't enough of her intestine to absorb the nutrients from the formula they're feeding her. The doctor at Kaiser didn't know what to do, except to begin feeding her intravenously."

"Then one day the doctor decides to introduce her to hyper-alimentation. It's a new medical technique used to provide nutrition intravenously, not through the digestive tract. They insert a tube through a large vein in her neck, right behind her ear. They run this tube all the way to her heart. It is a complicated procedure and very risky. Once the tube is in place, they start giving her two bottles of a special nutrient liquid per day. They were very expensive, one hundred and fifty dollars each, and my insurance with Kaiser is about to run out."

"This is the first of three of these operations. The first tube was only in her for a couple of weeks because she got an infection. One of the nurses in the ICU had taken a liking to us. One day she tells us she feels as though they were getting nowhere with her treatment and she encouraged us to find better help."

"We decide to research this on our own. My wife contacts the American Medical Association. The AMA tells her there are two doctors in the Bay Area who specialize in intestinal disorders. One is at Stanford Medical Center, the other is at Children's Hospital in Oakland."

"We decide to call them both. Each of them agrees to come to Kaiser for a consultation. They're both nationally renowned specialists."

"The Stanford doctor is the first to arrive. He flies in by helicopter. He checks her over, confers with the doctor at Kaiser, then gives us his opinion. He feels very strongly that they should be feeding her breast milk."

"My wife tells him that she has been freezing her breast milk and he suggests we turn those reserves over to the hospital to feed our daughter."

"The second doctor, Dr. Lane from Children's Hospital in Oakland, arrives at Kaiser a couple of hours later. He apologizes for the delay, but says that traffic was bad and it was slow getting there."

"No need to apologize, we're just glad you came."

"He then dresses in a gown to check her out. He spends a great deal of time with her. Much more than the doctor from Stanford. His bedside manner depicts the gentleness of his soul. I liked him best, the moment I meet him, as did my wife. His words display a deep passion for his work and a deep compassion for our daughter. These attributes set him apart from the other doctor."

"He knows the surgeon at Kaiser. After conferring with him, he gives us his medical opinion. He said that Kaiser is doing the best that they can, but they were not specialists. He told us he recommends that they feed her only breast milk, because it is easiest to digest."

"The doctor from Stanford had scared us regarding the costs of medical attention at Stanford. Dr. Lane tells us not to worry about the cost, if we decide to bring her to Oakland Children's he would see that everything was taken care of."

"He did suggest that we give Kaiser a chance to act on his recommendation before we make any decisions to move her."

"Kaiser does as he recommended, at least so we thought. We find out a couple days later, from the same nurse who suggested we look elsewhere, that they're giving her breast milk only when we're there. When we're not there, the nurses are instructed to feed her Enfamil."

"Three months have passed since she was born. I still haven't gotten to hold her. They let my wife gown up and go into the ICU to hold her hand for about ten minutes a day, but she never gets to hold her. Mom comes up to visit from San Diego and a funny thing happens. They move Natalie close to the window so Mom can see her. Mom tells her to put her thumb in her mouth. I can't believe my eyes, she does it!"

"Mom's been sucking her thumb her whole life. I've had many embarrassing moments when my friends would see her lying asleep on the couch, sucking her thumb like my baby. I don't say a thing to her for teaching her. That is a special moment between her and her granddaughter."

"During the same week Mom is visiting, Natalie gets sick with a high fever of 105-degrees. The Kaiser doctor is losing hope and tells us she's going to die within the next twenty-four hours."

"Mom has me call Pastor Thoeni, a dear friend, very close to our family. He's a Lutheran pastor in San Francisco, and the same pastor who married us. His daughter is Mom's god-child and his son John is named after me."

"Pastor 'T' can you please come to Walnut Creek right away to baptize my daughter Natalie? The doctors are saying that she won't make it through the night. Mom and I want to make sure she's baptized. She's here at Kaiser."

"Sure, I'll be there as quick as I can."

"Pastor Thoeni is here in less than an hour. The nurse prepares him with a gown and a mask. My wife is allowed in to hold her, while Mom and I watch through the window outside. We can't hear the words, yet I know what we're doing is important to her soul. The baptism takes less than ten minutes. Pastor 'T' puts water on her head. Natalie, too weak, just lies limp in her mother's arms. She barely has the strength to open her eyes. The coolness of the water strikes a nerve, and she kicks her feet, looks up at Pastor "T" and for a moment, she musters up a smile."

"He breaks out laughing. At that very moment, I know she's going to be okay."

"Pastor 'T' and my wife climb out of their gowns. They join Mom and I outside."

"We talk for a few minutes when the nurse, Natalie's new godmother, begins knocking on the door. We can hear her voice faintly as she yells through the window, 'She's okay. She's going to be just fine. Her temperature's back to normal.'"

"That is miracle number two."

"After her baptism, we make the decision to transfer Natalie to Children's hospital. The timing to move her is perfect. The insurance with Kaiser runs out the same day."

"We call Doctor Lane and he makes the arrangements. He arrives at nine o'clock in the morning, riding in the ambulance. A few minutes later, we're on our way to Oakland."

"I decide Doctor Lane is the most compassionate and dedicated human being I have ever met."

Bobby asks, "What is compassionate?"

I tell him, "The simple definition of compassionate is feeling or showing concern for someone who is sick. These feelings of concern are real and come from the person's heart. They don't just think it, they demonstrate it."

Then Bobby says, "I want to be a doctor someday, so I can be compassionate."

I say to him, "I trust you will be a great doctor and compassion will be your best attribute. Heal your patients from your heart."

"By the time my wife and I get to the hospital, there are six doctors surrounding Natalie. They huddle around her for close to fifteen minutes before Doctor Lane comes out of the room to talk to us. He tells us Natalie is in good hands and then asks us to go downstairs to speak with the hospital administrator."

"She has us fill out some paperwork and tells us, 'Don't you worry about a thing, including the money. Everything is being taken care of.'"

"We are ecstatic. She tells us because Natalie was born with this problem, she qualifies for the State of California's Crippled Children's

Fund. We qualify financially, and the fund will be picking up all her medical expenses."

"After we finish with the paperwork, we go back upstairs to Natalie's ward and the doctor then introduces us to the nursing staff. They put robes on us and for the first time after three and a half months I'm holding my little girl in my arms. This is a special moment, one that I've never forgotten. I just cuddle her little body close to my heart, lower my head and I whisper in her ear, 'I am so proud to be your father. Thank you for having a strong will to live and a deep desire to survive.'"

"She grabs me by the finger and grips it tight. I can feel her strength. She wants to live. I know it, I can feel it."

"The next five months, I'm allowed to go into the hospital anytime, day or night, it doesn't matter. I hold my little princess every chance I get."

"The hospital's on my way to work, so I'd leave early in the morning, stop and hold her before going to work. It is a wonderful way to start my day. Natalie is beginning to gain weight. They are feeding her breast milk and her body is reacting very well to her new diet. My wife is no longer able to produce milk and the hospital is getting low on reserves. They ask us if they can display Natalie on a TV commercial. They want to build up their mother's milk reserves. Of course, we said, 'Yes.'"

"The next day there she is on the five o'clock news, seven o'clock news, even the late news. This kid has personality. She smiles big for the cameras. The response is fantastic. Mothers from all over the Bay Area are bringing in their milk. They fill the hospital freezers up in one day, and when they got more than they could handle they give milk to the other hospitals in the area."

"Even one of my cousins who didn't even know I was living in the area, Marylin (from Dad's side) sees her on TV. She got my number from Mom, so she calls and the next day she comes to visit."

"This was our miracle baby, Natalie Jean. After a little more than nine months of hell and of heaven, she survives, and soon, we will finally be taking her home for the first time, in late November 1973."

"My faith in the universe has grown strong. During the stay at Children's Hospital we saw many happy moments and we saw some ugly moments. We were the lucky ones because our daughter survived.

There were others who weren't so lucky. It was then that I determine that will power and purpose are key to the existence of our life."

"There were two kids in that hospital whom I have never forgotten. One was born with a brain tumor. Her bed was on one side of Natalie's. On the other side, the baby in the bed is a crack baby. I watch the reaction of the parents of each of the babies. I witness the value of their souls. I see their hearts in action and I see their denial. The parents of the tumor baby are fabulous people. They know their child will never survive, yet they come every day to hold her, to love her every moment that she's alive. Their child lives for less than a month, but they hold her, they talk to her, and they love her. That baby knows she is loved, before she passes away."

"The crack baby on the other hand, never knows her parents. She's so doped up from the crack, she doesn't know if anyone is there or not. They show only one time and stay for only a few minutes. *This poor baby, I thought.*"

"When the State agency worker comes to take her away I can't help but think she's better off without them. Hopefully she'll get new parents who will give her what she needs to survive. We saw others born addicted to drugs and even a few born as alcoholics. No wonder sometimes it's hard to skip a generation."

"Is that the end of the story?" asks Christina.

"Not yet Christina."

"Natalie has two more hyper-alimentation surgeries while at the Children's Hospital. Breast milk wasn't enough to sustain her. When she finally gets strong enough, Dr. Lane does an exploratory surgery to see what is going on inside."

"The surgery takes over four hours. When he's done, Doctor Lane comes to tell us what he found. I detect he was a bit angry by the tone of his voice. Then he says, 'What I'm about to tell you is completely off the record. If you decide to file any lawsuits, I will not testify regarding what I found.'"

"He says, 'Natalie has two sections of intestine. One section is the diameter of a banana and other one, much longer, was just dangling inside. The first one is too short to sustain her life. I don't know what he was thinking, but he should have connected the smaller diameter section. He made a huge mistake. Lucky for us, the smaller diameter section still has blood circulation and is alive. What I did to correct things was to untie the longer, thinner section, disconnect the larger diameter section from her stomach and then I saddle the two together."

"What do you mean by saddle?" asks Charlie.

"I had not become a pipefitter yet, so I have no idea what the doctor was describing. He pulls a notepad from his smock pocket and draws it out for us."

"In simple terms, the smaller diameter section was sewn into the side of the larger diameter section of her bowel."

"Later in life when I became a pipefitter, I learn how to saddle a small diameter pipe to a larger diameter pipe, the same way the doctor had described," I tell Charlie.

"The doctor then tells us, 'The critical moment will be the first time we feed her. If the food passes the saddle without ripping the suture, Natalie should be able to sustain her life without tube feedings ever again. We'll wait forty-eight hours before we find out. Let's give her some time to recover from surgery.'"

"Forty-eight hours later, Natalie is given a few ounces of breast milk. She passes the first critical moment with flying colors. Then the next day she is given some solid food, mashed peas as I remember. When she finally has a bowel movement, they check for blood. Blood is an indicator that something is wrong. They find no blood."

"One week later our miracle baby, Natalie Jean, is going home."

"Is that the end of the story?" asks Christina.

"No yet, but it's an appropriate time to take a break. Why don't you kids take Rascal for a walk and a potty break?"

They all agree and fight for his leash. I convince them to take turns.

While the kids and Rascal are gone, I sit and talk with Vasiliki and Barbara. I ask how things are going between Barbara and Ray. I'm concerned for her and the welfare of her kids. "I apologize in advance for any impropriety on my part," I say.

"No, our situation is in no way your fault," Barbara responds. "Your father and Ray have many similarities. Hearing your stories is like seeing our life in the mirror. Your stories make me stronger. I'm learning how to gain my power back, just as your Grandma said. He's being nicer to me and the kids. Although he still hasn't stopped drinking. I'm not sure he ever will."

"Where is he today? I was convinced he was going to be here."

"He was across the street at the neighbor's house drinking his beer. When I ask him if he's coming, he just says, 'Have an enjoyable time listening to your damn stories.' He already had plenty to drink, so I grabbed the kids and came to Mom's."

"Yep, heard my dad say similar words many, many times. What a miserable way to live life. Is there anything I can do to help or to make things easier for you?"

"No, keep telling us the stories. They're helping my kids in so many ways. They're beginning to see their father very clearly now. They're learning what pushes his buttons and know exactly when to stay away from him. For this I am very grateful to you."

"Okay, I have a few magical stories yet to tell."

About that moment, the kids come in with Rascal and sit down in front me. I begin telling the rest of the story.

"This story is a short one, but I want you to hear how unthoughtful some people can be, even people of authority."

"Natalie's finally home. It's one week before December. The week before, I had notified the landlord that the heater was not working. I ask him to fix it because our daughter is coming home from the hospital for the first time since she was born."

"He says he will."

"We're living in a five-unit complex. Everyone's without heat. I see the landlord again the next day and ask him how the heater repairs are coming."

"'It's getting fixed,' he says."

"But I don't see anyone working on it. Two days pass, it's now December 1ˢᵗ and the rent is due. I type up a note explaining to the landlord that I'm not paying the rent because he hasn't fixed the heater. When he comes to the door to collect the rent, I hand him the envelope and say, 'It's all in here.'"

"Without opening the envelope, he says, 'Thank you,' and then leaves."

"He's only a few feet away as he opens the envelope and sees there is no rent. He knocks on the door. When I open it, he says, 'There's no rent money in here.'"

"Did you read the note explaining why not?"

"Embarrassed to say, he pulls the note from the envelope and reads it. Then he says, 'You can't withhold the rent because I haven't fixed the heater.'"

"At the same time, the neighbor next door is walking by. I say to the landlord, loud enough for him to hear, 'I'm not paying you a dime of rent until you fix the heater. My daughter spent the last nine months in the hospital and she came home to a freezing apartment. How dare you put her life in jeopardy?'"

"My neighbor walks over and tells him, 'You know what, we aren't paying the rent this month either. You want rent money, fix the damn heater.'"

"You guys don't know who you're dealing with. I work for the FBI."

"So that gives you the right to make people suffer and freeze?"

"He then walks away and I close my door."

"Two weeks later he comes to the door to inform me the heater has been fixed. He says, 'Because of the delay, you only have to pay half the rent this month.'"

"It so happens the neighbor is walking by again and the landlord tells him the same thing. 'You people only have to pay half the rent this month because it took so long to fix the heater.'"

Then I say, "There isn't going to be any rent payment from us this month. You took more than four weeks to fix the heater. I asked you to fix it a month ago, you need to be more diligent next time. Maybe this will teach you a lesson."

"My neighbor tells him he's not paying too. I then hand him a two-week notice stating that we were moving the first of January."

"He says, 'You still owe the rent for this month.'"

"Your rent is in your heater repair."

"After Christmas, we start packing. We move back to San Francisco and into a flat near the area where Aunt Clara lives."

"The day after we move in, a certified letter come from a law firm in the city telling us we need to pay the landlord the back rent for the place in Walnut Creek. The letter threatens to take us to court."

"I call my Mom and she tells me to call her lawyer, Mr. Friedenberg."

"I call him the next day. Mr. Friedenberg asks me to read him the letter. Then he asks me for the lawyer's name and his phone number. As soon as I tell him, he tells me he doesn't need the number. He knows the lawyer and has his number. Then he asks for mine."

"About twenty minutes later the phone rings. It's Mr. Friedenberg calling back."

"He says, 'Did you know the landlord works for the FBI?'"

"I did."

"That's how he found you so easily without a forwarding address. I spoke with his lawyer who was insistent that you should pay the rent. Then I suggest to him that we should go to court and let a judge decide. I tell him we will be counter-suing your client for more than just the rent. We're going to sue him for harassment and mis-use of his power. We might even throw in cruel and unusual punishment too."

"His lawyer asks me, 'On what grounds?'"

"Cruel and unusual punishment needs no explanation."

"What cruel and unusual punishment?"

"Then I explain to him that you'd asked the landlord to fix the heater two weeks before your daughter came home from the hospital. Then 'Did your client tell you that their daughter spent the first nine and a half months of her life in the hospital? She'd been there since birth and this was the first time she came home from the hospital? They brought her home to a freezing house. Wouldn't you call that cruel and unusual punishment?'"

"His lawyer says, 'I wasn't presented those facts from my client. I think this will be the last time you hear from us. I want to apologize on behalf of my client for any problems he may have caused.'"

"Mr. Friedenberg wasn't done. He tells him, 'That's not enough. I expect a letter of apology, accompanied by a check returning their deposit within twenty-four hours.'"

"The letter of apology and the check were delivered to us by courier that same day."

Then I tell the kids, Barbara and Vasiliki, "Now that ends the story for today. But before we leave I have a couple of questions to ask you."

"Question number one: Did you like the story?"

"Yes."

"Question number two: Did you learn anything from the story?"

Charlie snickers and then says, "Yes, don't pay your rent if the heater is broken."

"Not the answer I was expecting Charlie, anybody else?"

They all look at each other. No one wants to give an answer, but Christina says, "What is the answer?"

"The answer is this," I say, "When someone like this landlord, who was hiding under the guise that he was an FBI agent, tries to bully you, let them know that you aren't afraid of them. Let them know you expect to be treated just as you would treat them, with respect and dignity."

"Treating people myth respect and dignity," is one of Grandma's Secret Blessings.

"When would you like to hear the next story?"

Before anyone can answer, Vasiliki says, "How about next Tuesday, at my house at noon. I'll make lunch."

"Tuesday at noon is perfect." We say goodbye.

Chapter Fifteen

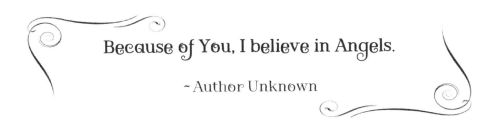

Because of You, I believe in Angels.

~ Author Unknown

Rascal and I show up at Vasiliki's house at noon. The kids come running out to get Rascal and take him into the backyard. I hand Vasiliki red roses from my garden.

As soon as I hand them to her, she says, "Lunch is ready. Why don't you go out to the table and join the kids?"

I grab a plateful of food and head outdoors. When I get to the table, I notice Ray's in the corner of the yard doing his usual, drinking beer and smoking cigarettes.

Vasiliki asks him to join us, but he says, "No thanks, I have what I need right here," as he taps the side of the can.

I finish eating and ask, "Who's ready for a story?"

Before I start, I ask Ray to come over to join us.

His response was as expected. "No thanks, your stories aren't for me." Then he walks into the house for another beer.

I give Barbara a quick glance and a wink, to let her know it's okay that he said no.

"As you'll remember, the last story was about the about the birth of my miracle baby girl, Natalie. It wasn't long after Natalie came home from the hospital that my wife became pregnant with our second miracle, my first son Brock, soon after we move back to San Diego. In December 1974, I become a Pipefitter apprentice and began working at the San Onofre Nuclear Power Station."

Charlie says, "Hey, isn't that the place you passed when your grandma died?"

"It is Charlie, that's the place I told myself that I was going to work at someday."

"Before the year is over, in mid-November, Brock is born at Tri-City Hospital in Vista, where we were living at that time. Brock was eight pounds ten ounces and twenty-two inches long. He's healthy and my wife is living her dream, breastfeeding our newborn baby."

"Working at the power plant was fun, exciting and different to anything I have ever done before. I work from Monday through Friday, and go to school Tuesday and Thursday nights in San Diego, at Mesa Jr. College. Within a few weeks after Brock is born, we move into our first home. It's a two-story condominium located in Vista. It's a brand-new complex, with a swimming pool, park and a place for the kids to play. It even has a garage. Every man's dream."

"Unfortunately, not long after moving in, our marriage crumbles. It's only been a few months since Brock is born, and we divorce for the first time. The welding class that I was taking for the apprenticeship was taught by her dad. He made things tough on me. The first welding test was proof that he didn't care for me. I thought I had done a pretty good job. But he tells me, with a Texas snicker, 'Well, one thing for sure, you'll never be a welder.'"

"Then one of Grandma's Secret Blessing came to mind. She always told me, *'No one can make you be who you are and no one can ever stop you from being successful except yourself. Always be careful and beware of the saboteur archetype.'*

Bobby asks, "What's a saboteur archetype?"

"I'm glad you asked. I studied archetypes through the writings of author Caroline Myss. She says that each of us has four main archetypes that are part of our character. One of the four is the **saboteur**."

"The saboteur archetype is the energy that undermines or sabotages our empowerment. It is the guardian of our choices. Remember the story I told you about the day I married my first wife. It was my saboteur archetype telling me to run and it was also my saboteur archetype that made the decision to stay and get married. One side of the saboteur protects us, and the other side undermines us. Does this all make sense to you?" I ask.

"I think it does."

But I detect otherwise from the hesitation in his voice. I give him another example.

"One of the things my father used to tell me was that I would never amount to anything. Those words could have sabotaged me if I had let them. But my protector guardian taught me otherwise."

"My dad tells me the same thing," he says, while looking around to make sure his dad's not there.

I do my best to simplify the explanation, "Bobby, you can be anything you want to be by making good decisions."

"Now I understand."

"My wife and I were legally divorced. However, neither of us signed the final papers. One weekend in June of 1977, I brought Natalie and Brock home from a weekend visit. Their mom coaxes me into the bedroom and before I know it, we've re-consummated our marriage and we conceived our next child."

Before anyone has the chance to say anything, "We were now married again." That seems to work, because no one asks what "consummated" meant.

"Just before the summer of 1977, I convince Mom to patch things up with Aunt Genevieve. I tell her it's ludicrous that they've gone this long, still angry with each other. I miss my aunt being here during summer. They were close for most of their life. It was a shame a quarrel between them kept them apart for so long."

"Mom thought about what I said and called Aunt Genevieve later that day to patch things up."

"As it turns out, it was a good thing they did. Toward the end of summer my aunt's diagnosed with breast cancer. They perform surgery and remove both of her breasts. Almost a year passes. When the chemotherapy treatments are over, her cancer seems to be gone, she's in remission."

"That same summer, while my wife was pregnant, we sold our condo for a profit. We doubled what we paid for it. My best friend Charlie, who also owns a condo there, two doors away, waits an extra six months before selling his. When he does, he sells it for double what we sold ours for. Then we bought the house in Lakeside, a three-bedroom house, two bathrooms, a large kitchen, large family room, dining room and the master bedroom itself is 600 square feet. The property is 1.86 acres, large enough to install a tennis court someday."

"We move into the house in late October 1977. We've barely moved in when in March, one month before Ryan is born, we have monsoon rains. It rains night and day for more than two weeks. One morning, as I step out of bed, my feet are in six inches of water. The house is flooded. Within an hour, the water's risen to fourteen inches. Everything on the floor is ruined, the water's dirty, full of soot and dirt."

"My wife, less than one month away from delivery, is having a tough time. The first thing I want to do is to take her and the kids to her mother and father's house. They live on Mount Helix, about twelve miles away. My wife insists she needs to stay to help save as many of our belongings as possible."

"The County workers came by with a truckload of sandbags. But they only left twenty bags per homeowner. I did my best to put them around our doors, but there were only enough to slow the water down, but not stop it. A couple of my friends, Fernando and Joe, show up to help. There's a large contention of Mormon's who live in the valley. A dump truck load of them show up. They're all carrying shovels or sandbags. One of the women notices my wife is pregnant and she tells her to sit and rest, while they take over. Our house is surrounded with sandbags in less than thirty minutes. Then the vacuum crew comes and removes every ounce of water. In less than an hour, the only thing left in the house is us and the damp floors."

"Then I convince my wife I should take her and the kids to her parents' house. As we drive down the street, we get as far as six houses away. We spot a little old lady and a little old man trying to sandbag their house. They were all alone, and look to be in their late 80's. We stop to help. My wife and kids drive down the street to find the Mormon's. Within minutes, they're there to help save the day. The elderly couple were so grateful for our help. Two weeks later, just before Ryan is born, they show up with a homemade apple pie to thank us. It was and still is the best apple pie I've ever had."

Christina says, "No it's not, Grandma makes the best apple pie, right Grandma?"

"I don't know if mine is the best or not? I'll just have to make one sometime so Yianni can tell us if he thinks it's the best."

"Goody, goody," says Christina.

Then I continue.

"I take my wife and the kids to her parent's house. It was hard driving out of the valley. Water's pouring over the dam up the road and copious amounts of water is coming off the mountain behind us. The roadway has more than two feet of water on it, just below the doorway to my truck."

"When I get back home, I check the rest of the property. I had knee-high rubber boots and I'm wearing a raincoat from the power plant. As I walk toward the back, I sink down into a couple of gopher holes, knee deep. The only dry spot on the property is about two hundred feet in the middle. Down the road everyone's property is under water."

"Ryan is born the first week in April, at El Cajon Hospital. He's born the largest of the three, weighing nine pounds, ten ounces, four more ounces than Natalie when she was born. But he's shorter than she was, at twenty-two inches like his brother. He's healthy and that's all that anyone can ask for."

"The clean-up from the flood continues for some time after he's born. The drywall and most of the electrical wiring is replaced. Most of the furnishings were ruined and had to be replaced. Homeowners insurance didn't cover anything. It was a natural disaster. The President declares it a disaster and FEMA show up to help out. The government provided us with $27,000.00. The first $10,000 at one percent interest and the remaining $17,000 at three percent interest. It's like getting free money. It's the best rates I ever got. The county of San Diego waives all permits per the direction of the President of the United States, as we rebuild our small community."

"We hire a friend of the family who's a contractor. He lives down the street from my mom and is a close friend of hers. He uses every bit of the money to complete the repairs. I wasn't paying much attention because I was working long hours at the power plant, mandatory six days a week. Monday through Friday ten hours a day and Saturdays eight-hour shifts."

"By December, the house is back in order but our marriage crumbles. Two weeks before Christmas, my wife announces she wants another divorce. She tells me, 'I want you to pack up your belongings and to be out of the house this weekend.'"

"As we talked about earlier Barbara, I wasn't going to leave the house my parents helped me pay for. So that weekend, I pack up the truck with their belongings and they leave."

"As she drives away, tears roll down my cheeks because I know my kids are broken hearted and I know I'm a failure as their dad."

"We divorced for the last time in 1979. It was a rough year. Not just because of the divorce, but that same year, my Aunt Genevieve dies. Her breast cancer came back and within months, she's gone."

"I saw her in the hospital one week before she passed away. I've never forgotten that day. When I walk into her room, her smile steals my heart and her eyes are sparkling with joy. The sad part about her cancer is that this time, it really took her down. She lost all hope for living. She weighed about sixty pounds and looked like a child. She's no longer that vibrant person who I grew up to love almost as deeply as I love my mother."

"One week later, after I have gone back to San Diego, my mom calls me to tell me that my aunt has died. I fly to San Francisco to attend her funeral. It's another typical family funeral, two days of viewing and then she's buried at the Greek cemetery along with her sister Margarite and her brother Alex. At the burial ceremony, twenty-nine years old, I'm crying like a baby."

"My mom clutches my hand and says to me, 'I bet you don't cry that much when I die?'"

"'How can you say that at a time like this?' I ask her. 'Of course, I'll cry when you die. I'll cry like a baby then too.'"

"The following year, 1980, is another bad year, it's raining cats and dogs. The rain is much harder than the rain in '78. I wake up one morning to find twenty-two inches of water in my house. However, this time, even though it's declared a national disaster, I'm one of two people in the whole valley that has flood insurance. I collect close to $45,000 and I'm able to put my house back together again for a second time. It takes two years to finish, but more shocking news is on the way. Death is among us."

"Who died?" the kids are all asking?

I continue, "One weekend in May 1981, I have my kids for a weekend visitation. I'm still working mandatory overtime on Saturdays. Mom agrees to watch the kids while I'm at work. She's busy doing someone's book-keeping and taxes. My dad is of no help watching the kids because he's too busy across the street drinking with his beer buddy. Mom didn't trust him with them anyways. Their relationship's on the brink of disaster. Little does he know, Mom's making plans to divorce him. She calls her godchild, Janet, to ask for some help. Janet, who is also the daughter of our family doctor, Doctor Hanson, is glad to help and goes to Mom's right away."

"Later that night, Janet tells her dad that my mom has a weird cough. He asks her to explain it to him and seconds later he's on the phone calling Mom."

"He tells her to meet him at his office at eight in the morning, Sunday morning mind you. Six months earlier he gave her a 'clean bill of health.'"

"Mom shows up at eight, just as Doctor Hanson asked. He examines her and takes chest x-rays. After the x-rays are developed, he walks into the examining room. Tears in his eyes, he tells my mom she has lung cancer and that she has about six months to live."

"Doctors don't cry, but this time was different. He was telling his best friend she is dying."

"Mom calls me when she gets home and asks me to bring the kids over to see her. She doesn't say a word about the cancer. I can tell by the way she's hugging her grandchildren that something's up. I notice she's been crying. Without saying a word, she takes me by the hand and walks me into her bedroom. She closes the door and says to me, 'I'm dying. Dr. Hanson says I have lung cancer and I only have six months to live.'"

"I start crying like a baby. Mom and I have a moment and then she says, 'Stop crying, clean your eyes and do not tell the kids I'm dying. But bring them here to see me every weekend that you have them. For your two summer weeks, I want them here with me. Don't talk about me dying, just bring them around more often, promise me,' she says."

"'Of course,' I tell her. 'I know how much they mean to you, I would never dishonor or deny your dying wish. But, it's going to be hard to keep this from the kids. They're smarter than you think. They're going to know something's up, if they don't know it already.'"

"Mom has one chemotherapy treatment. She hates how sick it makes her and she hates it even more when her beautiful brown hair starts falling out. That was it, only one treatment. For the next six months, she spends every moment she can with her grandchildren. My dad on the other hand, he's a real ass. He treats Mom like a piece of dirt. Ready to just throw her away. Sure, he takes care of her, but he goes out of his way to let her know he hates every minute of it. 'He's a real prick,' I say, forgetting the kids were there."

"How dare he. She has been the breadwinner of this family, the one person that put food on the table, made enough money to buy his beer, his cigarettes, everything. How dare he treat her that way during those six months. We all knew the love was gone. It was gone many, many years ago. The only reason he stayed around was because she took care of everything and he didn't have to work."

"Once Mom found out she was dying, there's no need for a divorce. Death was fine with her. It was the easiest way to get away from him she told me. In her loneliness, the times when none of us were around, Mom spent those six months reading every book she could find about death. She read parts of the Bible, the Book of Mormon, even the Jewish Torah. Mom wants to know where she's going. She spends that time preparing herself for death."

"Mom's very worried about me. She tells me every time she sees me how worried she is. We'd become very close after my divorce and even closer, as the time of her death draws near."

"One night when I'm visiting her, she makes the comment that she wishes someone would take over her tax business. I take the hint, because I was the only one in the family who has a background in accounting because of my college days. She lit up as bright as a firecracker when I tell her I'll take her business. Mom's an enrolled agent so she readies me for what to expect when doing taxes."

"What's an enrolled agent?" Barbara asks.

"An enrolled agent is a person who has earned the privilege of representing taxpayers before the Internal Revenue Service. She passed a three-part comprehensive test. An EA status is the highest credential the IRS awards. It is an elite status."

Barbara's satisfied, and the story resumes.

"I remember when Mom studied for the tests and how excited she got when she found out she passed. She represented a lot of my co-workers at the power plant. Many of them still talk about her today. I never took the exam. It was just more study than I ever wanted to take on. But I'm very proud of my mom for doing it. She taught me that we can do anything, if we put our mind to it."

"It was getting really close to the end for Mom. She was in a great deal of pain. One week before she dies, I was there visiting her. She's begging my dad to give her a shot of morphine."

"He refuses, tells her it's too early since her last one."

"She's begging again. He still refuses."

"I tell him, 'Give her a shot. She's in so much pain and if you don't give her the shot, I'm calling Doctor Hanson at home to ask him to come give it to her.'"

"He refuses. I go to the phone to dial Dr. Hanson's number. I know it by heart because he's my doctor too. I'm just about done dialing when Dad grabs the phone from my hand and says, 'Fine, I'll give her the damn shot. I just don't want to give her another shot and end up in jail for killing her.'"

"You're not going to end up in jail, she's going to die, but show her some sympathy and respect. Give her a shot and let her die with some dignity."

"He says nothing, but relents and gives her the shot."

"A few minutes later she's telling me, 'Make me a promise that after I die you'll make every effort to have a relationship with your father. Promise me?'"

"I tell her, 'Mom, it's not up to me to make sure there is a relationship between me and Dad. Relationships take two people. Not one.'"

"Then she tells me again, 'Promise me you'll make an effort.'"

"I can't make you that promise Mom. We both know he's hated me since the day I was born and he still hates me today. I can't make you that promise."

"She asked me one more time, but I give her one more response, 'Mom, you can't beat a dead horse into the ground. Please just let it be the way he wants it to be and stop worrying about me. I will be just fine.' Even though I know that once she's gone, life is going to be very lonely for me."

"One week later, on a Monday night, I drive over to see her. I knew the time was getting near. When I pull up out front, there is a darkness hovering over her house. It's an eerie feeling. I know her time of death is near. I decide not to go see her. I couldn't bear to see her again, so I drive away. It's the weirdest feeling I've ever had in my life."

"The next day, at exactly two thirty in the afternoon, I laid my head down on my workbench. I was talking to God. I said, 'God, take her away. She's in so much pain and she really doesn't want to be alive. Please take her pain away. Relieve her from the wickedness of my father, just take her away.' And then I said, 'Amen.'"

"That night as I walk into my house the phone's ringing. It's Dad. He says, 'So how was your day?'"

"It was fine."

"Then he says, 'What's new?'"

"'Nothing much,' thinking to myself how weird this call is. He never calls me to see how I am, so I know something's up."

"Then he says in a nonchalant voice, 'We lost Mom today. They took her away and she's at the mortuary. I thought you'd like to know.'"

"Even though I wasn't surprised, it was weird the way he told me. There was no sympathy, not an ounce of remorse in his voice, just calm and cool, very nonchalant, as if he's glad she's finally gone."

"What time did she die?"

"At two-thirty."

"He said the time I expected him to say. I knew it, but had to hear it to make it so. And then I hung up. Mom died as I was praying to God to take her away. She was just waiting for me to let her go."

Tears start rolling down my cheeks. I was doing my best to brush them away, when Christina says, "Mr. Yianni, don't cry. Your Mommy is right here with us now. I can see her."

I look at this little angel, dumbfounded by what she just said. I ask her, "What do you mean she's right here, Christina?"

She points to the back door of the house as she says, "She's right there. She's smiling at what you said and she's standing there with my grandpa."

Before I can say anything, her grandmother says "What do you mean you can see your grandpa standing next to her? How do you know that's Grandpa?"

"Because he told me the first time I saw him, that he was my grandpa."

"You've seen him before? How come you never told us?" she says as she looks at her daughter Barbara, then puts her attention back to Christina.

"I don't know, I guess because he asked me not to tell you."

Vasiliki's crying too. She comes over to give her granddaughter a big hug.

As soon as I gather my composure enough to say anything, I tell her, "Oh you precious angel Christina, you know just what to say to make me feel better. Thank you. I'm really glad you can see her," all the while wishing I could see her too. But, the way Christina describes her smile, I do see her in my own way.

Then Christina asks, "Is that the end of the story Mr. Yianni?"

"Not yet, there's a very magical story I have to tell you."

However, I suggest that we take a break. I need a few minutes to regain my composure and I think Vasiliki does too. For a few minutes, we sit there dumbfounded about what has just happened.

Vasiliki says, "Is it possible she really sees her grandpa? I'm in shock and I don't know what to think."

"You know Vasiliki, in the New Age spiritual beliefs, it is said that our children can see things that we can't see until they pass the age of three. Many children have what is believed to be imaginary friends. I think that those spiritual believers are right and that our little ones are still connected to the spirit world until fear takes their independence away. That's why the latest studies say to let them have their hidden friends. It's highly possible these made-up friends are not really made up, they are spiritual beings helping the child adjust to the physical realm. It's one of those mysteries I keep seeking to know the answers to. What happened today with Christina puts some validity to it."

While the kids take Rascal for a long walk, I take the opportunity to ask what happened to Ray. "How come he isn't here with us?"

"I think he's too embarrassed. Remember when you and Bobby were having the discussion about the saboteur and you told Bobby that your dad used to tell you that you would never amount to anything."

"I do."

"We had no idea that Ray was sitting in the kitchen close to the window listening to everything that was said. When Bobby said his dad tells him he won't amount to anything, Bobby's words struck a chord with him. It's really bothered him since he heard him say that. I think he's too embarrassed, ashamed or afraid the kids might point out more of his faults. He didn't tell me why he wasn't coming, he just gave his usual response by saying 'No thank you, not my cup of tea.'"

"It's kind of strange though, he didn't respond with anger like he has in the past."

About that time, the kids walk up with Rascal and announce they're ready to hear the rest of the story.

"One of the last things Mom told me before she died, was not to be surprised if there is a blonde lady sitting on my dad's lap when she's gone."

"I thought she was a bit crazy and silly when she said it, so I tell her, 'Mom, don't be ridiculous, that's not going to happen.' After all, who would want him anyways?"

"Well guess what? I was wrong. Mom's only been dead one day, when her best friend Ginny, Grandma Lil's daughter, shows up to help Dad. She's not really a blonde, but she was at one time. Her hair has changed from blond to white. She's a southern girl, but it becomes obvious she's Dad's girlfriend. They didn't do much to hide their affection."

"During the six months before Mom's death, she made her funeral arrangements with the local mortuary. She bought her casket and she arranged for the Hearse to take her body to the airport after the service at St. Luke's Lutheran Church. She made arrangements with Pastor Hoffman to hold her burial service for those family and friends in San Diego. Yes, she even made the arrangements for her flight to San Francisco, along with the arrangements at the Greek cemetery to be buried with the rest of her family. She paid for it all. No one had to do a thing, except be there."

"Incredible," says Barbara.

"But that's just who my mom was. She spared us from the pain. She had a lot of experience making funeral arrangements. After all, she had made the arrangements for Papa's, Grandma's, Uncle Alex's and Aunt Genevieve's funerals. Mom died at fifty-one years of age, November 10, 1981. It is a day I can never forget."

My story resumes...

"After the ceremony at St. Lukes, the family gathers at Mom's house. I pick up the boys from their maternal grandparent's house. Natalie was with me because she wanted to go to the service. It was kind of strange too, because Natalie is the same age I was when Papa died. The grandkids were in the front yard playing. The rest of us were inside. My brother and his wife, my sister and her husband, my dad with his future wife and me. Suzy, my sister-in-law, and Ginny are in the kitchen preparing supper."

"When supper's ready, Suzy asks me to get the kids. When I open the screen door to tell them to come in, I notice the kids are playing with a pigeon. It evidently flew down to join them. I ask them to put the pigeon down and come into the house. Ryan, my youngest was the last one in the door. Before I can close the door behind him, the pigeon flies into the house and lands on my brother's lap. It sits there for a moment and then jumps over to my sister's lap, then to her husband Brad's."

"By this time, Suzy's yelling and saying, 'Someone get that damn bird out of here.'"

"I take the bird with both hands and walk to the doorway. Once I get past the screen door, I throw the bird into to the air suggesting that it fly away. But that didn't happen. The bird flew for a brief second and then lands back on the grass. The pigeon just sits there in front of the house."

I happen to look over at the kids as I'm telling this part of the story. I can see they are all anxious to hear what I say next. They're sitting in front of me, their legs crossed, arms perched on their knees, and their hands tucked under their chins. They were intrigued, I can tell.

Charlie says, "What happens next."

"After the kids finish dinner, they ask if they can go back in the front yard to play. Not paying attention, we tell them 'yes,' without making sure they put on jackets or sweaters."

"About thirty minutes later we realize it is getting a bit cold, especially since it is November. We decide it's time for them to come in. When I get to the door, I notice they're playing with this pigeon again. I ask them to set the pigeon down on the grass and to come in."

"Once again, Ryan's the last one in. As he walks past me, the pigeon flies into the house again. This time it lands on my brother-in-law's lap, jumps to my brother's, then to my sister's, then to my dad's and then it flew over to mine. I stroke its head and then I shock them all by saying, 'Hello Mom, how nice of you to join us.'"

"They're shocked by what I said. My sister gets angry. She says, 'Why would you even say such a thing? You know that's not Mom.'"

"Before I can say another word, my sister-in-law's yelling at me. She's French, she's loud and she's being a bit obnoxious when she says, 'Get rid of that damn bird.'"

"I walk to the door, holding the bird gently with both hands. I stroke the top of its head. My brother-in-law opens the door for me. Just before I throw the bird in the air, I say, 'Thanks for stopping by Mom. Now it's time for you to fly away.' The pigeon hovers over the house for a couple of minutes and the lands on the neighbor's garage eve. It's perched dead center at the arch of the roof, sitting on the edge. I stand there for a few seconds and just watch as tears roll down my cheeks."

"Brad grabs me by the arm and says, 'Come on, let's go back in.'"

"As I walk inside, I'm wiping tears from my face. My sister says, 'I can't believe you said that bird was Mom. I'm really mad at you for putting a blemish on today.'"

"Then I call the kids into the living room. I ask them to sit down so I could tell them a story. My kids are sitting right in front of me, while my brother Donald's kids are sitting with him and Suzy."

"When I was young, about fourteen years old, Tony from across the street and I bought homing pigeons from a guy down the street. When we bought them, the guy told us to feed them good, clean up after them daily and to talk to them. His dad made him a beautiful cage for his birds. I didn't have a cage, so I kept mine in a wooden box covered with wire. Every day I fed my birds, I watered my birds, I cleaned up after them, I held them each one at a time and I talked to them."

"Tony on the other hand just put his birds in the cage and barely fed them food and water. He only cleaned up after them when his mom or dad told him the smell was getting too strong. He never held them, he never talked to them. Three months pass. We decide it's time to see if our homing pigeons would come home. Tony's mom drove us with our pigeons to the east side of the city. Tony opens his box waiting for the pigeons to fly away. I open mine and hold them one at a time, saying goodbye. 'I'll see when you come home,' I say to them."

"We're home less than an hour, when Tony's first bird flies into the cage. Then the second, the third and before we know it, all his pigeons are home. I wait, and I wait. I see a pigeon fly by, but none of them fly into the box. I wait and watch for two days. Still no pigeons have come home."

"In the afternoon of the second day, Mom tells me, 'Come with me to the grocery store. Your birds aren't coming back and we need some food for dinner.'"

"I get into the station wagon, in the front next to Mom. As she's backing out of the driveway, she spots a pigeon on the eve of the neighbor's garage and says, 'Look son, there's one of your pigeons.'"

"I snap at her and say, 'Mom, knock it off. That's not funny.'"

"Then she says, 'When I die I'll come back as a pigeon to visit you.'"

"The adults are all shaking their heads in total disbelief. The kids sit there with smiles on their faces. Then I invite everyone to go outside. We gather on the lawn and I point at the neighbor's garage eve, 'Look for yourself, the pigeon sitting on the eve.'"

I notice they're all smiling, as I continue.

"Later that evening when it's time to take my kids home, as we get into the car we look across the street and say goodbye to their Grandma, my mom. She's still perched on the eve of the neighbor's garage, waiting for us to leave. I say a silent goodbye. Then I begin to drive away. As soon as I do, I see the pigeon fly away."

Without saying another word, Christina says, "Is that the end of the story? That was the greatest story of all. Your mommy is a special angel."

Within seconds after she says that, another song pops into my head, "My Special Angel," by Bobby Vinton.

"Yes, that's the end of the pigeon story. But there's still more story. We have to bury Mom."

"Oh, goody!" they all say in unison.

"Mom's funeral was scheduled for Thursday. I went to work the next day, Wednesday, and flew to San Francisco that night. But that afternoon, something mysterious happens. I'm at my workbench working. My co-worker John, also a tax client of Mom's, is there with me. We're doing some instrument calibrations. At exactly 2:30, this picture that John had on the wall above his workbench comes flying off the wall and lands behind us. As we're looking at each other, two pieces of stainless steel tubing, about ten feet long come flying over our heads. There's no earthquake, no sudden movement in the building."

"John looks at me and says, 'What the heck is all that?'"

"Only one thing came to mind. Spotting the clock at 2:30... 'That's Mom telling us goodbye.' There's no other explanation for what had happened."

"The following day we're at the Greek cemetery burying Mom and saying our last goodbyes. I cry like a baby at her funeral, just like I had at the other funerals. What can I say, I'm just a big blubber baby. Saying goodbye is not an easy thing to do."

"My dad, standing behind me at the grave, does something very uncharacteristic. He reaches out to touch me. It was the first time he touched me in a very long time. And I could tell it would be the last time he ever touches me again. I wasn't just saying goodbye to Mom but I'm also saying goodbye to my dad. I could feel it in my heart. His days as my father were over. My tears vanish soon after that."

"And that my dear friends, is the end of today's story."

Everybody comes to hug me and thank me for telling them such a beautiful story. Then they ask when the next story day would be.

I suggest Thursday at the park, but Vasiliki says, "How about dinner at my house on Friday at four?" She said she is really enjoying my stories and it's much easier for her at home than it is sitting on the bench in the park.

I agree, because it's easier for me too.

As we walk toward the door, I turn to Vasiliki and Barbara and whisper to them, "Let me suggest you don't ask Christina too much about what she saw today. Let her come to you, otherwise she might stop seeing them or turn inwards to avoid any confrontation. Little ones need acknowledgement, not skepticism or doubt."

I then grab Rascal by the leash and we head for the car. As we're driving home, all I can think about is what Christina said today about seeing my mom. I feel really good about the outcome of today's story.

Chapter Sixteen

To forget one's ancestors is to be a brook
without a source, **a tree without a root.**

~ Chinese Proverb

Friday finally comes. We prepare ourselves for the evening dinner with Vasiliki, Barbara, the kids and hopefully Ray. I pick up some roses and off we go.

As we drive up, the kids are waiting in the front yard. They grab Rascal by the leash and take him through the gate to the backyard. I go to the door and let myself in. I feel comfortable enough to do that now, and announce myself as I enter.

I hand the flowers to Vasiliki, who kisses me on my right cheek and then my left cheek. Barbara on the other hand gives me a big hug. I can really feel the love from this family. I ask about Ray and they tell me he's in the other room taking a nap. He said he had a rough day at work and wants to be left alone.

Vasiliki asks what I've been doing since last week. I tell her about our hike, about Rascal feeling sick and my phone call with my brother. She asks about my relationship with my brother and wants to know if it's good.

I explain about my relationship with my brother.

"There was a time when things were strained between us, and for about six years after Mom died, we didn't have much to do with each other."

Barbara asks, "What happened to strain your relationship?"

"When I was divorcing my first wife, his wife Suzy, who is still good friends with my ex, got involved with something regarding our divorce that I thought was none of her business."

"What did she do?"

"One Saturday I went to visit Mom. I walk into the house, she and Mom are in the kitchen preparing dinner. As I'm walking to the kitchen I hear her to say to Mom, 'John should be paying more child support and alimony than he is.'"

"Hearing her say that enraged me. She pushed my button, so I tell her to mind her own F'ing' business. My brother came into the living room at the time I said it. Without any knowledge as to why, he gets really mad at me for using the 'F' word with his wife. We argue and I said, 'Your wife needs to stay out of my divorce and mind her own business.'"

"Then Mom jumps in to back me up. 'He still has to live too. He's only protecting his future. You would do the same thing if you were in his shoes.'"

"My brother didn't disagree, he was just mad that I used the 'F' word with his wife. Back then, I wasn't about to apologize for what I said. After that they didn't invite me or my kids to family functions. I only saw them while Mom was alive and at her funeral, but after that, not much at all. I stopped by his real estate office once or twice to say hello."

"So how did you get back together?"

"That came about Christmas, 1987, as my memory serves me. Natalie's back living with her mom and is almost fifteen. Brock just turned twelve and Ryan is nine. It's my turn to spend Christmas Eve with the kids. They were spending the night with me and the next day I'd bring them back to spend Christmas day with their mom. Under the terms of our divorce, we switch every year."

"I had worked earlier that day, but they let us go home for Christmas a couple of hours early. I had made no preparations for dinner expecting the kids would have eaten with their mom and their grandparents."

"As it turns out, they didn't have any dinner because they were expecting to have it with me. We drive all over town looking for an open restaurant. Nobody's open."

"I had two presents in my car for my nephews, my brother's kids, and decide we should drop them off. Afterwards, I would take my kids to my house. I knew I could find something to cook, but it wouldn't be as special as eating out in a nice restaurant. When we get to my brother's house, my sister-in-law answers the door. She's caught by surprise seeing us standing there. She has a house full of guests and they're gathered at the dinner table getting ready to eat. Even my dad and his wife Ginny are there. First time I'd seen him for a couple of years."

"I'm embarrassed for intruding, so I reach out to hand her the two gifts. 'We were in the neighborhood looking for a restaurant, so we thought it would be a promising idea to drop the presents off and then continue looking for a place to eat.'"

"My sister-in-law was born in Nice, France. She says in her deep French accent, 'You're not going to find any place open for dinner tonight, you guys can have dinner with us.' She wouldn't take 'no' for an answer."

"Tears came to my eyes because I wasn't expecting this at all."

"She quickly grabs a plate for me to sit with the adults and three plates for the kids, who were sitting with their cousins at their table. She sits me at the opposite end of the table away from Dad. We have too much history to jeopardize ruining Christmas. There's no way I was going to risk that."

"Dinner was fabulous. I met Don and Suzy's closest friends and said hello to Dad and Ginny. He said nothing, but he still has that same sour look that he always had, especially when I'm around. He just looks right through me. Doesn't turn his head at all, just glares."

"After dinner, the women are in the kitchen cleaning up. The kids are having a blast playing with their cousins. I notice Dad sitting on the couch with no one next to him, so I sit down beside him. Remembering that my mom told me it was up to me to keep the relationship going, I made an attempt to hold a conversation with him, by asking how he was."

"Short and to the point, he says, 'I'm fine'."

"What's new, Dad?"

"'Nothing new to tell you.' By the tone of his voice, I know I've asked enough so I get up to talk to my nephews. As I get up, he wants to start an argument, but I just walk away. I didn't want to ruin their Christmas."

"A little while later, my kids are in the other room with their aunt. At some point Dad walks up to them and makes an attempt to give them each five bucks for Christmas. When he attempts to hand five to Natalie, she says, 'You didn't care for us before, what makes you think we want your money now. You've missed all of our birthdays and all of our Christmas's since Yiayia died. Keep your money.' She hands it back, then her brothers do too."

"Seconds later she's looking for me. When she finds me, she walks up and says, 'Dad, take us home.'"

"I turn to my nephews to give them a kiss and a hug goodbye. The kids greet their aunt and thank her for dinner. This is the second to last time I've seen my father. Then we walk out the door with my brother following behind. The kids hug him, then get into the car. My brother and I spend a few moments alone talking and I apologize if I said anything wrong or spoiled their Christmas dinner, even though I knew I didn't."

"As I drive away, I say, 'What an A-hole.'"

"Natalie says, 'No he's not. He's a nice uncle.'"

"Not him, I'm talking about your grandfather."

"They tell me he tried to give them five bucks. Natalie tells me what she said."

"I'm very proud of her for standing up to him, but there's is a bigger part of me that's sad he doesn't care about them or about me."

"Then they ask me to drive them back to their mom's parent's house. They didn't want to spend Christmas Eve with me because they were too upset. I didn't try to talk them out of it. I just obliged and took them to their grandparents."

"Something good did come out of that Christmas. My nephews said to their mom and dad afterwards, 'Why don't you invite Uncle John and the kids for Christmas from now on. We would rather spend it with them than we would with Grandpa. He's always so sour.'"

"From that year, and most every year since, Christmas has been spent with them. Sometimes it's just me and sometimes it's Natalie and my grand-daughter Kalista who show up, but no longer do Brock and Ryan. They stopped coming for Christmas more than ten years ago. Recently, Brock has been inviting me to spend Christmas at his house with his wife and step-children. Of course, most every opportunity I'm asked, I spend it with them."

"In the mid to late 90's I had season tickets to the San Diego Padre baseball games. I took my brother to quite a few games. We spent time in between innings talking about life. Most of the time I did all the talking, but every now and then he surprised me with something constructive to say."

"Early in 2001, just after 9/11, I help my brother get a job at the power plant as a laborer. The following year he makes the second highest annual income in his lifetime, working long hours at the plant doing security upgrades because of 9/11. He's getting a small pension from the laborers union today, because of working at the power plant. But most important of all, we have become much closer."

Barbara says with a laugh, "I always thought it was the big brother who was supposed to take care of the little brother, not the other way around."

"I've never thought about it either way. I'm just glad I was able to help. I'm sure he would have done the same if the tables were turned."

A few seconds later, Vasiliki announces, "Dinner is ready to be served." But just before we converge on dinner, Vasiliki asks me, "So when was the last time you saw your father?"

"I believe it was 1991 when my nephew Robin graduated from high school and the following week at my nephew Dimitri's baseball game. We gathered at the ball park. My dad walked in with his wife Ginny, said hello to my brother and his wife, my sister and her husband, and then walked past Natalie and I without saying a word, as if we were 'dead to him.'"

Vasiliki lets out a shameful sigh as she says, "Ah pasha," just like Grandma and Papa used to say. It's as if they were using her to let me know it's okay, that he's the loser, not me.

Then she says, "Okay, time to eat. Let's not let the food get cold."

187

Her timing's perfect. I'm done talking for now, so I help carry the food outside. The aroma smells fantastic and once again it is a feast to be remembered. Vasiliki is really a great cook.

Most everyone is quiet while we eat dinner. Even the kids are not their usual selves. I wonder what might be going on, so I ask Barbara why they were so quiet.

"Just before you got here, their dad was really tough with them. He drank a couple of beers and he snapped at them more than once and because of that they're being quiet. They don't want to wake him."

Thinking to myself, "I've seen that picture, too many times, way too many times."

Then Vasiliki says, "Would you like dessert?"

"Not right now, I'm stuffed from dinner, but for sure after I tell the story."

"But Grandma made something special. She...."

Christina's cut short, as Vasiliki raises her finger to her mouth, asking her not to give away the secret.

She giggles, then says, "Can you tell us a story now?"

"Yes, that's a clever idea, why don't we begin?"

"Oh goody, what story are you going to tell?"

"Tonight, I'm going to tell you how I found my family from the Old Country."

"By now you've heard most of the important stories related to my life. In my early forties, I met another woman who seemed to love me. But I never felt that spark, that moment where you feel goosebumps when you think about her. The one that captivates your mind and you can't wait to see her again."

"She's a very spiritual individual. I've never met anyone like her before. She has a one-on-one relationship with her spiritual guide, whom she calls Anne. She shares amazing stories with me related to meditation sessions with her guide. Meditation came naturally to her. She could meditate anytime she wanted. All she did was close her eyes and breathe and Anne would appear. Her favorite time for meditation was in the shower."

Charlie interrupts, "What is meditation?"

"That's a great question. When we pray, we're sending our thoughts and requests to God and the universe. When we meditate, we silence ourselves so that we can receive the answers. To say it in simpler words, in prayer we ask for answers and in meditation we receive the answers."

"How?"

"It takes practice to receive the answers Charlie. Our minds are cluttered with noise. I call that noise chatter. We receive messages and answers every day as thoughts in our mind. We have more than 60,000 thoughts each day, and 40,000 or more of these thoughts are the same ones we had yesterday. Because there's so many, our mind becomes cluttered. We have to learn how to get rid of those thoughts that are clutter. Once we learn, we're able to hear the important messages. People with great minds knowingly or unknowingly invent such things as cars, computers or even the television just to name a few examples. These people were open to receive and take actions. Who knows, you might be the creator of the next invention that saves the world."

"I want to learn how to meditate so I can be the one to save the world. I can be a super-hero," says Charlie, as his brother Bobby punches him in the arm.

"Other people receive the same messages that you do. Just remember this, Charlie, there is one secret ingredient you must put into play when you receive messages that inspire you to create. You must put the 'Law of Action' to work and create it, not just think it."

"So how do we meditate?"

"I like to use the dark closet method."

"What's that?"

"Take a chair and place it into your closet. Close the door, because the darker you make it, the easier it is to shut things out. Make sure no one is around to disturb you. Make sure you can't hear any noise such as the noise from a television, a radio, or even the cars that drive by. Close the windows and doors to your room. When you're sitting quiet in your closet, thousands of thoughts are going to come into your mind. Tune into everything you hear. Recognize the thoughts that are there, then ask them to leave. Each time you do, silence your mind. Do this until your mind becomes completely silent."

"Is it easy or does it take practice?"

"Like anything we do, it takes practice, Charlie. Over time, your mind will become silent. All good things take time. Don't give up, because there are great benefits that you'll receive when you learn how."

"What're the other benefits?"

"I'm glad you asked. Take a look at me. I'm a big man. My doctors say I am obese and of course I agree. But my doctors are amazed that I have the best blood pressure in the world. That's because I control my blood pressure with my mind. Dr. Boone and Dr. Garcia are amazed that I have no diabetes, no high cholesterol, no sodium issues, just obesity. And that one is my fault, because I like to eat! Who doesn't? But I don't let negative thoughts control my mind, especially letting the thoughts of illness of any kind take over. When you say the words, 'I have a cold,' for example, what you're really saying is 'I own having a cold.' Instead, next tell the cold to leave and don't take ownership of it."

"What else can you do with meditation?" asks Barbara.

"Meditation brings clarity into our lives. It addresses questions related to our relationships, finances and of course, health. When you meditate you just feel good afterward. Most of all, your mind, your body, your heart and your soul feel cleansed."

Vasiliki asks, "Can you heal yourself?"

"In my opinion, I think it helps with visualization. When I go to my doctor's I go to get a diagnosis or confirmation as to what's going on with my body. I've never taken pain killers because I've learned to manage pain with my mind. Plus, I have a philosophy regarding pain. When it's gone, I know I'm better. If I take a pain killer, the pain is gone, but I never know when I'm better."

"Have you done any healing with your mind?"

"Yes, I healed Bell's palsy twice. No drugs, no anti-biotics. Just with my mind. The most recent time I beat it in less than three weeks. Ever since I was a little boy, I watched both of my parents killing themselves with pain killers and other drugs. They were always dealing with pain and trying to heal their backaches, headaches and so on. I've always thought there was a better way. I adopted the use of my mind for healing most anything."

"Now don't get me wrong, sometimes an antibiotic is necessary if we let things reach the point of infection. We can't always fix an infection with our mind, or maybe I just haven't gone deep enough to learn how. A positive outlook helps the most in my opinion. We can control pain with our mind. I have a high pain threshold because of it. I've had four surgeries in the past twenty-one years. Each time I came out of surgery there's morphine attached to an IV. Not one time did I push the morphine button."

"The very first surgery, when my appendix burst, the surgeons came to see me the day after. We had the following dialogue;"

"Are you in pain?"

"Yes, I'm in pain, I'm in a great deal of pain."

"Then push the morphine button, your pain will go away."

"No thanks. I'd rather deal with the pain than inject my body with drugs."

"What, you don't want the morphine?"

"No, I don't want the morphine. I don't want to mask the pain, because I'll never know when I'm better. Plus, taking it increases the chance I might want more."

"He's shocked by my answer, then he says, 'I wish all of my patients shared your philosophy. I agree with you completely.'"

"Then he turns to the nurse and says, 'Take the morphine away.'"

"Jokingly, I tell the nurse, 'And don't charge me for it, either.'"

"You are an amazing man," says Vasiliki. "I don't think I have that much will power or strength when it comes to pain. But you have definitely given me something to consider."

Barbara says, "Is there anything else you can tell us about any of this?"

"Consider the reason your husband drinks. Is it because he likes beer or is it because beer is his drug of choice? What pain is he covering up?"

"Food for thought."

"My gosh, we sure digressed from today's story, didn't we?"

Charlie says, "Yes, we did. But we learned something valuable and important."

I knew he was right. This was an important digression.

"Back to the story. I think we've covered enough regarding meditation and guides for now. I'm sure there will be more in future stories."

"I hope so," says Charlie.

❧

"This story is about finding family from the Old Country. In 1994, I begin to write a book about my Papa. He was my superhero. I wanted to know all about his war days, but I've already told you everything I know, and that wasn't much. If only he would've told me more."

"I gave up writing the book and shifted towards fulfilling my promise to go to the Old Country. Papa told us he was an orphan, so I never expected to find any family from his side, only Grandma's."

"For nearly two years, I work like a detective searching for clues. I still don't know where the Old Country is. In 1994, the computer wasn't sophisticated, and the internet wasn't so easily available."

"I start with the National Cemetery where my grandparents are buried. I call asking for my grandfather's military ID number. The woman I'm talking with suggests that I contact the Military National Archives. She gives me the name and address for two of them. I send letters off to with my grandfather's name and his military ID. I know was from San Francisco."

"A few weeks later, I get information back about Papa from both. At the time he joined the military, he was living in Philadelphia. He had a cousin listed as his next of kin. I try to find any one related to him, but have no luck. One of the archives suggests I try three other archives, so I send out three more letters. That's when I received the stories about the battles his division fought in, along with his military pay records. That's how I'm able to trace his steps in the war. One recorded listed him as being from Arta Greece. But there are no other clues related to relatives."

"Then one of my friends from work suggests that I should go to the Mormon library. The Mormons have been gathering all of the family tree records, dating back hundreds of years. Which I do, but find nothing. A woman at the San Diego Mormon library suggests that I go to the census bureau for information."

"The census bureau gathers information about us every ten years, so I look for information from 1920, 1930, 1940, and 1950. I find information from 1930. It lists both of my grandparents as being from Albania, but no cities, towns or villages are mentioned. What it did mention is how many languages they both spoke. That was intriguing information. Grandma spoke nine languages and Papa spoke seven. I had no idea."

"Next, I send off for their immigration records and death certificates. I send for the birth and death certificate for the first-born child, Spiro from Philadelphia. I send for my mother's birth certificate. All of these records cost me money, but I didn't care. I am doing my best to find out all that I can. I'm like a detective trying to solve a crime."

"Some of the information I find is interesting and curious. I discover that although his whole life Papa said he hated the Turks, his death certificate states that he was from Turkey. His immigration record said he was from Arta, Greece, and his census bureau record says he's from Albania. No wonder I have no idea where the Old Country is, I don't know which country."

"I continue to look. Mom used to receive a letter from a cousin from in Tirana, Albania. But the letters stopped coming after she died. Discouraged and about to give up, I decide to keep looking."

"My girlfriend is encouraging me to give it up. She keeps saying, 'Why is it so important anyhow? What do you expect to gain from all of this?'"

"I don't know, but there's something deep inside of me telling me not to stop."

"She begins interacting with her guide, Anne, asking such things as why this is so important to me? Her messages send me into a tizzy. I begin to feel as though she's twisting things to make me stop. I don't say anything to her, but deep down, I get the sense she's not telling me the truth of what her guide is saying. But I continue looking."

"I decide to go to my Uncle Victor's house in Danville, California. I think he might have the key to the missing information. We spend the first couple of days catching up on the years we missed seeing each other. We share stories and memories about Papa, Grandma, Aunt Genevieve, Mom and Uncle Alex. Victor wasn't born yet when Margarite was alive.

Our only memory of her is the picture that was hanging on the wall in Grandma's house, which Victor has on his wall now."

"Then I ask him if he has any records that might help. We spend nearly eight hours the next day rummaging through every box in his garage. We find nothing of interest related to the Old Country. We're upstairs in his bedroom rummaging through one the last box. Still no answers. As Victor's putting the last box on the top shelf of his closet, he catches a glimpse of an old suitcase lying on the floor. He says, 'Hey look, Yianni, there's Grandma's old suitcase.'"

"He grabs it and sets it on his bed."

"We stand there staring at the suitcase, gathering the courage to open it. It's the suitcase Grandma called her pain box, the one she took to 'Queen for a Day.' We weren't surprised to find the dress she wore that day lying inside. Even so, neither of us could hold back the tears."

"As we share our memories, something strange and mysterious happens right before our eyes. A large envelope flies out of Grandma's suitcase and lands on Victor's bed. It was hidden in the lid of the suitcase, tucked inside the cloth pocket lining."

"We look at each other, amazed and confused."

"Victor says, 'What the heck was that?'"

"That was Grandma making sure we find this envelope. Obviously, there's something inside she wants us to know."

"Aw go on. Grandma didn't do this. That's a crazy notion. This is just a coincidence."

"'Then you explain it,' I tell him. 'By this time in my life, I have come to the realization there's no such thing as a coincidence. Everything happens for a reason.'"

"Victor's not open to believing it. We open the envelope to see what's inside."

"There it is, all of the clues as to who was family. Letters, old letters dating all the way back to 1924 according to the postmarks. But there's one slight problem? We can't read them. They're written in a language we don't understand."

"I convince Uncle Vic to let me take the letters. I tell him I would find someone who could translate them. But I have no idea how hard that is going to be."

"At the time, I'm a member of A.H.E.P.A. It is a Greek men's organization, American Hellenic Education Progressive Association. It's their mission to promote Hellenism, education, philanthropy, civic responsibility along with family and individual excellence within the Greek community in the states since 1922. Papa was a member and Grandma for many years was a member of the Daughters of Penelope."

Vasiliki asks, "What's the Daughters of Penelope?"

"It is a woman's organization founded by Alexandra Apostolides, also a San Franciscan, founded November 16, 1929. Their mission is the same as that of AHEPA, to promote Hellenism, Education, Philanthropy, Civic Responsibility, and also family and individual excellence within the Greek community."

Then Barbara says to her mother, "We should look into that and become members. That would be fun, and we can teach the kids more about our heritage."

Vasiliki says, "Yes we should."

Anyhow, that was just a bit of Greek American history, as I continue with the rest of the story.

"I take the letters to some of the old timers in AHEPA to see if they can translate them. They have a tough time because they're written in the Old Greek language as they call it. Some of the writing is totally unrecognizable to them. They figure it might be the Albanian language. They suggest that I contact some of the guys who were members of the church in San Diego who are from Albania. They give me phone numbers for a couple of people, one man and one woman."

"I called them. I find they live in La Mesa, ten miles from my house. They're happy to meet me and to help me out. Unfortunately, they have a tough time reading and understanding the letters too. 'They're just too old and the language has changed,' they tell me. They recognize a mixture of the Greek, Turkish and Albanian languages."

"About to give up, an idea pops into my mind. Remember at the beginning I mentioned the importance of listening to inner messages? This one turns out to be an important message for me to hear."

"I ask them, 'Is it possible to determine the family names from these letters? The city, town or village and if they were from Albania or Greece?'"

"That was it. For the next hour, we look at each letter, each envelope, looking for names, addresses, towns, cities or villages. We find thirty-one different names, no addresses, but we're able to determine what town, what city or what village they're from."

"It is now too late that night, so the next night, I wrote one letter and sent it to each of the thirty-one family names at the determined town, city or village and country."

❧

Vasiliki says, "So what happens?"

I laugh and tell her, "That's a story for another time."

To which she responds, "No way, we want to know the answer now. We can't wait for another story to find out. You tell us now," she demands with a smile.

How could I refuse? "Okay, okay I'll tell you." I had every intention to anyways.

"For two months, every day I check the mail but there's no response. After exactly two months, I pull into my driveway from work. Seconds pass, when the mailman pulls up with a registered letter from Albania."

"This is the first of many more to follow. I can't wait to open it. My heart's beating like a drum. I'm so excited, I'm about to pee my pants, so first I rush to the bathroom."

"The letter's from Qirjako Dako. He's the oldest living son of Kostandina Spiro Meta, my Papa's sister. The letter's difficult to read because the person who wrote it is not well versed in the American English language. I call Uncle Victor and I read it to him."

"Tears roll down my cheeks as I am reading. For us, it is a revelation to find that Papa is not an orphan, as he always told us. He's the oldest and only son born to Spiro Meta and Varvara Kozmai, her birth name before she married my great-grandfather Spiro. The letter goes on to say that he has another sister whose name was Polie Spiro Meta, and they were born in the village known as Zverness."

"Two days later, the second letter arrives. This one is much easier to read. The person writing the letter is Enkeleida Bisha, the granddaughter to Vasil Panajot Stefa, the oldest son of Papa's sister,

Polie Spiro Meta. This letter gives me their ancestral bloodline as it relates to their family tree. It explains that my great-grandfather, Spiro Lambro Meta, came to the village of Zverness from Greece sometime in the early 1880's. He settled in the village of Zverness with his wife Varvara, who had their three children. They go on to say that they do not know the date of birth or the date of death for Spiro, but he died before his wife Varvara who died in 1909."

"A few days after, I receive the first letter from Grandma's side. By the end of 1994, I receive numerous letters from both sides of the family from Greece and Albania."

"That my dear friend's is the story about how I found our family from the Old Country," I say with honor, as they clap for my success. And then, "How about that dessert? I'm so ready for a break."

Vasiliki says, "Let me bring out the surprise."

While she's gathering the dessert, Barbara asks, "Can you explain your philosophy about coincidences? You said everything happens for a reason and there's no such thing as a coincidence. Please explain."

"Absolutely Barbara. I have a simple example and a question for you."

"Okay," she says, somewhat puzzled.

"Do you think it was a coincidence that I met your Christina? Or, do you think there's a higher force that brought us together? I believe there was. Which one do you believe?"

"I agree there's a higher force at work."

"Watch for new, different or extraordinary things to happen this week. With a keen sense of knowing and expecting things to happen, you'll notice them. You'll see things happen that you never expect. You'll see, some amazing synchronistic events will follow."

"Okay. Now give me an example of synchronicity."

"Sure. When I first started my search for family and my expansion to a higher awareness was in its infancy, one day while at work, I was sharing the stories about finding family with a friend. I shared finding the letters and then sending letters to family in the Old Country."

"She says, 'That sounds like what's described in the book, '*The Celestine Prophecy,*' have you heard of it?'"

"Funny thing is, I had, vaguely from TV, but couldn't remember where. It was one of those subliminal messages that remains somewhere deep in our subconscious until the time is right to remember them."

"A couple of months later I'm at the Barnes & Noble bookstore. I decide to go to the spirituality section. Before I have the chance to look at any of the books, a book comes falling off the shelf. I reach down to pick it up. It was the *'The Celestine Prophecy'* written by James Redfield. Instead of thinking of it as a coincidence, I took at as a message from the universe that this was my next book to read."

"Soon after reading the *'The Celestine Prophecy,'* besides completing my search for family, book after book opens my eyes. I read everything I can get my hands on. I was like a sponge filling up with water, but I was filling my heart, my mind, and my soul."

Seconds after that explanation, Vasiliki returns carrying the best-looking and best-smelling apple pie I've ever seen. She hands out the plates and forks, then cuts the pie.

Everyone waits for me to take the first bite. I take a few moments to ignite my senses as I smell the apples, then I take a bite and savor every ounce of it in my mouth. Afterwards, while rubbing my belly, I announce, "This is the best apple pie I've ever tasted, seen or smelled."

As we finish with the apple pie, Ray comes out of the house and says without even mustering up a hello, "Where's mine?"

Everyone's astonished at his entrance. He sounds and acts so much like my father. He shows up just in time for the dessert. I stand up to tell them all goodbye. We agree to meet again next Tuesday at two.

Ray turns to me and says, indicative of the sound of my dad, "Don't leave on my account."

"Not on your account, just time to go, thank you."

They hug me and say goodbye. Christina's the last one to reach me. She reaches up and jumps into my arms to kiss me. Then she tells me loud enough for everyone to hear, "Mr. Yianni I really love you and you tell the best stories."

Little does she know, as I wipe the tears from eyes, I'm thinking *I wish this was my granddaughter, Aubrey Rose.*

Christina has found a special place in my heart. I realize I love her like she's my own granddaughter, but deep down, I know she's not.

As we head to the car, Vasiliki comes out her front door carrying a plate covered with foil. "I thought you might enjoy this for tomorrow." She hands me the plate and says one more thing, "You have no idea how much we appreciate you coming into our lives. Thank you so much from the deepest part of my soul. You are helping to fill a void for my grandchildren after the loss of their grandfather."

"The pleasure's all mine." Then I drive away.

Rascal jumps on my left knee to his favorite spot. He then shoves his nose under my left hand, expecting me to take it off the steering wheel to pet him. Which I do, as I say "It was an awesome day today, buddy. Don't you think?" His tail beats the side of the door like a drum.

Chapter Seventeen

It's not a coincidence,
it's a synchronistic event that nudges
you to find your purpose.

~ John£greek

Around one thirty in the afternoon I prepare Rascal for the trip to the park. He's coming with me all the time now, especially since he knows not to disturb me whenever I'm telling stories.

We get to the park precisely at two. They're all there waiting for us, except Ray. Rascal's jerking on the leash trying to coax me into letting him go. I jerk him back just enough to let him know that I want him to slow down, "We'll be there soon enough."

Half way there, Charlie runs to greet us first. I hand him Rascal's leash for being the victor. But before he takes it, he hugs me, he's more excited to see me. I'm in awe about this sudden change and mark in our friendship. Then I thank him for the nice greeting and for the presence of his spirit. About the time I finish, Bobby and Christina arrive. They greet me in a similar fashion. I'm shocked and speechless for a moment by all of this. These kids have stolen my heart.

When we reach Barbara and Vasiliki, they hug me too. I feel a different sense of spirit, a warm and deep feeling of love. I can just feel it.

How deeply touched I am by their love and their kindness. I have no idea as to the depth I have touched their hearts, but it's more than evident to me how much they've touched mine. I take time to wipe away the tears. Then, "Who's ready for a story?"

"I am," they all say.

"Keep today's story stowed away in your mind, because I can only tell you part of it. The other two parts will come in future stories. They're too long to tell in one day."

"Before I begin, I want to share a cute poem that a dear friend sent me by email over sixteen years ago. I don't know who wrote it, because when I researched it on the internet, I found the poem written three or four different ways. One person declared it his, but that was in the 1990's and I found this version of the poem listed as 'Author Unknown' from the 1950's."

"Here's that cute poem my friend sent to me called 'Pennies from Heaven.' It reminds me of Papa every time I read it. I've changed it up a bit to make it more understandable."

Pennies from Heaven

˜Author Unknown

I found a penny today, just lying on the ground.
But it's not just a penny this little coin that I have found.

Found pennies come from heaven, that's what I have been told,
By angels watching over us, from their clouds of gold.

When an angel thinks of you they toss a penny down,
Sometimes just to cheer you up, to turn a smile from your frown.

So don't pass by that penny when you might be feeling blue,
It may be a penny from heaven, that an angel has tossed to you.

202

"In God, We Trust" is not just a phrase printed on a penny,
It's something to remember, when your troubles seem like many.

When you're down and it seems, your life has a blue tint,
That penny on a sidewalk may truly be "heaven-cent."

❧

"It's a cute poem fitting to today's story. By the way, I've been picking up coins my whole life. Mostly pennies, but one day I found a collection of Indian-head nickels lying next to the highway where I was doing my daily run."

Charlie, with his profound sense of humor says, "You run?"

"Funny Charlie, I do like your sense of humor and your keen sense of timing. No, I don't run anymore. But I used to run thirty-five miles a week. I wish I never stopped, but I did and that's why I'm so fat today."

Charlie has a giant smile on his face, knowing he got my goat.

"As you know from earlier stories, Papa died in 1959 when I was only eight years old. You also know now that his death was the most tragic experience of my young life."

"Papa was very private about his life in the Old Country and his life during World War I. He always said he was an orphan, but now I know that he wasn't. Sure, his parents died when the three of them were young, but Papa was twenty-three years old when his mother Varvara, my great-grand-mother died."

"Finding out he has family is a revelation to me, which gives me cause to look for more answers related to his life. Vasil's letter contains a great deal of information regarding his family and Papa's family, which validates that he's my mother's first cousin. Qirjako's letter did as well. They knew so much about us that they named their kids after Papa, my uncles and my aunts. Why we didn't know about them is the bigger question."

"A few days after receiving their letters, one morning, while driving to work, totally consumed by this experience, I start talking to Papa."

Charlie, the wise guy, says, "You talk to dead people?"

"I do. I've been talking to those who have departed most of my life. Sometimes it's on Mom's birthday or the date of her death. Sometimes on Grandma's birthday, April 1ˢᵗ, who could ever forget that Grandma was born April Fool's Day? And then there's Papa in that picture in my living room roasting a lamb for Greek Easter. It's pretty hard not to talk to him. So yes, I talk to the dead."

"Do they talk back to you?"

I take a few seconds to gather my thoughts before I respond to his question. I don't want to scare them, then say, "Yes, they answer me in ways some people might not expect. I mean think about it. When I told you about those letters flying out of Grandma's suitcase, don't you think she was talking to me?"

They nod their heads in agreement.

"While driving my car I'm talking to Papa, 'So Papa, is this really your family?' I say it over and over two or three times."

"After getting to work, most of the morning my mind wanders to the conversation with Papa. I'm consumed by it. Throughout the day, I keep wondering why Papa never told us about his family."

"That afternoon, I go across the highway to a meeting. The engineering staff works there, and they were having a meeting regarding a project that I was responsible to plan."

"Most of the day, my thoughts have been elsewhere. I keep wondering what the answers are. My boss tells me to drive my car over to the meeting. He tells me it's okay to head for home from there, afterwards."

"About two in the afternoon I drive to Mesa to attend the two-thirty meeting. As I pull into the parking lot, I glance around for a good place to park. I look for a fast get-away spot. I notice one near the exit. I do a complete circle around the lot to get there. After turning off the car, I grab a notebook and a pen. As I open the car door, I notice a coin laying on the ground. Another Penny from Heaven,' I'm thinking."

"But something looks different with this coin. After picking it up, I'm bewildered as my eyes spot that it's a Greek coin, dated 1959."

"No way," Vasiliki interrupts.

"What were you thinking after you saw that it was a Greek coin dated the same year your grandfather died, Yianni?"

"Probably the same thing you're thinking Vasiliki. My grandfather sent more than a just a penny from heaven, he sent the answer to my questions."

They just stare at each other in total disbelief or maybe in awe as to what had happened.

"See what I mean about getting answers to our questions. The answers come in different forms, unusual ways. But they do come, maybe not on our time but on heaven's time, messages are sent from heaven."

Charlie says, "How would you describe heaven?"

I'm caught off guard by Charlie's question. I stand before them, befuddled and feeling awkward about how to describe heaven. But, in seconds, the answer falls into my lap.

"Heaven is described as a 'higher place,' almost like paradise. It's where we'll be one day. Simply put, it's known as the other world."

"What's paradise like?" asks Charlie.

"I think if I were to describe paradise it would be a place where there's no anger, guilt, fear or sorrow. No judgements, no disgust, only friendship. That's paradise to me."

"I like that explanation," says Charlie. "That's good enough for me."

I can hear Grandma saying. "This is another one of Grandma's secret blessings for Yianni, Yianni Capedoni."

"Is that the end of the story?" asks Christina.

"It is the partial end to this story, but there's more to this story that I will tell you in future stories."

Then Bobby says, "Is that all for today? That story took less than a half hour to tell us. We want more."

"Yes Bobby, I do have another story. I'm not ready to leave you guys just yet. I enjoy your company more than that. The next story is about the preparations for my trip to the Old Country and about something that happens to me, one week before my trip."

"In late December, 1994, I begin planning my trip to the Old Country."

"My daughter, Natalie, a flight attendant for the American Eagle, arranged my flights. The first leg of my journey was to fly first class to

New York via American Airlines. Because she's a flight attendant, 'parents fly free.' The only drawback to flying free, it's standby."

"What's standby?" Charlie asks.

"Instead of going to the ticket counter for a ticket, I ask to be put on a standby list. Paying customers have top priority and are seated first. After all paid customers are seated, then those on the standby list are seated last."

I ask Charlie if he understands and he says yes, so I continue.

"When I signed up for standby, I asked to be placed in first class seating. To get the shot at first class seating there are two requirements. First you must wear a suitcoat and a tie, second is they take parents in the order that they sign up. First person signed up, first person to determine what seat they want on the plane."

"Natalie planned the second and the third legs of my trip, too, flying from New York to Greece via Olympic Airways. The arrangement for that round-trip ticket was different than the flight on American Airlines. It was purchased as an I-90 ticket. I-90 tickets are for parents and other family members of flight attendants internationally. I was required to pay ten percent of the highest fare for the destination which in my case, it was $2540.00. I only had to pay ten percent, so round trip New York to Athens Greece cost $254.00."

"Wow," says Vasiliki, "I want to go to Greece with you."

I look at her and smile.

"Natalie arranged for the third leg on Greek Airways, too. Flying from Athens to Ioannina in Northern Greece. There's no discount for that fight, it cost $60.00 round trip."

"I didn't make any hotel reservations for Greece. I'd decided to wing it, figure it out when I get there."

"Two weeks away, I begin packing and gathering my belongings for the trip. In the middle of the preparations three things happen to me that almost put my trip in jeopardy."

"First, the woman who I'd been dating and living with the past four years informs me that she's moving back to her condo while I'm gone. At this stage of our relationship, I have no more fight in me to convince her to stay. It's been a constant battle as to why the trip to the Old Country is so important to me. She doesn't understand the impact of the promise that I made to my grandparents. I suggest she not wait for me to leave, but to start packing now."

"Second, a couple of days later I'm taking my annual physical at work. One of the tests requires the use of a breath aspirator. The nurse tells me to take a deep breath, blow into the aspirator tube, unloading all the oxygen from my lungs. As I'm exhaling, the nurse is motioning to me to give more. This test is tough for me, because I'm a shallow breather. I'm standing there with no oxygen left in my lungs. I'm light headed and I fall over backwards, like a tree that had just been cut down."

"What happens? Did you get hurt?" asks Christina.

"Let me tell the story Christina. You'll find out soon enough."

"The nurse panics. She tries desperately to break my fall. But she isn't quick enough and down I go. My head's about to hit the tile floor, I feel someone reach behind and slow me down. But how can that be, there's no one there. My head snaps backward and taps the floor only slightly, just strong enough to open up a small cut. There's very little blood. I remember thinking afterwards, it should have been worse."

Charlie asks, "Who caught you from behind?"

"It had to be Grandma. There's no other explanation."

"Right before the test, the nurse and I exchange words. We felt as if we had met before, but we couldn't figure out from where. While I'm lying on the floor, momentarily unconscious, she's crying and I can hear her say, 'Mr. Hodgkinson, are you okay?'"

"Seconds pass and I come to. Realizing how scared and panicked she is, I hear a whisper in my ear, 'You know what to tell her.'"

"You may not have known me before, but I'll bet you never forget me now."

"She laughs, while her tears are swept away."

"By now the doctor and two other nurses are at my side helping me to my feet. She tells me how much my fall scared her, and I tell her not to worry. Then I say, 'I am going on a trip of destiny next week, fulfilling a promise I made to my grandparents.'"

"Then I shock her, 'Who do you think slowed down my fall? It was Grandma protecting me.'"

"We look at each other and she shakes her head, but I hold steady to what I said."

Then Charlie says, "Who caught you?"

"His Grandma caught him," says Christina.

"How do you know Christina, this is too confusing for you to understand," Charlie stated.

"No, it's not, his Grandma's shaking her head up and down telling me it's so."

"You can't see his Grandma, Christina."

"Yes, I can, she's standing right behind Mr. Yianni and I can see her."

Then Bobby says, "If Christina says she sees her, then she sees her, Charlie. I believe her."

"It was either Grandma or an angel, but someone from outside the realm of our universe caught me. I choose Grandma because she's the one who agreed to watch over me."

"Your Grandma says you're right."

"Thank you, Christina."

"The count-down begins. It's one week before my departure when something magical and mysterious happens again."

"More magical and mysterious than your dead Grandma catching you when you fall?" Charlie says with a snicker of cynicism.

"Yes, more magical and mysterious than that. One week before I leave for the Old Country, I have an epic dream."

"What's an epic dream? Is it one that you have over and over?" asks Vasiliki.

"Similar, but an epic dream is one that you remember when you wake up and you never forget every detail. It was the most vivid dream I've ever had and I can still remember it today. Grandma is in my dream."

Christina screams out, "I know, it was your grandma. Because she just told me."

That's the second time she's said that Grandma told her something. I do my best not to say much about it, but, "Thank you for sharing that Christina." Then I throw her a wink to let her know that I believe her.

"Today's story is about my epic dream."

The Epic Dream

"It's one week before my trip to the Old Country, Sunday night. I'm sound asleep..."

"I'm in Greece, at the border crossing into Albania. Grandma's standing by the gate. As I enter Albania I need to pass through customs. When I'm done, Grandma takes me by the hand. She says, 'Come myth me, we have a long walk.'"

"Grandma's dressed in her favorite black-and-white floral dress, the one she wore on 'Queen for a Day.' She's barefoot. She hates to wear shoes. She takes me down the mountain, through the valleys, until we reach a river. It's a long walk, but we make it there in dream speed. When we reach the bridge, we cross the river. There's a cloud like fog hiding the sun and the trees are veiled in the lightest of mists."

"As we're crossing the bridge, I can barely see through the mist and fog. But I catch a glimpse of the silhouettes of buildings in a town as they appear right before my eyes. As we walk to the middle of town we come upon a large four-story building. It's rectangular in size, brown in color, and one city block long."

"Grandma knocks on the door. A young girl answers and Grandma introduces her as my Aunt Margarite. She's the one I never met, because she died before I was born. She died one day after her thirteenth birthday from a burst appendix. 'Do you remember her picture hanging on my wall?' Grandma asks."

"'Yes,' I say, as I embrace Margarite. She's just a tiny thirteen-year-old girl, somewhat frail, with hardly an ounce of fat on her body. Yet, she feels alive."

"When we finish our embrace, she and Grandma take me into the building. There's a large number of people dressed in the garb of their day. They take me through the first floor of the building, Grandma in front, Margarite following close behind. Everyone is joyous, exuberant about the fact that I'm there. It's as if they knew I was coming. They're hugging or kissing me."

"Grandma says, 'They are your family.'"

"As we continue through the building, at some point I wake up because I need go to the bathroom."

"Ah shucks. That ruins the dream," says Charlie.

"Let me finish sport, there's more to this story."

"Within seconds after crawling into bed, I fall asleep and continue where I left off with the dream. Grandma takes me to the second floor. There's still lots of people. I notice some of them dancing like they did in the roaring '20's, just like I'd seen in the movies."

"But something interesting happens when we got to the next two floors. The people seem too quiet, they don't even notice we're there. When we get to the fourth floor, it's dead silent. There's no interaction between the people, most of them are sitting with their eyes closed. I ask Grandma, 'Are they alive?'"

"Yes, they're silent because they're reflecting on their life when they were alive."

"In a moment, we're back to the first floor. Everyone's still hugging and kissing me. But something's different. I realize Grandma's gone. She and Margarite are nowhere to be found. I'm searching everywhere for them, standing on my tiptoes looking over the heads of everyone in the room. I ask a couple of people if they've seen them. No one says a word."

"By now I realize the only time I touched Grandma was when we held hands walking through the countryside. I never even gave her a hug. At that moment, I realize how much I have missed her and I just want to give her a hug. Seconds pass, but it feels like an eternity and Grandma is gone."

"Then a loud buzzer sounds. It sounds like the same noise my alarm clock makes, but it's not loud enough to break the trance I'm in. I look around to see what's making the noise. A few more seconds go by while I keep looking for Grandma and this noise keeps getting louder and louder. All of sudden, I squint out of the corner of my eyes and see the numbers on my alarm clock flashing, as I realize it really is my alarm. Seconds later, I'm awake."

"I remember this dream as if it just happened today."

Both Vasiliki and Barbara say, "Not me, I have never remembered a dream that vivid before."

"For some time, afterwards, I keep wondering what it is that Grandma was trying to tell me with this dream?"

"Did you ever figure it out?" asks Vasiliki.

"I did. It's a long story, that I will tell you someday soon."

"Tell us, tell us," demands Christina.

"I can't, sweetheart. There's things that happen before I know the answer that I have to tell you first. Trust me, this is a story for another day. I will tell you, that during the last week before going to the Old Country, I had a grumbling pain in my stomach for a few days before going. It surfaced the day before the dream. I figured it was nervousness and tension related to the break-up with my girlfriend or because of anxiety related to my trip. After all, I was going to a country barely out of communism for a little over three years. There won't be other Americans there, and I have no idea what to expect when I get there."

"For the next couple of days the pain increases. Just when I'm about to call off my trip. I decide to pray for some relief. I ask God to take away the pain."

I pray, "Whatever the cause of this is God, just take it away. I'm ready to go on this trip. It's planned and paid for. I may never get this much time again in my life to go. Let me fulfill the promise I made to my grandparents, I'm pleading with you God. Make me healthy. Amen."

"That night, I share the prayer with my ex-girlfriend before she leaves. She meditates on it, and her guide, Anne, tells her that prayer will be necessary for the success of my trip, and that she was to give me a message to always end my prayers with 'Thy will be done.'"

"'Thy will be done.' I've said it for years with The Lord's Prayer. It seems to have new meaning to me now. You've heard me say 'Life is what it is.'"

"From now on I'm saying, 'Life is what I will it to be.' This is the end of the story for today."

Christina asks, "Can we take Rascal for a walk?"

"Of course."

While they're gone, both Barbara and Vasiliki are still buzzing over the dream that I had. They still can't believe it's possible to wake up, go back to sleep and then continue on with the dream. But hearing me tell them it's possible, makes them want to know what happens next.

While the kids are gone, they ask when we can meet for the next story.

I suggest Thursday afternoon again here at the park, but Vasiliki says, "No, how about my house for lunch on Thursday?"

By the sound of her voice, I know not to disagree and have no desire to anyhow, because she is a great cook. It's always nice to have a home-cooked meal now and then. About the time, the kids get back with Rascal.

We share hugs then head off to our homes.

Chapter Eighteen

Grandma, someday I will go to the
Old Country.

~ JohnEgreek

Thursday came faster than I expected. I gather Rascal and some food for him to eat, because today's story is going to take some time.

As usual, we arrive at Vasiliki's at noon. I'm a stickler about time and appointments. If you're not going to be on time, you shouldn't say you will be there. Honesty and integrity are the cornerstones to life.

As we pull up to Vasiliki's house, I'm surprised, because the kids are usually there waiting for us. When we get to the door, I knock, but nobody answers. I look at Rascal and I'm thinking, *did we have the wrong day?* But I look at my cell and find that it is Thursday and it is twelve midday.

I start to walk down the steps, when the door comes open and Charlie yells, "Fooled you."

"You big tease, Charlie. Just so you know, there is such a thing as payback. I'll get you."

In seconds, everybody's at the door greeting us as we walk in.

We head outside and once again I notice Ray is nowhere around, but I choose not to say anything about it. I figure at this stage of our storytelling, he obviously has no interest.

I catch up with the kids, Vasiliki and Barbara. Then my favorite girl, Christina, starts asking about today's story. I tell her and the rest of them to sit back, today's story is going to be a long one. Then I begin where we left off on the last one.

ॐ

"Even though my girlfriend and I've officially broken up, she insists that she should take me to the airport. She sends me off with an obligatory hug, then utters into my ear, 'Remember to end your prayers with *'Thy will be done.'*"

"She then offers me good luck and kisses me goodbye. There's a bit of sadness in my heart, knowing that I'm experiencing another failed relationship. I just know in my heart, however, that what I'm about to do holds a higher priority in my life for now."

"I walk up to the ticket counter and announce to the agent that I'm the father of an employee and I would like to be placed on the stand-by list, requesting first class."

"She finds Natalie's name on the employee registry and says to me, 'You're the second parent to sign in, so they get first choice for seats. The plane isn't full, so there should be no problem finding you a good seat.'"

"I decide to stand next to the other parents and make small talk with them, hoping to position myself for a first-class seat. 'Do you use your free flights often?'"

"The wife tells me, 'We use them every chance we get. We've had the opportunity to fly just about anywhere that American Airlines flies. We've even gone to Europe a couple of times.'"

"This is the first time I'm using this great perk."

"Her husband asks, 'Did you tell them you want to be seated in first class?'"

"I did, but you folks have first dibs. Chances are I might get business class or coach seating. It really doesn't matter that much to me, I'm just happy to be flying for free."

"Then she asks, 'Where are you going?'"

"I'm flying Greek Airways to the Old Countries, Greece and Albania. My daughter arranged an I-90 ticket, are you familiar with those?"

"Oh yes, we're very familiar with I-90. We use it every time we fly out of the country. It's even better than the free flights we get here, because those seats are guaranteed. However, we never get a shot at first class. Have you ever flown first class?"

"No, never."

"Seconds later, the agent calls their names. They walk up to the counter and I hear the agent tell her there is one seat available in first class, one seat available in business class and multiple seats in coach."

"She points in my direction, then tells her, 'Give him the first-class seat. He's never flown first-class, and everybody should fly first-class once in their life. I'll take the business class seat and my hubby will take a coach seat.' He consents without argument."

"I'm impressed that she gave me the first-class seat, but surprised she didn't choose to sit with her husband in coach. When the agent calls my name, she tells me, 'I am so glad I'm giving you first class. I really can't believe she didn't sit in coach with her husband.'"

"My sentiments exactly."

"As I walk past them, I thank them for their generosity."

"Seconds later, the flight attendant asks me for my boarding pass and escorts me to my seat. She asks for my jacket and I whisper, 'I'm a parent, so I'm supposed to wear it while I'm on the plane.'"

"She giggles, then says, 'Only to get on the plane silly. Now you're mine and I'm telling you it's okay to take your coat and your tie off.'"

"I'm sitting next to the window with my head turned to the side so no one can see that I have tears in my eyes. I'm thinking about my grandparents and how proud they must be of me, knowing that I'm about to fulfill my promise. It's a quiet moment we share together. I can see their smiles. I hear Grandma saying, 'Enough of the tears, no more tears.'"

"Thank God, I stop crying. Another first-class customer's taking his seat next to me. I recognize him right away, but say nothing. He's a famous world champion tennis player from Australia."

"He sits down and says to me, 'Hello mate.'"

"Hello Rocket."

"You know who I am, do you?"

"Yes, sir, I do, you're Rod Laver, but I promise to leave you alone and not tell anyone else you're here."

"No worries mate. By now I'm used to being recognized everywhere I go."

"Then the flight attendant walks up to hand us a warm, wet wash cloth and asks for our drink order."

"I order a fresh squeezed orange juice and Rocket orders something a bit stronger."

"He starts wiping his face and hands with the wash cloth, so I follow suit. I have no idea that's what I'm supposed to do, so thanks to him I have it figured out. I clean the tears from my face, so it was perfect. Just before the pilot announces we are heading to the runway, the flight attendant hands us our drinks. Mr. Laver clutches his drink with his right hand and reaches over to tap my glass and says, 'Cheers mate, here's to a safe trip. Are you sure you don't want anything stronger?'"

"No thanks, I don't drink."

"Say again, you don't drink. What's up with that, mate?"

"My dad was a mean bastard drunk and I swore I never wanted to be like him, so I just never drink."

"He raises his glass again, then says, 'Good on you mate. That takes a lot of tennis balls.'"

"Subtle way of putting it, a very fitting response for two tennis players."

"He lets out a good laugh, as the pilot announces its time for takeoff."

"As we take off, I swear to myself that I won't bother him anymore. As it turns out, it wasn't me bothering him, it was him chatting with me. He made the five-hour non-stop flight trip fly by. The time went fast. He figured out I was a tennis player, so we start talking about tennis. I share a story about a special time I had at the San Diego Sports Arena when he was playing team tennis there."

"I tell him about my daughter Natalie being displayed to the crowd by the KGB Chicken. 'As you remember he used to do his patented voodoo hand signals to you players. The crowd loved it. That night, in between the Chicken's voodoo hand waves, he held my daughter high into the air telling her to do voodoo to the players. He really had a knack at getting the crowd into things. Those were some fun times. I would go watch whenever you players were in town."

"He laughs, then says to me, 'You know, I think I remember that time. He held that little girl up for a long time. The crowd loved it and so did I. That was your daughter mate?'"

"It was. She's responsible for getting me this first-class seat. She's twenty-two and works as a flight attendant for American Eagle, sister company to this airline."

"You sound very proud of her mate. Good for you."

"I'm absolutely proud of my daughter and my two sons. They've turned out to be great kids and are very successful in their endeavors and their responsibilities."

"Before he has a chance to say anything else, the pilot announces that we're about to land in New York. When the plane lands, he reaches up for his carry-on luggage, opens it up and hands me a white tennis warm-up jacket. 'Here mate, this is to commemorate our trip together and thank you for not asking for my autograph.' He then turns and walks off the plane."

"I wasn't paying much attention when they announce where to find our connecting flights. I knew I had a little over an hour to get to the Greek Airways terminal. I had no idea how gigantic the New York airport is and when I find out I need to board a bus to get to terminal eight, I start to panic because I am at terminal one. Then I find out that terminal eight is on the far end of the airport, a few miles away from where we landed. You can only get there by a bus which takes passengers to one terminal at a time."

"By the time I get to terminal eight, the plane's already boarding. I ask for non-smoking, so the flight attendant seats me in the middle section of the plane. I have a row of seats all to myself. Non-smoking, how silly is that when I find out there are only five rows of seating in the middle of the airplane that are for non-smokers. I might as well have been a smoker. The majority of the people on the plane are Greek or other European ethnicity and they all smoke. I'm trapped in the middle."

"I'm glad they don't allow smoking on airplanes anymore," I tell my audience.

Vasiliki says, "Me too. The Europeans are worse than Americans when it comes to smoking."

"Yes, because the tobacco industry is dying in our country, so they have addicted all of Europe and other parts of the world. If the world only knew how it bad it is for them?"

"Then again, how guilty was I? I bought a carton of cigarettes to bring along in case I need them for a bribe. Figured I'd give them to a relative who smoked."

"It's night-time now and the flight to Greece from New York is an eight-hour flight. After eating the dinner meal, I decide to sleep. I spread my body across the three seats, the flight attendant hands me a pillow and a blanket and I sleep for almost five hours."

"By the way, in 1995 I was only one hundred and seventy-five pounds. I was in great shape, still playing tennis and running."

Then Charlie the comedian says, "What happened?"

But I'm wise to his sense of humor by now, so I continue telling them about the flight to Greece, ignoring his question.

"I arrive at the Athens Airport, Greece airport at 11:30 in the morning. A shuttle takes me to the hotel section in Athens and I get a room in the Brittani Hotel. The hotel was suggested by one of my AHEPA friends back home. What he didn't prepare me for was the bathroom. There's no toilet! There's only this porcelain pad on the floor with foot pads and an uncovered hole. I had never seen one before, but I remember Papa talking about Turkish toilets when I was young."

"How do you use it?" asks Charlie.

"For boys or men, when you have to pee, you stand on the pads facing the hole in the floor and you do your best to hit the target. If you have to go number two, you turn and face away from the hole, you squat and go. That's how women use it, too."

Then he says, to no surprise, "What happens if you miss?"

I chuckle, then say, "If you miss peeing, it's okay. The urine goes into a lane, similar to a bowling alley, but narrower, as it finds its way back into the hole. But if you miss going number two, you better be prepared to clean up your own mess."

"The hotel is a four-star hotel, at an affordable price and it's close to the Parthenon. My friends warned me to be aware of thieves."

"Thieves?"

"Yes thieves. They told me they work in twos. One guy will walk up to you and acknowledge you're an American and then suggest you might like to check out his Taverna. He might tell you there are beautiful women there, but you need to be aware of your surroundings. Because if you walk down any side streets with this guy, there will be one more guy down the street ready to jump you and rob you of your belongings."

"As it turns out, that night while in Athens, around nine o'clock I decide to walk around Athens to look for the Parthenon. Everyone's out late at night. Nightlife actually starts about nine in Europe. I was told it was really beautiful at night. I was two blocks away from my hotel when this guy approaches me and says, 'You American?'"

"Yes."

"Then he asks me if I'm in Greece for any particular reason. I tell him I've come to meet my Greek family."

"Where do they live? I can take you there?"

"No, I fly to Ioannina tomorrow?"

"Oh, your family is from Ioannina?"

"Yes."

"Would you like to go down the street to my Taverna? It's a new place and we have beautiful Greek women there."

"I look down the street and I notice a McDonald's hamburger joint on the next corner. I'm thinking to myself that'll be the perfect place to ditch him. I knew he was a thief, so I say, 'Sure, let's cross the street.'"

"As soon as we get across the street in front of the McDonalds I notice a guy crouching behind a car, two buildings away. It's obvious they're working together. I tell him, 'You know, I think I'm going to stop for a hamburger instead of going to your Taverna. Thank you for the invitation, but I'm hungry for an American hamburger.'"

"He tries to convince me otherwise, but I just turn and walk into the McDonalds side entrance, walk through the store and out the front door. Then I head up the hill directly across the street."

"Were you scared?" asks Charlie.

"No, I was on a trip of destiny and Grandma was watching out for me. I knew what was happening. I stayed away from the dark streets. There was plenty of light and lots of people. I wasn't about to let my trip get ruined."

"Did you worry about pick-pockets?" asks Barbara.

"I didn't have to worry about pick pockets because I didn't have anything in my pockets, except ten bucks. I carried my passport in a carrier that hung on my neck, under my shirt and my money was tucked away in my waist pocket, between my underwear and my pants."

"You had everything figured out," says Vasiliki. "Bravo."

"I haven't heard that saying for a long time. My grandparents said 'bravo' all the time."

"I walk up this hill looking for the Parthenon. I knew it was in the area, but I couldn't find it. At some point, I decide to turn right and go up another hill. When I get to the next corner, I look up the street ahead and I look down the street to my right. I see a line of people waiting to get into a bakery, so I thought I'd check to see if they have baklava and maybe I could ask someone where the Parthenon is."

"When I get inside, the girl behind the counter says something to me in Greek. She has a really strange accent though, so I'm curious about that."

"'English, I only speak English,' I say, hoping that she did too."

"Oh, you're American. You look Greek."

"I'm second generation Greek-American."

"She giggles, then says, 'I'm first generation Greek-Australian.'"

"We share a few more words. I order some baklava and then I ask her how to find the Parthenon."

"There's a trick to finding it. As you walk up the street, I want you to look at the roof-line of the buildings and notice the beautiful architecture. When you get to the next street, turn right and walk up the hill. Keep looking at the top of the buildings, all the way to the top of the hill."

"Then what?"

"'Just walk and keep looking up,' as she waves her hands as if to tell me to scoot."

"I walk up the first hill admiring the architecture, just as she said. She's right, it's beautiful. When I get to the first street, I turn right, continuing to walk up the hill admiring the architecture. I'm nearly to the top, when my eyes catch a glimpse of this massive structure. I'm awestruck. The light cascades up the columns. It's the Parthenon. It's massive and I stand there enjoying the moment. I'm astonished and amazed. I'm aghast at how giant this structure is. I wonder, *'How in the heck did the Greeks build this?'* I close my eyes for a minute and take it all in."

"I was thinking I'd come back the next day to see it up close, but some tourists standing next to me tell me that it's closed for renovation. I stand there a bit longer, enjoying the view, then head back to my hotel to enjoy the baklava. However, I'm disappointed. The baklava was very dry and bland. They didn't use honey. It wasn't sweet. Earlier in the day, I had a similar reaction when I ordered moussaka. They make it with potatoes, not custard like we do here in the states."

Vasiliki says, "You poor man. I can see the disappointment in your eyes. I'll make you moussaka and baklava again very soon."

"The next morning, I check out of the hotel and take a shuttle to the airport for my trip to Ioannina. My plane's scheduled to leave at 8:10 in the morning."

Vasiliki says, "I'm jealous. I would like to go to Ioannina to meet my family. But I don't know who or where they are. I have no idea if there's even family there?"

"I'll help you find them. We have the internet now. Even Facebook is a wonderful place to look. I have cousins I communicate with on Facebook from Greece, France and Albania all the time."

"I'm at the Athens airport ready to board the plane. They're announcing everything in Greek and I have no idea what they're saying."

"There's a guy waiting to board who looks over to me, and says, 'Do you understand Greek?'"

"No."

"He sticks out his hand right hand and says, 'My name is Kostas, follow me, I'm flying to Ioannina too.'"

"We board the plane together and it's open seating. The plane takes off and I have a new friend to talk to. He asks me why I'm going to Ioannina. When I tell him that I'm going to Albania to meet family, he's deeply impressed to hear my stories."

"The flight is fifty minutes. Halfway there, air turbulence becomes very strong. It feels like we're on a roller coaster. The plane is bouncing up and down. A couple of times the drop is intense, even with seatbelts on it felt like we were flopping around. The flight continued to be rough. Even the flight attendants were strapped in. At one point, one Yiayia stands up and goes toward the door to open it. The flight attendant grabs her, scolds her and then makes her strap back in."

"How did you know she was a Grandma?" asks Charlie.

"By her age. Calling her Yiayia is giving her respect. It's a term of endearment."

"I look about the plane and notice people are scared. Not me, I know I'm on a trip of destiny. Nothing's going to happen to us, Grandma just won't let it. For some odd reason, it crosses my mind to wonder if they have earthquakes in Greece. Not sure why at the time."

"The pilot says something to the passengers that I don't understand. Kostas tells me, 'We're turning around, going back to Athens.'"

"The pilot didn't say why, but seconds later we're back in the turbulence."

"We've been flying for two hours when I notice we're flying over the sea really low. I can see small islands above and below the water. This is the most beautiful clear ocean water I've ever seen. Then it dawns on me, that we have flown over the same islands three or four times. One hour later, the pilot announces we're going to land."

"When we've landed, I see they're removing our baggage from the plane. As I reach the ladder to head toward the terminal, I see our pilot lying on top of the suitcases with a bottle of wine, drinking and yelling something."

"Kostas tells me, 'The pilot's happy to be on land. He's yelling, we were flying on fumes. Thank the God's we made it!'"

"I guess that explains why he's drinking a bottle of wine."

"When we get into the terminal, it's total chaos. Everyone's yelling and screaming at this poor ticket agent. I have no idea what they're saying."

"Then there is an announcement, Kostas tells me, 'There was an earthquake in a village just outside of Ioannina. It did some major damage and a lot of people may have died. They didn't have the time or the resources to inspect the airport landing strip. That is why they brought us back to Athens.'"

I stop telling the story for a minute to tell them about the earthquake. I researched it years later on the internet. "That particular earthquake happened May 13, 1995, at 8:47 in the morning and was measured at 6.6 magnitude. At the time, it was the strongest earthquake of the decade. Only twenty-five people were injured, but 5,000 homes were destroyed, and 7,000 others were damaged, but there were no deaths."

"Thank God I was in the air and not on the ground. But after all, I was on a trip of destiny."

"Kostas tells me they're going to fly us back to Ioannina in five hours or we can ask for our money back. Then he tells me he's going to wait the five hours and take the next flight, and says to me, 'If you want, we can wait together and go to the restaurant across the street?'"

"Sounds good to me. Five hours later, we're flying to Ioannina, arriving there around five o'clock."

"On the way, Kostas tells me which hotel to stay in. He says, 'The lady who runs the hotel speaks English. I will call you there tomorrow.'"

"When we land, I notice there's plenty of daylight. I grab my suitcases and go to find a taxi to take me to the hotel. I have the strangest feeling. I'm having a déja vu, something I've never encountered. I've heard of them, but never had one. I feel as though I've been to Ioannina."

"Seconds later, Kostas walks up just as I'm climbing into the cab. He tells the driver where to take me. Then he tells me, 'Don't give him any more than five bucks.'"

"I get to the hotel and sure enough this beautiful Greek woman standing behind the counter speaks English. She tells me her name is Genevieve and the odd thing, she actually looks just like my Aunt

Genevieve. The room is only $29.00 for the night. I get settled into my room and then decide to go for a walk. I'm hungry, so I thought I'd find some place to eat."

"I walk out of the hotel and head toward what looked like downtown. I still have goose bumps on my arms, thinking I have been here before. I feel like I am home for the first time in a very long time. I notice the people look just like me. Most of them have brown hair, brown eyes, dark olive complexions and they're all in great shape. There's very few cars. I'm finding restaurants, but none of them are open. Even the markets are closed. I notice one bakery open and I almost settle for a loaf of bread, but instead I go back to the hotel."

"When I get there, I ask Genevieve where I might find an open restaurant. As I do, an old Greek song pops into my mind, *'Never on Sunday.'* Maybe it's true, nobody's open."

"Genevieve tells me, 'Go up the hill across the street. Stay on the right side. When you reach the top, there should be a restaurant open there.'"

"I leave the hotel and walk up the hill just as she said. As I get around the corner there's the restaurant, their door is open, but nobody's inside. I walk through the door, then up a small flight of stairs. As I get to the top, I swear the guy that greets me is my Uncle Victor. I can't believe my eyes. This guy could be his twin."

"He greets me and is talking to me really fast in Greek. I tell him, 'No speaka the Greek, only English.'"

"Then he says, 'No problem, I learn to speak English when I live in New York. I live there for nine years. That's how I get the money to buy my restaurant.'"

"Then he holds out his arm and bows as he says. 'Choose any place you like to sit.'"

"For the next ten minutes, I'm his only patron. But that changes quickly, within twenty minutes the place is full of Greeks. They're talking so loudly, I can hardly hear myself think. But I enjoy it immensely because that's how it was with Papa and Grandma on Greek Easter. And the lamb, the lamb was out of this world. I really enjoyed the meal and the atmosphere. Afterwards, I wasn't ready to go back to the hotel, so I walk from one end of the city to the other, until halfway back again, I reach my hotel. I feel at home."

"At precisely noon the next day, the phone in my room rings and it's Kostas, calling as promised. He gives me the name and phone number of a guy he knows who has a taxi and speaks a little English. He tells me to pay him only ten dollars for the ride and not to lose his number, because I'm to call him when I'm ready to go to Albania. He'll drive me to Kakavia, where the border crossing is between Greece and Albania. His name is really easy for me to remember, because it's the same as mine, Yianni. Kostas tells me to keep his number and to call him when I come back to Greece."

"I'm enjoying Ioannina. I decide to stay the rest of the day, so I pay for one more night in the hotel. I have a phone number to call in Albania, so I call the number to tell them I will be there tomorrow, Tuesday. Then I call Yianni to arrange to pick me up the next morning. He tells me he'll be there at exactly eight in the morning. Then I spend the rest of the day walking from one end of the city to the other, enjoying Ioannina. At the far end of town is a banner that says Tennis Tournament or something in Greek, so I go down to check it out. But there's no one there. It was the day before. Too bad I missed it."

"The following morning, at precisely eight o'clock, Yianni pulls up in front of the hotel in his taxi. He helps put my luggage in the trunk of his car and we drive off. But I have to tell you, his English is very, very weak, he hardly speaks it at all. The scenery as we drive to Kakavia is breathtaking. I'm enjoying the countryside, the villages and the homes are very old. I guess that's why they call it the Old Country."

"At one point, we pass another village. Yianni points and says, 'boom, boom,' shaking his body at the same time. I knew he's telling me it was the place of the earthquake. There is lots of fallen rocks and rubble. We could see the damaged homes."

"The ride to Kakavia took about forty-five minutes. When we get there, I notice there's a lengthy line of people waiting to get into the building. Yianni motions me to stay put, while he goes inside. He's only gone five minutes when he returns to tells me, 'Come.' He insists that I leave my baggage in the car."

"We pass everyone standing in line. When we get inside, we continue past everyone to the front of the line. I feel awkward doing that. When we walk up to the counter, this man standing behind says, 'You are the American going to Albania?'"

"Yes."

"He asks for my passport, stamps it and says, 'Good luck. Have a wonderful time.' I notice him shaking his head from side to side as we walk away. The thought comes to mind he must think I'm crazy."

"Then Yianni and I go to the car to get my luggage. I hand him ten bucks just as Kostas told me. He kisses my right hand and says, 'Thank you.'"

"I tell him, 'Ef-hari-sto.' Which means thanks. One of the few words I know how to say in Greek."

"Then the Greek guard at the border crossing opens a really large iron gate and I walk through. On the other side of the gate is a broken-down dirt and cobbled road, just like the one I saw in my dream. I'm dragging two suitcases on wheels and one shoulder bag across my chest. It's a struggle and I'm thinking to myself, 'How stupid is this? I brought way too much luggage, typical me, always bringing too much when I travel.'"

Barbara laughs, but Vasiliki says, "How many days were you staying?"

"Including weekends and time off from work I have thirty-two days. The most days I've ever had for vacation in my entire life and my longest vacation ever."

"When I get to the border building in Albania, there's a line with about nine people in front of me. This is exactly how it was in my dream, so I begin looking around for Grandma. Of course, I don't see her, but I know deep inside she's standing right there beside me."

"In line for less than a minute, a policeman comes from the building, walks up to me and says, 'You American?'"

"Yes."

"He calls over another policeman to watch my luggage, then walks me inside. There's a guy sitting at a four-legged table, no drawers, just a simple table and he says to me, 'Passaporte.' He almost sounds Italian."

"I hand him my passport. As he stamps it he's asking me where I was going in Albania and he asks me why."

"Vlore and Zverness, I'm going there to meet my family."

"He smiles at me, hands back my passport and says, 'Enjoy Albania.'"

"Then the other policeman who brought me inside, walks me to my baggage. He tells me to go with the guy who was watching my bags to the swing arm, adjacent to the building in the center of the roadway."

"We walk over to the swing arm, standing in the middle of the roadway, stopping cars on both sides and he says, 'We wait.'"

"A couple of cars pull up and the drivers ask me, 'Taxi, you want taxi?'"

"I just shake my head. They say taxi in Greece too, so by now I'm realizing it's a universal word everywhere around the world."

"We stand there for nearly fifteen minutes, when a small man, dressed in a brown suitcoat, sweater underneath, a hat on his head, walks up to me and says in a soft-spoken tone, 'Jhon, Jhon Amerik?'"

"Yes."

"He motions me to follow him, as he turns and walks away, without even offering to help with my luggage. We walk to this white Jeep Cherokee. There's two guys standing outside waiting for us to get there. I was a bit apprehensive because I have no idea who these guys are. I turn back to see if the policeman's still there, and I notice he's watching me every step of the way."

"As I get closer, one of them starts yelling at the guy who's bringing me to them. I don't know what they're saying, but I figure out that it has to do with him not helping me with my luggage. When I'm almost to the car, they walk up to me and gently push me aside as they grab my luggage to throw into their car."

"Seconds later, they're patting me on the shoulder, shaking my hand and telling me their names. The little guy is Joseph, the other is Stefan, who keeps saying 'Gjenovefa, Gjenovefa,' as he points his finger to his chest. The driver's name is Yianni, same as mine."

"But that's it. We couldn't talk because we didn't know each other's language. They motion for me to get in the car, insisting I sit in the front seat. Then the driver starts the engine, puts the car in gear and off we go. We go about five hundred feet when he stops the car and parks under a tree. For close to twenty minutes, no one says a word."

"By this time, I'm a bit apprehensive and nervous. They're talking amongst themselves, but I have no idea what's going on. We sit and wait. We sit there forty-five minutes when another guy comes running up to the car. He's smiling and really happy to be there. He's shorter than Joseph but he takes my hand to shake with him, as he says, 'Nikolla, I Nikolla.'"

"I'm recognizing them by name from the letters that I received. I begin to feel better and more relaxed. After Nikolla gets into the car, we drive away. Nikolla is laughing and making everyone else laugh as we drive down the mountain. I can tell he's the comedian of the family, because they're all laughing when he's talking."

"The countryside has a beauty of its own. But there's an ugliness about it too. As we pass this one area, the mountainside is full of oil wells, pumping oil. When we come alongside a lake, the water is covered with oil that's running off the mountainside. They have ruined the ecological aspects of this lake and their countryside. I'm in shock. There's no way anything like this could happen in the states, at least not anymore. The other thing I notice all through the mountainsides and the valley are these mushroom-like concrete structures. I'm curious to know what they are, but since I can't ask, I only hope to figure it out later."

"Farther down the road we come to a complete stop. There is a huge herd of sheep blocking the road. Cars going upward are honking their horns, and cars going downward are honking their horns. The trip to Vlore is only 89 kilometers, which calculates to a little over 55 miles. It takes us nearly six hours to get there."

"When we get to Vlore, they stop the car at a market. I really need to pee. It's been close to eight hours since I left the hotel. But I don't know how to ask them. I send out a prayer, asking to take away the desire to pee. I end with, 'Thy will be done.' I put it to a test."

The kids are laughing because I said pee. Bobby asks, "What happened?"

"It worked. Low and behold, within seconds after saying the prayer, I didn't need to go to the bathroom anymore."

"Wow, it really works," Bobby says.

"It really works."

Then I turn to Vasiliki and say, "I need to use the bathroom. Why don't we take a break, and may I please use your restroom?"

I suggest to Vasiliki when I get back, "This is a really long story, so maybe we should break here for lunch."

She agrees and heads into the kitchen with Barbara to bring out lunch.

They surprise me with a treat for lunch. They made gyros sandwiches.

I ask how they made the meat, but Vasiliki tells me, "It's a family secret. If I tell you, it won't be a secret anymore and only the women in our family know the secret, not the men."

I laugh, nod my head in agreement and say no more until I finish eating.

Only seconds after I finish, Christina's asking me to get back to telling the story. I'm done eating so I agreed.

Chapter Nineteen

Hoxua could take away our Bibles,
our crosses, our priests and our church,
but Hoxua could never take God
from our Heart.

~ JohnEgreek

Vlore and Zverness

"We sit for twenty minutes, waiting for the sheep to clear the road. To distract myself, I spend time gazing at the people. I can't believe how much these people look like the average everyday American. They dress and look just like we do. I believe these people are sisters to America."

Bobby asks, "What do you mean by sisters to America?"

"It's just another way of saying they look just like you and me."

"Joseph comes out of the market carrying a large tray of lamb shoulders. As soon as he gets into the car we head to the village where my great-grandparents settled years ago. It's the home village of my grandfather."

"I have no idea how long it's going to take to get there. I've lost my sense of direction. I get the feeling we're traveling southwest, only to figure out later we were actually traveling northwest to a peninsula that borders the Ionian Sea. It isn't far, but there came a point in the drive where Yianni has to put the car in four-wheel drive. We're traveling on the beach, right next to the sea. Minutes later he turns what I think could be east for about a mile on a dirt road, then makes a left-hand turn onto the final road to the village of Zverness."

"People are standing in the doorways of their homes, yelling and waving at us as we drive by. I have no idea what they're saying, but I'm guessing they're all welcoming me to the village. As we drive a bit further, I see some kids playing soccer in a dirt field and an older man standing in a field with a couple of cows eating weeds nearby."

"When we reach the village, people begin to swarm both sides of the car. Those on my side are reaching through the window to touch my arm. They just can't wait until we stop. I notice a gathering of women around a free-flowing spout of water. They stop what they're doing and follow the rest of the people behind us."

"We finally reach Joseph's house, the home of Qirjako, my mother's first cousin, who I find out later is the man I saw in the fields with the two cows. He lives here with his wife, their daughter Donika and son Joseph. I'm barely out of the car and everyone is greeting me. Everyone kisses me on my left cheek and then they kiss on my right cheek, men and women alike. I figure out pretty quick this is the custom, so I return two kisses to each of them, one on the left cheek, one on the right."

"There's close to a hundred people standing there cheering and applauding me. I've never felt such a deep feeling of love and gratitude from so many people in my whole life. I'm overwhelmed, and tears are rolling down my cheeks as each of them greets me while telling me their names. I have no idea as to what they're saying. None of them speaks English and I have no idea if they're talking to me in Greek or Albanian."

"At some point when it seems everyone has greeted me, Donika takes me and points me in the direction toward the house. About twenty of us go inside and the rest of them stay outside."

"Within seconds we're inside. They fill shot glasses with alcohol. I have no idea what it is, but it most definitely smells and tastes really strong. I find out later it's called Raki."

"Once everyone's glass is full, they raise them to the air, tap each glass, and then they say, 'goszura.' After all of this, the elder of the family, my mother's oldest living cousin, Vasil, (a small man, no taller than five-feet, maybe ninety pounds, eighty-one years old), raises his glass and toasts me with many words. Then they down the whole drink in one swig. Not being a drinker, I take a small taste and then do my best to chug the rest of it. I feel it burning all the way down."

"They fill everyone's glass again. One is enough for me, so I put my hand over the top of my glass to signal no more. By now I need to pee. Not knowing what to say, I use the only other words I know, similar to the Spanish word, with a Greek twist, 'Toe, Bano.' As it turns out, it's the Albanian word and the Greek word for bathroom."

"Donika grabs me by the arm, takes me back out the front door, around to the right side of the house, into the backyard to a small hut. As she opens the door and motions for me to go in, I can't believe what I see."

"I'll do my best to describe it to you. It's a hut about four feet square and just under six feet tall. The door itself is about five and a half feet tall, less than three feet wide. Inside is a concrete floor with two bricks on it. There's a pipe at the back side that protrudes through the wall, which leads directly into a body of water the size of most local harbors, behind."

"So how did you go the bathroom?"

"Well my little friend Charlie, you either pee on the concrete floor or you drop your pants, squat and go."

"Everything you do, stays right there?"

"Yes, but only for a brief minute or two. It's the responsibility of the woman of the house, in this case Donika, to take a pail of water and clean the concrete floor."

"I'm in culture shock."

"What's that?" Charlie asks.

"It means I'm in a third world country Charlie, doing something totally different than what I know, something most people in our society have never and may never see or do. But most people in their society don't know anything else. It's their culture to go to the bathroom in this way. It's all they know."

"It seems most everyone in the village has come down to get a peek at me. I'm the first American they have seen in the village in a very, very long time. Papa was the last one there. Some of them have never seen one at all. So here I am, 1995, three years after communism has ended and I am the second American to come to Albania."

"You'll never guess who was the first?"

"Who?" asks Vasiliki.

"James Belushi, the famous actor and comedian. Both of his parents were immigrants from Albania. He was in Albania one year earlier when he opened the 'Blues Brothers' establishment in Tirana, the capital of Albania."

"The first night in the village it gets dark about nine o'clock, but we still haven't eaten dinner. I'm totally exhausted and hungry. The women are outside cooking the lamb in an earth stone oven. It takes them close to three hours to get it hot enough to put in the meat. The inside walls of the oven are fire red. At eleven o'clock we finally sit down to eat dinner. Just like in Greece, these people are late night eaters."

"The main course is lamb, rice, tomatoes and cucumber salad, feta cheese, Kalamata olives, bread and string beans. For dessert, we eat apple and orange slices. The food is fabulous, but I'm just not used to eating dinner this late at night. I'm usually in bed at this time. It's the European culture to eat late. I notice something, only the men are sitting at the dinner table, while the women and children are eating in the kitchen."

"Soon after eating, I motion that I want to go to sleep by laying my head on my hands, so Donika shows me to my room. It's Joseph's room. Because I was their guest, he has to sleep on the couch and they insist that I sleep in his room. Then I learn another interesting custom. Just before I pull off my pants to climb into bed, Donika appears with a large pail of warm water, and sets it down next to the bed in front of me. Then she pulls up a chair and sits in front of me. She grabs my right leg, pulls up my pants and sticks my foot in the pail of water. Then she washes and massages my feet and my calves. First the right, then the left, the whole time stroking them with a gentle, yet strong stroke. When Donika is finished scrubbing my feet, she grabs the pail of water and motions to me to crawl into bed. I fell asleep in seconds."

"My second day in Albania starts off late in the afternoon. Jet lag finally hits me. I didn't wake up until after two. I slept over twelve hours. Soon after I get up, they are feeding a delicious breakfast meal which consists of hard boiled eggs, Greek cheese, olives, cucumbers, and bread. However, this meal gets my bowels going and soon after eating it's time to make another trip to the bathroom hut."

"It's my second experience with squatting while standing on the two bricks. However, I'm not as successful this trip. I make a mess of my clothes. I'm embarrassed and I do my best to sneak into the room to change. I hide my pants and my undershorts in the liner of my suitcase."

"That afternoon while I'm taking a walk with Joseph through the hillsides of the village, Danika finds my clothes and washes them. There was no trace of the bathroom incident on my clothes. Even our best laundry soap couldn't have gotten those stains out. I learned from that experience. Each time I use the bathroom hut, I remove my pants. It's a bit difficult because there's not much room to undress. However, I don't want to embarrass myself again. Maybe that's what the nail hanging above the door is for. I found it one morning when I stepped inside. It scraped the top of my head and cut my scalp pretty bad."

"The humility of the second trip to the hut causes me to consider cutting my Albania trip short. I'm still in culture shock. No one speaks English and the bathroom conditions, no running water or toilet is too much for me to bear. I really don't want to insult them, but it's just too much for me to handle. I decide to tell them that night I need to go back to Greece, but I just don't know how."

"Dinner is at Vasil's home. As I said before, he's the oldest of my mother's first cousins. His house is a short distance away from Qirjako's, just before the top ridge of the hillside above the village. I find out later this land where Vasil's house sits is land that was once my grandfather's. He'd given him the land in 1937, the last time he saw him."

"When I get to his home, I'm greeted at the front door by his granddaughter, who says, 'Welcome to our home.'"

"It takes a few seconds for me to respond. I'm awestruck by her likeness to my Aunt Genevieve. Then it strikes me, 'Hey, you speak English?' Within seconds, my thoughts about leaving Albania disappear."

"She responds in a soft, gentle tone, 'Yes. My name is Enkeleida but you may call me Kela, everyone else does.'"

"We then go through the custom of kissing each other on the cheeks. I've got the greeting down pat."

"She introduces me to her mom Kleanthi, dad Telemak, brother Dorie, Uncle Kristaq, Uncle Panajot, and Aunt Gjenovefa. I have already met her Uncle Nikolla and his wife, Gjenovefa's husband Stephan, Panajot's wife and all of the kids."

"Kela tells me she will be in the village for most of the remainder of my trip. She'll be gone during the week in the morning while she's in school. She has no idea how relieved I am that she's there and that she speaks English."

"The majority of the evening we share stories about our families. They want to know so much about Papa. It's so hard, he died in 1959. My vision of him is strong, but my childhood memories are only a glimpse of who he really was. What stories I tell them are the stories about my beating, my parents telling him lies and his death. All sad stories and each one makes me cry as I tell it. The only happy ones are the memories of Greek Easter and about the homes he built."

"'He was very secretive about his life and I'm sad to say, he never even told us about you,' I tell them. They couldn't conceive of the difficulties I've faced in my life. Their family is the most important thing in the world to them. Not like so many families in the Western world who face turmoil and dysfunction, total family destruction."

"Partway through the evening, something magical yet disheartening happens. Before leaving Joseph's house, I had checked my wallet to make sure the 1959 Greek coin was tucked inside. It's become my good luck piece, a very special keepsake that I've kept tucked away in my wallet since I left California."

"I decide to tell them the story about finding the coin. I had written Vasil and told him about finding the coin, but the others hadn't heard the story. This would be their first time."

"They sat in amazement as Kela translates my every word. Part way through the story, I pull my wallet from my front pocket. I reach into the middle pocket, between my credit cards, to find the coin. But it's gone. I'm distraught by what has happened. I start frantically looking on the couch and then the floor below me, thinking it might have fallen as I pulled my wallet from my pocket. Kela is on the ground helping me search, yet there's no coin to be found."

"After giving up the search, Kela's grandfather, Vasil, walks over to me and puts his hand on my shoulder. He tells Kela in a softly spoken Albanian tone that she's to give me the following message: 'It doesn't surprise us he no longer has this coin. This coin was sent to him as a message and to bring him here. He's returned the coin to its homeland. To us, this is the miracle message of the coin.'"

"His eyes and the intent in his voice convince me to believe him. But there's a hole in my heart because I've lost it. During the course of the next two weeks, I'm constantly looking for the coin. I just knew it had to be there somewhere. I'm having a tough time letting it go. I begin to realize there might be a higher meaning as to why it's gone."

"Vasil sees that I'm disheartened by the loss of the coin. He changes the subject and asks if there is anything else that I want to know."

"I have lots of questions. 'I'm curious to know what it was like living under communism, Especially, in 1967 when Enver Hoxua, the dictator of Albania, declares the country atheist. He takes away your religions, your churches, your priests, your Bibles and your crosses. How did you live without your religion? What did you do?'"

"Vasil provides an answer to a lifelong question, one that I've had ever since Papa died. 'Is there a God?'"

"Vasil says, 'Hoxua could take away our churches, our crosses, our Bibles, all of the icons of our religion, including our priests. But there's one thing Hoxua could never remove-GOD from our heart.' He's patting his heart as he's talking."

"Wow. I just sit there with tears in my eyes thinking to myself: *'Such powerful words. We don't need a church, Bibles, crosses or even a priest to tell us how to commune with God. God is with us everywhere that we go, because God is located in the energy source of our soul, which is our heart.'"*

"He continues, 'God's always with us. Whenever we're down, we go to the top ridge of the village and look down at the Monastir. Come, go with us,' he says as he leads me to the door. We walk about 150 feet to the top of the ridge. As we reach the top, I instantly see the Monastir of Zverness and the living quarters that were one time the homes of the Greeks priests."

"Their memories of their religion were buried there. 'When communism ends in Albania, that was the day all of the people of Albania's prayers had been answered,' Vasil says."

"Vasil tells me that soon after Hoxua's death, the people of Albania destroyed many statues and icons associated with him. He was a mad dictator and his ego was evident everywhere, even still in Albania. I took a picture of the mountainside that bore his first name as we passed it on the way into the country. The beheaded monuments were the people's way of showing retribution, much like he took away the icons of their religion."

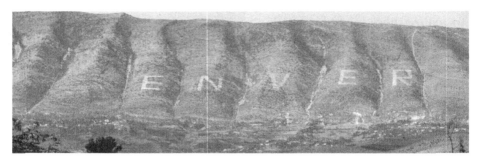

"The following morning, Joseph and Kela take me for a stroll through the hillsides of the village. We see the olive fields, the lands of my great grandfather Spiro. I see those mushroom like concrete huts along the hillside and down in the sand near his land. I ask Kela what they are. It turns out they are bomb shelters. Each family in the village had their own. In this particular area, the military was present and they used them as quarters."

"I then saw the gravestones of my great-grandparents. My great grand-mother bears my mother's name, Varvara. Next to her gravestone is the gravestone of my mom's grandfather, Spiro Lambro Meta."

"They take me to see the Monastir Zvernec again. It's even more breath-taking in the morning. It's an awesome sight. On a small island, on the backside of the village along the Ionic sea to the west and southwest along the Adriatic Sea, nestled in the pines to the north is the Monastir Zvernec. It's an old Greek monastery, built hundreds of years ago. I stand there for a great deal of time. I can feel the presence of God. The beauty of this monument is beyond explanation."

"I spent the third night at Joseph's brother, Lambro's house. Lambro was named after my grandfather. He'd come home for the first time in a very long time just that afternoon. He heard I was coming, so he came to meet me. He's a merchant marine. We ate dinner and of course there came a time I needed to use a bathroom. Their house is like the rest of the houses in the village. They have no toilet, but they have the closest thing to one. They have a stoop above a hole that you sit on, instead of crouching down to go. Yet there's a drawback. They have no toilet paper. There's a school book, with pages like a newspaper that you rip out to clean yourself. Before I use the bathroom, I run back to Joseph's house, where I grab a bag of toilet paper from my suitcases. I thought I had prepared for the worst, but the worst was a school book for toilet paper."

They're laughing. Charlie says, "You thought about everything Mr. Yianni."

"Not quite everything."

"That night, when it's time to go to bed, his wife starts gently scrubbing my legs and my feet. By now, three nights in the village and I'm feeling pretty spoiled, I do look forward to going to bed. It feels good. Almost sexual even, especially as she's stroking the backs of my leg. Then Lambro says something to her and she abruptly halts. I think he saw how much I was enjoying it. He wants his turn, so she washes his feet for less than two minutes and with less enthusiasm than she had with mine."

"They have three daughters. Two of them were the ones I help pull the weeds and the little one, Kostandina, is about five years old. 'As cute as you Christina.'" I say.

"Whenever I stay at Joseph's house, I'd stand by the gate and tell her good morning as she walked on her way to school. It was a struggle remembering the Greek word for morning and the Greek word for afternoon. They're similar. Then I figured a way to associate them. "Kalimera" means good morning, so I associate the "m" for mera with morning. "Kalispera," means good afternoon or good evening, so I associate "pera" to "PM" with afternoon, evening and nighttime."

"Two days after spending the night at Lambro's home, Kostandina walks past me with her notebook hiding her face. I say 'Kalimera,' but she ignores me. I say it again, but she ignores me. By now she's in front of Aunt Gjenovefa's home and she hears me say Kalimera again. Aunt Gjenovefa runs out to Kostandina and pulls the notebook from her face, telling her to respond to me. As she pulls the notebook away, I notice Kostandina has a black eye, then she starts to cry."

"When I get to her, she jumps into my arms and hugs me, like she's afraid to let go. For a moment, I feel like I'm three again, just after being beaten by my father. Her grandmother and I bring her back to her house. I find out later from Kela, that she'd told her grandmother that her father beat her the night before. Her grandmother's angry, just like my grandma was when my father beat me. Lambro left that morning and we never saw him again. I can't help but think, she'll be the lucky one if he never comes back again."

"The next ten days in the village I spend meeting a different family. They're all related to my great-grandparents. In each home, they toast me with raki, they feed me at least one meal and wherever I am at night-time, I spend the night with them. The only thing expected of me is to tell about our family. By this time, I'm hardened enough that I drop no more tears."

"During the course of my trip, I take a walk up the hill almost every day, to the high grounds to see the Monastir. I'm beginning to realize there's a higher reason for me being there and I'm constantly going there to listen to my inner thoughts. There's a feeling of serenity that engulfs me."

"One day, the family takes me to the Monastir by boat. The water's really shallow, so the oarsman uses a long wooden pole to push the boat forward. He goes from side to side as necessary to keep the boat in line with the destination. We pass the left-over stanchions from the bridge that once linked the Monastir with the village."

"When we reach the island, I hear magic in the wind as the sound rustles through the pines. It's summer, so the trees are healthy from the winter rains. We walk through the quarters where the priests once resided, then to the Monastir itself. Inside is a large rotunda that has the design of a religious painting from the Bible. But there's only faded remnants of paint, most of which is gone. I can only imagine what must've been there at one time. There's the faint outline of a few faded figures. No one could describe what it looked like before, because it'd been many years since they'd been there."

"When we go into the courtyard in the back of the Monastir, we find a tomb laid in the ground. I'm told it's a tomb of an Austrian prince who used to come to the Monastir for times of silence and retreat. He requested that his body be buried there when he died. When Hoxua began looting the churches, the homes, and taking away the religious icons, the people of the village hid their religious artifacts in the tomb of the Austrian prince."

"We board the boats to go back to the village for lunch. There are six boats full of family. On the way back, they begin singing. Their voices are like angels. I can hear the joy in their voices whistling through the pines. The beauty of their songs leaves me speechless. Kela tells me this is the first time they've gone to the Monastir since 1967. The children had never seen it because of Hoxua. There's a generational gap. It feels good to know they see it for the first time because of me."

"Just after lunch, I decide to go for a walk on my own. I wander about the village, wondering what my grandfather's life was like living in the village. The answers come. I notice they use olive oil for everything. Besides cooking, they use it to keep their lanterns burning, for skin care and protection from the sun. They use it to wash their hair. What is the magic behind olive oil? I discover it was the family business. Right before my grandfather left the Old Country, he was working in Arta, Greece where his father was born. He was picking olives. When his father moved to Zverness with my great-grandmother Varvara, he planted olive trees in the village lands. Most of them are still there now."

"Is that where our olive oil comes from Yianni?"

"It does Vasiliki, but most of it goes to Italy to be bottled there. They put Italian labels on the bottle. Check it out sometime when you're in the store. You'll find that most of the oil comes from Italy, imported from Greece, Albania, and Italy."

"Twelve days have passed. I'm stuck in the village without transportation. There's no telephones. I'm wondering if I will ever meet Grandma's side of the family."

"On the thirteenth day, a car arrives in the village. There are four people looking for me. They are my cousins from Grandma's side. They knew I was in the village and found their way to Zverness. None of them had been here before. Stefan, my mother's first cousin, and his daughters Mimosa and Vitjana were there, along with one of their cousins who was driving the car. They are the Sinjari family and they came to take me to their home."

"I promised Kela and her parents I would go to Vlore that night and stay with them for a couple of days. I didn't want to hurt their feelings. I talk them into picking me up in two days, in Vlore, at Kela's flat. I was really excited about going to Kela's because they have a shower. I was going to shower for the first time since I left Greece. I'm tired of sponge baths in the hut. Plus, I would feel much better being clean when I meet the other side of the family."

"What, you had to bathe in there too?" says Charlie.

"Yes, with a sponge and a bucket of water."

"If they didn't have running water, where did the bucket of water come from?"

"It came from an artesian well down the road. I mentioned it earlier, when we drove into the village I noticed the women were washing their clothes from water coming out of spout. That is the only source of fresh water. My cousins would go down two or three times a day with five-gallon plastic gas cans to fill them with water. Most of them carried the water on their heads. I was amazed when I saw them do that."

"My, the woman of that village had to do everything."

"Yes, they did Vasiliki. I felt for the women because they were subservient to the men. One day, two of my younger cousins, fifteen and sixteen years old, were pulling weeds in their grandmother's garden. I jumped the fence to help them. They're laughing and enjoying me being there. When their grandma sees me, she starts yelling at me to get out of the garden. I ignore her and keep pulling the weeds."

"When Kela came later, she told me I wasn't supposed to do that. I told her to tell their grandma, 'Too bad, in my country both men and women pull the weeds.' I really have a lot of compassion for the women in the village."

"Oh, and marriage. In 1995 it's still custom to marry someone from the village. A single man, much like my grandfather when he came to the village, is shown available women from age fifteen up. Some are spinsters, never married. I was scared for my younger cousins. I want to bring them all back to America to save them from this way of life. Of course, I know that's impossible, but my heart's telling me otherwise."

"I have a cute story to tell you about Kela's flat," I tell them.

"It's a two-bedroom flat located on the fifth floor. Her mom and dad sleep in one bedroom, Kela sleeps in the other room while her brother and his grandmother from her father's side sleep in the living room. That night her mom, Yolanda, the name she goes by instead of Kleanthi, tells me that I'm to sleep in their bed. She and Telemak are sleeping in the living room, on the floor. We argue, but it's an argument I lose."

"The following morning, I woke up about ten o'clock. I went into the bathroom to prepare for the morning shower. I'm so looking forward to that shower. I turn the valve on the tank that Kela had shown me the night before, but there's no water. Being a pipefitter by trade, I do my best to get the water running, but no water. I then stick my head out the door to call for Kela. I'm standing behind the door with no clothes on as I tell her, 'I can't get the water to come on in the shower.'"

"Kela laughs, 'That's because we only get water in the morning from seven to nine, and then again in the afternoon from four to six. You were sleeping when we had water.'"

"The whole family's laughing. But they had never told me there's a certain time to get water. After I finish dressing, when I came out of the bathroom, her father Tele's still laughing. He's quite the comedian. Things get better with breakfast. Yolanda fixed the best French toast I'd ever eaten. Masked with butter, dipped in sugar. Never had it this way before. It was to die for."

I stop telling the story long enough to ask Vasiliki for a glass of water. I suggest we take a ten-minute break. My mouth's really dry from all of this talking.

Lushnje and Berat'

"Two days passed. As agreed, the cousins show up around noon to take me to Lushnje. Grandma's family is really excited to meet me. We eat some great food, dance, talk and share most of the same stories I've been telling over and over. On the second day, they take me to the town of Berat', Grandma's hometown. Berat' is an interesting town. Nestled in the hillside, blended in with trees were the homes of Berat'. It's picturesque. I take a few shots of the town, but later when I have them developed I realize I don't have much of an eye for photography. I missed the mark. The pictures were quite different in my photos than they were in person. I believe there's another blessing from Grandma on this one. She once said, '***Yianni, life is not always how we envision it to be, sometimes reality is really hard to see.***"

"I realize now what Grandma meant when she said it."

The Castle of Berat

"High above the town is a Castle. It was built hundreds of years ago. Many of the perimeter walls are still standing. As we tour the inside of the castle we come to the religious museum. Before my eyes are the most beautiful gold and silver embossed Bibles, crosses, chalices and urns that I've ever seen. No wonder the people hid these artifacts from Hoxua. He probably would have turned them into gold and silver bars."

"We walk around the castle for a couple of hours. When it's time to go, as I'm climbing into the car, Mimosa tells me to take a picture of the statue of the man who designed and built the castle."

"I take the picture and then I ask her who he is?"

"Onofre, this is St. Onofre."

"I take two steps backwards, my legs get wobbly, and I travel back in time. I'm having another flashback to 1967 when Grandma died. I see myself passing the San Onofre Nuclear Generating Station, and I remember telling myself, 'I'm going to work there someday.' Which I did, for thirty-eight years."

"Then I think, *'Who says we aren't guided by saints, guides, grandparents or even angels.'* Most likely, another one of Grandma's Secret blessings."

Onufre (St. Onofre)

"That night, when we're back in Lushnje, my cousins take me to a restaurant built high above the town. It's called 'Panorama,' so named because you can see a full panoramic view of the city. We walk up a giant stairway, 900 plus stairs to get there. The longest staircase I've ever walked. As soon as we get to the restaurant, I need to use the bathroom. Mimosa tells her cousin, the waiter, that I need to use the bathroom."

"He shows me to the executive bathroom. When I get inside, I can't believe my eyes. They have a toilet. I never thought a toilet could make me so happy. But it's the first one I've seen since I left California. I stay sitting there for a very, very long time."

"When I get back to the table, Mimosa asks, 'Yianni, are you okay?'"

"I whisper to her so no one can hear, 'I'm okay, they have a toilet in the bathroom and I was so comfortable sitting there, I didn't want to get up.'"

"She laughs and of course tells everyone what I said."

"That night I got, 'Montezuma's revenge.' My gut's wrenching. I was in their bathroom most of the night."

"The next morning, Mimosa, also a doctor, writes me a prescription and takes me to the pharmacy to get it filled. By the end of the day, the problem's gone."

"The following morning, it's time to go back to Vlore. I say goodbye to each one of them."

"Evis, one of the younger cousins, says to me, 'I will remember this day for the rest of my life.'"

"I'm choked up. Her words strike a chord in my heart and I can't hold back the tears. The love these people express makes me feel like I'm part of their family. I feel as though Grandma's using them to help to heal my soul."

"A little over an hour later, were back at Kela's house. We stay for a few minutes at Kela's and then we go back to the Village to say goodbye to Papa's family."

"While saying goodbye to everyone in the village, I sneak into their kitchens, one house at a time. I place a hundred-dollar bill in their refrigerator. I do it when they're not watching me. I don't want them to catch me. The last stop is at Kela's grandfather's house. I sneak into the kitchen and I leave two bills in theirs. Vasil and his wife are sad that I'm leaving. His wife surprises me with a kiss on the lips and two pinches on my cheeks. She then hands me a bag with four bottles of Olive Oil. As she does, she rattles off a couple of sentences in Greek. She throws me one last kiss, as I wave and say goodbye."

"On the way down the hill, Kela says, 'Do you want to know what my grandmother said?'"

"Not necessary, I understood everything."

"Kela looks at me a bit dumbfounded. 'Your grandmother told me thank you for coming. I will miss you and you have made my husband Vasil very happy. You're welcome in our home anytime. We love you.'"

"Kela's astonished. 'That was her every word. But you don't speak Greek.'"

"You're correct, I don't speak Greek, but I do speak soul talk."

"What's that?"

"That's what happens when two souls are joined together and they speak the language of love with their heart. Your grandmother was speaking to me with her heart."

"Kela shakes her head. Just before I climb into the jeep to leave, I say my last goodbye. As Yolanda's hugging me, I sneak another hundred-dollar bill into her smock. Then we take the eighty-nine-mile drive to the border, back to Kakavia."

"And this my dear friends, is the end of the story for today."

"Do you have more stories to tell us?" asks Bobby, who surprises me with his question.

"Oh course, Bobby, this is the end for today, but there's more to tell."

Vasiliki says, "I know your grandparents are really proud of you, but we're just as proud and grateful that we know you. Your stories are like magic. We talk about them all the time. I feel the presence of someone other than us in the room when you're talking. I'm not sure if it's my husband, but in my heart, I certainly feel it is."

I tell her another one of Grandma's simple, yet profound secret blessings, simply put, *"Just believe."*

I tell her that I will expand on this one in a future story.

"When will we hear the next story?"

"Well, let me see, today is Thursday, so how about next Monday?"

Vasiliki says, "No, that's too long to wait. How about Sunday after church? Maybe you would like to go with us? It's the Greek Church here in El Cajon and we could meet here at nine-thirty and be there by ten."

Not being much of church person these days, more spiritual than religious, I'm a bit apprehensive, but finally agree and say, "Sure why not?"

Chapter Twenty

You can't treat your kids like crap,
then expect them to love and
respect you.

~ John&greek

When Sunday morning arrives, I leave early enough to stop at Von's grocery store. There's just enough time to pick up some treats. I know Vasiliki well enough to know that she has other plans in mind, but I want to add something as my treat.

When I get to the store, I head toward the bakery section, right next to the beverage section. Out of the corner of my eye I spot Ray reaching up to grab a 24 pack of beer. I do my best to avoid him, but he spots me.

Within seconds, he comes over. I great him with a cordial, "Hello."

His response grabs my immediate attention. Without even acknowledging my hello, he says, "I really wish you would leave me and my family alone. Things were a lot better before you came along. Why don't you just stay away?"

I begin to shudder a bit because of what he said. I take a few steps backwards and attempt to walk away. But he's nearly forty years younger than I am and a bit stronger, so he grabs me by the arm and twirls me around.

Feeling the jerk of his arm, twirling me around, I see don't see him, I see my dad. He'd jerk me around with the same force and motion. I clench my fist just like I did when I was a kid. I didn't like it then and I surely don't like it now. The minute we're face to face, I look at him and say, "You're as much of a bastard as my father was. You think you can manhandle me and get away with it. You're a disgusting human being, no different than him."

Without giving him a chance to say anything, I turn and walk way. I go to the checkout lane. As I lay the food on the belt he walks up behind me. I act like I don't know he's there. I wasn't about to let him make a bigger ass out of himself than he already has.

When I get to my car, I attempt to open the door. Before I have time to get in, he's there. He twirls me around once again. His fist is rolled up tight, holding it up toward his head, ready to strike me when I say, "Go for it. If you think I'm going to fight you back and start a few lifetimes of karma between us, forget it. Take your best shot and leave. I've lived with this BS my whole life and I'm not about to start living it again. You're so much like my father it makes me sick. You drink because you're a miserable human being. You've got a beautiful wife and some really awesome kids, but you're losing them and you don't even know it. You're a lost soul. Who the hell broke you?"

My words stop him dead. I open my car door to get in, but he begins apologizing. He says, "I'm so sorry, I don't know what came over me. I'm just so angry every time I see you around my family and the thought of you being there today just made me snap. I wish you would just leave us alone. But my daughter adores you like a grandfather and my sons look up to you more than they do me."

"Why do you think that is, Ray? It probably has something to do with your passive-aggressive attitude."

"I don't know and I'm really not sure I want to know."

"You'd rather drown your sorrow with alcohol? Does it really make you feel that good?" I realize these are questions I always wanted to ask my dad, but never had the guts to ask.

"I just like the taste of beer."

"Oh, I've heard that before, that's BS. My grandma liked beer too. But she never got mean when she drank. Plus, she only drank one or two beers a day. I remember her savoring the taste, but never did she get falling down drunk or mean. It's a choice. And you've made the choice to drink and to be a mean bastard as a result of it."

I then look at the clock on my dash and notice it's too late to make it to Vasiliki's house in time to go to church. "I need to go. I have a phone call I have to make before I leave, and you've put me in an uncompromising situation that I've been in way too many times."

"I know who you're calling. You were supposed to go to church with them. I'm sorry I ruined your day and I would appreciate it if you don't tell them I was the one who ruined it for you."

"My day's not ruined, it's just been re-arranged." I start my car and begin to back out of the parking spot without acknowledging his request for anonymity.

On the way home, I dial Vasiliki.

"Hello Yianni, are you going to make it to church with us?"

"I was on my way to join you, but stopped at the grocery store to pick up some treats. While I was there, something came up to way-lay things for today. I need a rain-check. Can we reschedule for next Sunday? I think I'm going to need some time to figure things out."

"Sure, I know the kids, Barbara and I will be disappointed, but I know things happen to change the course of our day. I hope everything's okay?" she says, with a sense of knowing things were not.

"Everything's fine. See you next Sunday. Have a wonderful week. Goodbye."

Seconds later, my phone rings again. "Who's calling me now?" I say to Rascal as I notice it's a number I'm not accustomed to having on my phone.

I answer with a crisp hello.

"Hello, Mr. Yianni, I want to apologize again for what transpired at the grocery store this morning. I didn't mean to ruin your day."

"Oh, it's you Ray, no bother."

"I wonder if we could meet for lunch on Wednesday?'"

"Sure, where and what time?"

"How about 12:30 at Applebee's in El Cajon?"

"That works for me. By the way, I have one request?"

"Okay?"

"No alcohol before lunch and no alcohol during lunch. If that's agreeable, I'll see you Wednesday?"

Slow and deliberate he says, "Uh, okay. Any particular reason why?"

"Yes. There's no reason to be distracted because of alcohol. This is not a social occasion. If I detect any alcohol on your breath or a sense that you've been drinking, I'll be leaving for home, that's a promise."

"Okay, I'll do my best to keep that promise. See you Wednesday."

Without saying another word, he hangs up.

❧❧

As Wednesday rolls around, I take the time to clear my day and prepare myself for the lunch meeting with Ray. I haven't had much of an appetite lately, so I'll probably just have a light salad and a glass of water with lemon.

I'm not sure how I got into this habit of preparing my food menu in advance of my meals. I know it's not healthy to live your life around food. No wonder I have a weight problem. Everything revolves around food.

I have no idea why I'm so nervous about meeting Ray. I believe the universe is using me as an instrument in some sort of way. I'm sure I will be telling him things I wish I had told my dad. I never had the guts to tell him. That's probably why I'm so nervous. The knot in my stomach is a strong indication that something needs to be done to untie the knot. Just looking at him reminds me of my dad when he was his age. I was never able to talk to him and I'm apprehensive as to whether I will be able to talk to Ray.

Sitting here in my comfort chair I begin to think about how to present myself with Ray. The words of the ancient poet Rumi, ring out in my head as I remember reading them from a book of his quotes and poems, *"Raise your words, not your voice. It is rain that grows the flowers, not thunder."*

I've always had this bad habit of raising my voice when I'm talking to someone when I'm giving words of advice. I usually play it off to the fact that I can't hear when there's background noise. There's going to be plenty of background noise at Applebee's. That's the biggest downfall about going there, but I will do my best not to talk down to him.

254

Throughout my life, I know my daughter has taken my tone to sound like I am talking down to her, rather than talking with her. I know it's something I learned from my dad and it's been a very hard thing to change. However, I know that's the advice that Rumi is giving me now. "Talk with him, not at him." It's a tricky thing to do, because my dad always talked at me, not with me.

I know my kids resent it when I'm talking to them, but I've toned things down a great deal.

As I'm sitting here, I remember a time when my daughter was living with me. She and a couple of friends took off for an afternoon and told none of us where they had gone. When I found her, relieved as I was, I began yelling and screaming at her. I was doing my damn best to get my point across. At one point, I recognize my daughter's no longer looking at me, but looking through me. I knew at that very moment, she wasn't listening to a word I said. I stopped talking and just walked away. It was an eye-opening moment for me. I realized it was time to find a better way to talk with her, rather than talk at her.

Unfortunately, soon after she went back to live with her mom. I walk away when things turn into an argument. Walking away isn't the fix. The key is to recognize when things are heating up. Then, make a course direction change, by changing the tone of my voice.

It was a tough thing to learn. Today I do my best to speak from my heart, not from my mind. Back then, I always had to be right. I'm sure it was from living with a father who never let me right about anything. That set the pattern for most of my adult life. It's not an excuse, but now that I'm older and a bit wiser, I know I'm not always right. I will be careful with my word selection with Ray and do my best to talk with him, not at him.

It's now ten minutes after noon, I decide not to wait any longer, so I leave for the restaurant. I arrive there at precisely 12:30. Ray's not here. I take a seat on the bench just inside the door. I wait fifteen minutes before Ray walks in.

He apologizes for being late, says he hit some traffic on the way over.

The host takes us to our table and asks us if we'd like anything to drink?

"I'll have water with a large slice of lemon, thank you."

Ray says, "I'll have a beer on draft."

Without saying a word, I stand up and tell the host to cancel my water.

Ray says, "I can't eat a hamburger with fries and not have a beer. I'm sorry, I just can't do it."

Seconds before I walk away, I suggest, "Your demons are much greater and obviously more important than the welfare of your family. David Cook once said, 'Alcoholism is a well-documented pathological reaction to unresolved grief.'"

"What's your grief, Ray?"

And then I walk out of the restaurant.

Chapter Twenty-One

Dreams are today's answers
to tomorrow's questions.

- Edgar Cayee

When Sunday rolls around, I tell Rascal the sad news that he won't be coming today. He lies down in front of me, his body completely stretched out and puts his front paws together, his chin on top as if to be praying. I can't help but laugh, but I still insist he has to stay home.

I get to Vasiliki's at nine thirty as agreed. There's six of us going to church. Ray has no desire to join us.

"Church has never been his thing," Barbara tells me.

I can't help but think how much he's like my dad. He never went with us to the Greek Church. I think he resented the fact that we had a heritage and he had nothing. If only he'd realized it, his heritage could have been built with us. We could have been his heritage, just as Ray's family could be his.

When we get to the church in El Cajon, I'm surprised to find the mass is not the traditional Greek Mass I remember growing up. Parts of it were in Greek, but the majority's in English. The priest is quite the character. He calls himself the Cowboy Greek Priest of the East County. At one point during the service he asks if there are any guests. About three of us raise our hands. The other two were not Greek, but they were there because they were curious. I told him I was baptized Greek Orthodox when I was six years old.

He then asks me about my parents, curious to know which one was Greek. I tell him it was my mother's side. Then he asks for my name and our family name. I tell him, "My name is Yianni and the family name is Meta."

His response is amazing. "That's a very powerful Greek family name. There are so many names in Greek that are derived from Meta, but the most empowering thing I can think about regarding Meta is metaphysical, the spiritual aspect of connecting with the universe beyond the physical." Then he thanks me for coming and says to the congregation, "Yianni has brought a great subject for a future sermon regarding the metaphysical. Everybody stay tuned in and make yourself ready for a whirlwind of information."

I'm mesmerized by the character of this Greek priest. When he calls himself the Cowboy Priest of East County, he pulls up his robe and shows us his cowboy boots. Everyone in the church is laughing. I'm really impressed.

After church is over we gather outside for coffee, tea, milk and cookies. The Priest comes up to Vasiliki to ask about our friendship and he's curious to find out how we'd come to know each other.

Vasiliki explains that I have been telling her family stories about my life and the secret blessings from my grandmother. I hear her say, "He met my dear granddaughter Christina in the park one day. She's the same age as his granddaughter, Aubrey Rose, whom he's never met. While he's telling us these stories, there is something magical and mysterious happening that is having a positive effect on our family. It's hard for me to explain. I believe it's either God or some magical forces from the universe that's working behind the scene to make our family whole. My dear grandchildren just adore him."

The priest is impressed by what Vasiliki's telling him, so he comes up to talk to me for a few minutes. He's curious to know where I was baptized and where exactly my grandmother was from.

I explain to him that I was baptized in San Francisco in 1956 and that my grandmother Christina was from Berat' Albania.

Then he shocks me by saying, "I know of that town in Albania. Its roots are Greek and the majority of the people from there came from Greece. That explains why all of your family names are Greek."

"Yes, even though our family is from Albania, there has never been a doubt in my mind that we are Greek. My grandparents loved the fact that they were Greek. They were proud Greek-Americans and I believe that's why I am proud to be a second-generation Greek-American."

Then he thanks me for coming and tells me, "I hope you'll come back to our church again real soon."

I tell him there's a strong chance that I will. Then we go back to Vasiliki's for lunch and the afternoon story.

Vasiliki made a simple lunch, one that I find enjoyable and refreshing, yet fit for a summer's day, watermelon, cantaloupe and honeydew melon.

I tell her about the first time I had honeydew melon.

"I was with my grandparents for the weekend and my Uncle Odysseus was in the city visiting from Philadelphia. I remember he came into the house carrying two honeydew melons and said, 'Ma, you should try these melons. They're called honeydew and they have a fabulous taste.'"

"Grandma cut them up and placed them on the table in front of us. My uncle, who was wearing a zoot suit and a shoulder holster carrying a gun, is sitting on one side of the table and my grandfather's sitting on the other side."

"Papa notices the gun and tells my uncle, 'Get that damn gun out of my house. You don't bring a gun into my house when Yianni's here. Take it away or get out.' Papa's tone was adamant, he meant what he said."

"My uncle went to his car and put the gun in the trunk. Then he came back to join us for breakfast."

"Papa felt my uncle hung with gangsters. He told me to stay away from gangsters."

"While we're enjoying the honeydew melon, my uncle says, 'John, you should be a tennis player someday. You look like you have the makings of a great tennis player.'"

"It's amazing how someone can plant a seed in your mind. I believe the law of action is the most important aspect to success. Seeds are planted in the minds of the world and when someone takes action, mountains are moved. I believe that's why Jesus, the master of all masters, said to the people of the world, 'You can do as much as me and more.'"

Then we enjoyed the melons for lunch.

When everyone's done eating, Bobby's the first to ask for a story. I tell him we'll begin just as soon as we help your grandma clean the table. Then I get up, grab some plates and head for the kitchen. The kids follow behind doing the same. It's all about being a role model.

Vasiliki thanks me, then says, "Okay, we're ready for your next story."

However, before we begin, there's a knock at the door. It's the priest and one of the parishioners from the church. Vasiliki introduces me to her friend and says, "This is Simone. I've been telling her all about you and your stories."

Then we begin...

❦

Back in Greece

"It's four days before it's time to fly back to the states. As I walk back into Greece, passing the iron gates of Albania behind me, I notice Yianni the taxi driver sitting in his car waiting for me."

"He drives me to Ioannina, to the hotel where he had picked me up weeks before. I make arrangements with him to pick me up in two days. I spend time walking around the city saying hello to everyone as I pass them by. I just feel in my heart, I really have been here before. I feel like I'm home."

"I have dinner at the restaurant up the hill the last night. Yianni picks me up and takes me to the airport the next morning."

"When I arrive in Athens, there's a taxi waiting for me. Kela's mom had called ahead to let them know when I'd be in Athens. My cousins live in Megara, a town about fifty-five minutes away from Athens. The taxi driver takes me to a house in Megara, owned by a godfather to one of my cousins. His name is similar to mine, pronounced, Yannis."

"His wife shows me to my room and I place my luggage there. Then I go back upstairs to meet the rest of his family. His daughter Alexandra, a gorgeous twenty-year-old young Greek girl, speaks English. She tells me she will be my translator for the next two days."

"While sitting in their living room with her family and my closest cousins, Panajot, Nikolla, and Stefan, they ask about my experience in the village and how I enjoyed my visit. When I tell of my experience with the bathroom hut, they get a good laugh, especially when I tell about the mess with my pants."

"Then I start telling them the story about the lost coin. Panajot wasn't there the second night, so he didn't hear the story. I tell them I believe the spirits of my grandparents were with me the whole time I was there, and even now. I know now the coin was sent to me as a message from Papa, and it was instrumental in me meeting them. Then I tell them the coin disappeared, it was lost and gone."

"After the story, I make the comment as to how special this coin was to me and it was a special keepsake. I wish I had it to show them."

"Before I could say any more, my cousin Panajot walks over to me and places his hand on my shoulder, just as his father Vasil had done in the village. He says, 'This does not surprise us that you no longer have this coin. This coin was sent to as a message. It served the purpose by bringing you to our homeland where it and you belong. To us, this is a miracle and we are very proud of you for coming.'"

"You know what they say about messages from heaven when you receive them? *'If you hear it once but do not get the message, shame on us, but hear it twice and you still don't get the message, the shame is then on you.'* I've learned that messages come in mysterious ways, but I always listen or watch for them now, more than ever before."

"Yannis tells Alexandra to tell me not to worry about not having this coin. He was a coin collector and he tells me that when I leave to go back to America he will see to it that my coin is replaced by coins from his collection."

"That night my cousins insist on taking me to a local restaurant on the waterfront in Megara. It was an awesome restaurant. They placed us on the patio outdoors, next to the water. There were twenty-nine of us, including Alexandra my translator, and her father Yannis, the contractor. They serve us the best tasting lamb chops I've ever had, along with potatoes, Greek salad, string beans, bread and all of the beer or soda pop we could drink."

"During the course of the meal, Panajot tells Alexandra to tell me that he wants to give me some land in the village, land that was my grandfather's, and build me a home there. I'm totally taken back by his offer. Tears roll down my checks as I thank him for his generosity. I tell him that someday maybe I'll take him up on his offer."

"The second afternoon and evening I meet more cousins who weren't able to be there the day before. They came from Athens. My cousin Vlorra and her husband are both surgeons from the hospital there. I'm blown away by the heart of these people. They love me as if they've known me their whole life."

"That evening they suggest that we go to the same restaurant. There's no argument from me about going there, except they have to let me pay for the dinner. I noticed the night before they were all digging into their wallets to come up with enough money to pay the bill. I still had close to three thousand dollars with me, so I didn't care how much dinner cost, but I was paying."

"They keep telling me, 'No' that I am their guest and they would be paying."

"We argue in a friendly manner for about five minutes, until I finally put my foot down and say, 'If I don't get to pay for dinner, I'm not going.'"

"They agreed. When we arrive at the restaurant there's thirty-two people instead of twenty-nine. We enjoy the same food, a couple of bottles of their favorite wine, some have beer and others have soda. When the bill's brought to me, I do my best not to show any emotion, but I'm in shock at the price. The whole dinner, drinks and the tip was $129.00. A meal like that for this many people in the states would have cost me close to two thousand dollars."

"The following morning my journey home begins. The last two days of my journey are complete. As I leave his house for the last time,

Yannis hands me a special bottle of his homemade wine and a paper wrapped full of coins."

"I thank him for his hospitality, say goodbye and then climb into the Mercedes Benz taxi, which he has kindly arranged and paid for."

"On the way to the airport, we stop to pick up two nuns who need a ride to Athens. While they're putting their belongings in the trunk of the car, I decide to look at the coins he'd given me to see if one of them was a 1959 coin. One by one, I look at each coin. I'm very thankful for his gesture, but I'm disappointed to find out that none of the coins is dated 1959."

"When I get to the airport I have close to three hours to wait before my flight. After spending some time reading, I decide to go into the gift shop and buy a statue of Alexander the Great to commemorate my trip to the Old Country. After all, my Uncle Alex was named after Alexander the Great, so I thought it would make a nice memory of my trip. As I look at the different statues in the store, my eyes glance down on the counter in front of me. In front of my eyes is a collection set of coins. One set, but the complete set of 1959 coins."

"I can't believe what had just happened. I couldn't pay for them fast enough. Even though this coin is not the one I found, I feel that this set of coins validates the thought that my grandparents have always been with me."

"Holding the coins in my hand, it comes to me that there's one more lesson to learn related to the coins. And one day soon I will figure out that message. But for now, I know that even though my grandparents' deaths were traumatic to me, I no longer feel alone without them around. I believe one day they'll be there waiting for me. I just know it."

"Like I said before, this was one of many spiritual things that happened to me. As we continue to get to know each other more, I will undoubtedly share the rest of them with you. I hope you enjoyed the story. I have shared it with a few others, and it seems to come in handy for those who might be in pain, especially when it comes to losing a loved one."

"Is that the end of the story?" asks Christina.

"No, that's end of my trip in the Old Country. There's still more to tell you."

Chapter Twenty-Two

Leaving Greece

"As I make my way up the ladder to the plane, I take one last glimpse at the sunset as it surrounds Athens. A bit of sadness comes over me. Just before the plane takes off, I move to a less crowded section and find three seats untaken."

"Once I'm settled, I look out the window and I see my beloved grandparents looking back at me. I can see their smiles as they say, 'Our Yianni, Yianni Capedoni, he kept his promise to go to the Old Country.' There's a knot in my gut that's telling me it was much more than the promise. There's something missing and I just can't put my finger on it. I see their smiles brighten, as if to tell me there's still more to come."

"I wipe my tears as I continue to reflect upon my trip. There are many highlights that come to mind. Such as The Monastir Zvernec, the loss of the coin, the coin set at the airport and the miracle words from the family. I remember Vasil's magical words about Hoxua never being able to take God away from our heart. My thoughts flash back to each relative. At last, I know all about Papa's life."

"I remember the words from Kristaq when I handed him the carton of Marlboro cigarettes, 'How did you know I smoke?' Then Panajot offering to give me land and build me a home in the village. Oh, the heart of these people."

"Then there's Grandma's side of the family, especially beautiful Mimosa who said, 'So Yianni, you're not married and I'm not married. Why don't we be married?'"

"Then the day I'm about to leave Lushnje, when Mimosa's sister Evis says, 'I will remember this day for the rest of my life.' I leave with fond memories. I will now never forget them or the Old Country for the rest of my life."

"As I reflect, although this leg of my journey is over, there's something gnawing at me that says, there's more to come. I've changed, my heart is heart is open. I want to connect with my odigo, my spiritual guide."

"This experience taught me that Grandma was right, when we learn about anything, *'First we knock on the door, then we ask and be open to receive, and as we seek, we will find.'*"

"I see things more clearly. Even the power of prayer, especially the power of 'thy will be done.' Through this all, my faith in life has grown and that, my friends, is the end of this part of the story."

"Really? Is that the end?"

"Not yet. Fast forward to when I go back to work. Everyone's curious about my trip. My friend Cecil, one of the foremen, had put a collage together to commemorate my trip. It was quite humorous and it made everybody laugh as he read it at the morning meeting. Funny thing, some of the things he has in the collage actually happened."

"After the morning meeting, I was talking with one of the instrument technicians about the dream I had before I left. I was telling him about meeting Grandma at the border between Greece and Albania. That she took me down the mountainside, through the valleys, where we came upon a bridge that crosses this river. Just on the other side, as we walk through the morning fog we come upon this town with a four-story building one city block in size. We knock on the door and a young girl answers."

"Before I can say anything more, Paul stops me. He says, 'I don't need to hear any more. I have a document that was given to me eleven years ago and there's no doubt in my mind it was given to me to give to you. It's called 'A Patriarchal Blessing.' I have it in my safe at home. I will bring it to you tomorrow. You will find the meaning behind the visit your Grandma made to you in your dream. But you have to promise me that you'll never share the document with anyone. It's okay to talk about it, but only your eyes are allowed to see the Blessing. You must keep it in a safe place and never tell anyone who the author is. These things are very important for the well-being of our Church records and it belongs to the Mormon Church.'"

"I promise you, Paul."

"The next day, still a bit apprehensive, Paul tells me that I can take it and read it, but he wants the original back before the end of the shift. He didn't say I couldn't copy it, so I put it on a copy machine and did just that. Then I returned the original back to him later that day. This document is very hard to read and, in some aspect, very hard to understand."

"I put it under the microscope of my eyes. I dissect it and I believe I understand exactly what's in this document that made it important for me to know. I'm keeping with the promise I made Paul not to share the exact contents or the author's name. I have changed some of the words to make it more understandable. Due to the timeframe in which it was written, the English language has changed."

"Here is a synopsis of what I found."

"I hope that you still remember the dream I had when Grandma met me at the border, just before my trip to the Old Country. This document's not a duplicate to my dream, but it comes very close. Because the blessing was brought to me in the dream, by Grandma, this is not a Patriarchal Blessing, it's a Matriarchal Blessing. There's no coincidence that Paul was saving this document for me all these years. I pulled the following excerpts from the document to show how it matches up. The person in the blessing is having an out-of-body experience;"

"Come, go with me. Up we go a short distance above the trees and then over hills, valleys, cities, seas, and passing over a great distance in just a few moments. We come to a large city. As we enter the city, I know the city is where spirits live who have not been resurrected. The city is beautiful. The streets are bordered with trees, flowers and ornamental shrubbery. The buildings are not ornate with the fancy trimmings we add for decorations today. But it has a beauty with simple grandeur beyond description.

Deep in the middle of the city, we come to a large building covering an entire block and it is four stories high. A door is opened by a young lady, who asks us to enter. I wonder who the young lady is, as I look upon her as if to say, I have seen her before. Then my attending angel says, 'This young lady is a relative of yours, who, while living in the physical world, was killed. She is now doing missionary service among your relatives who have died without the knowledge of their spirituality.'

Then we pass into two other departments in the same building, also containing the spirits of your relatives who are in this spirit-prison. The first group was arranged in classes in groups of thirty to forty souls with one teacher for each group. They are being taught how to read, write, and spell, etc., like our common grade schools, by efficient teachers, except that each class does not have a separate room. They do not seem to be intimidated by the spirit scholars, but are intent to learn. It seems like they are being prepared with sufficient education to learn about their spirituality.

Then we pass into a third room. It too covers an entire city block. Inside there are thousands of spirits. Here however, there is chaos and confusion. They're quarreling, fighting and arguing. Those spirits who are attending them are trying their best to pacify them. Many seem to refuse to calm down and some require force to keep them from acting in violent or disruptive ways. I'm told that these too are my relatives who lived on earth during a period of dark ages, when there was so much sin, ignorance and blatant disregard. It was at a time when men were held as slaves to cruel masters and wicked potentates.

Thus, was the promise of the Matriarch fulfilled 'that at the touch of my guardian angel' my spiritual vision would be quickened so that I could look into the spirit world and behold its beauty and order and commune with my dead for their redemption."

"I have goosebumps thinking about how much this document lines up with your dream. Do you understand what it's telling you?" asks Vasiliki.

"I have a hunch."

"Maybe that's why your grandma and your aunt disappeared before you got to hug them. Maybe by you being there you released them and they were able to move on."

❧❧❧

"Let me continue with the lessons from the Blessing as I relate it to my visit to the building."

"Sounds good," they say.

"The Blessing says, 'Like the Patriarchs of the Old Testament period, our Patriarchs of today, by the inspiration of the Holy Spirit, *place their hands upon our heads and tell us of the future that lies before us.'*"

"In my case, there's no irony that the Matriarch of our family, Grandma, is the one who placed her hands upon my head to tell me of the future that lies ahead."

"Times have changed and women are at the forefront of the world more now than ever before in history. And why not, they are equal to men. They work just as hard, if not harder than men. Remember the parable of the Castle. Here are the blessings I derived from the document:"

"Thou shall receive knowledge of science and of literature. Your soul shall delight in learning, and you shall be qualified to teach both in the field of Spirituality and that of common learning."

"Your faith shall increase and you will learn how to command sickness to depart."

"You shall receive the gift of prophecy and you shall see remarkable things that are in the future."

"At the touch of your guardian angel, your spiritual vision shall be quickened; you shall look beyond this world of the flesh into a world of spirits and behold its beauty and order and commune with your dead who have departed, while freeing their immortal souls."

"I'm no longer the person I was before all of this, and a new, exciting challenge is in front of me. And that story I shall continue after we take a break."

During the break, Barbara says, "You have lived through such a horrible and miserable life. It seems like the last phase of your life is lining up to be very magical and exciting. I'm envious."

"Don't be envious Barbara. I think envy is a dis-ease like anger, guilt, fear and sorrow, only to name a few. Climb aboard, because anyone can have a magical and exciting life."

"How's that possible? I feel trapped."

"If you think back, in some of my earlier stories I said, '**Life is what it is.**' Then later in life I said, '**Life is what it will be.**' But neither of these are correct. '**Life is what we make it.**'"

"One week after my return from the Old Country a significant aspect of the dream becomes apparent to me to me, related to Aunt Margarite who had died from a burst appendix. The dream was a warning regarding my health. If you remember I was having stomach issues the week before my trip. I prayed for them to go away. As it turns out, home just eight days, Sunday night at eleven o'clock my appendix burst. I call 911 and the paramedics take me to the hospital. After six hours of testing, early Monday morning I'm on my way into surgery."

"When the anesthesiologist gives me the anesthesia, he says, 'Envision a place of serenity.'"

"I envision being at the Monastir Zvernec. Within seconds, I'm gone. Before I know it, I'm in the recovery room tearing the oxygen mask from my face. And that my friends, is the end of today's story."

"When do we get the next story?"

"I'm at the point now Vasiliki, you tell me what works best for you."

"How about tomorrow? I'm anxious to find out what happens next."

"Tomorrow works fine for me."

"Okay, here at four and dinner afterwards?"

"Sounds great." We exchange hugs. The kids are tired, so I help Barbara load them into her car. I thank the priest for coming and tell Simone it's a pleasure meeting her.

Barely home, the phone rings, "Hello Vasiliki."

"Hello Yianni. I wanted to call and thank you for coming into our lives. You've done a fabulous job filling the gaps in our Greek heritage and I'm thankful to you. You've given me cause to open my eyes and to see life in a way I never dreamed possible."

"Tomorrow's stories should give you some useful insight into what I did to heal my soul. Do you have a CD player?"

"Yes, why do you ask?"

"Tomorrow I'm bringing a couple of guest singers."

Chapter Twenty-Three

> As I walked out the door toward
> the gate that would lead to my freedom,
> I knew if I didn't leave my bitterness
> and hatred behind, I'd still be in prison.
>
> ~ Nelson Mandela

When 3:30 rolls around, I grab my CD and Rascal. As we pull up to the curb in front of Vasiliki's house, Rascal goes crazy. He's yelping and before I know it, he jumps out and runs to the front door. Thankfully, the kids are there to greet him.

I grab the CD and walk to the house.

After greeting Vasiliki, I notice Ray, Simone and the Priest are there. I go over to shake their hands and greet Simone with a kiss on the cheek.

"After hearing your stories yesterday, we had to come for more," the priest confided. "I believe you're doing good service to one of my favorite families. We've been here for a couple of hours. Barbara and Vasiliki have given us some background about your life and everything you've gone through. I feel as though I've known you for years. It's sad how much you've had to endure. No one should endure a lifetime of pain and suffering."

Simone says, "He's absolutely right, no one should have to suffer the pain that you've suffered. But I'm here to tell you, thank you." She then wraps her arms around me and says to me, "I love you for telling your truth."

The next words I hear, "When do we start? When do we start?"

"I'm ready now, Christina." I think to myself how great it is the priest is here. I think Ray might refrain from drinking or leaving. I don't think he'd want to embarrass himself or his family.

I turn to Vasiliki and ask, "What time will dinner be ready, so I can gauge how long to talk before we eat?"

"Dinner is prepared, so we can take a break whenever you're ready."

Before we get started I ask Vasiliki to lead me to her CD player. I put the CD in the player, but before I hit the start button I ask them to close their eyes.

"Nobody peek. Keep them closed the whole time the music's playing. I promise you'll have a fantastic experience if you do."

Then I turn it on, take a seat myself and close my eyes. When the song ends, I look around the room. I see the adults have tears in their eyes.

Vasiliki's the first to ask, "Who's the angel singing that song and what are those sounds in the background?"

"The person singing this version of *'Amazing Grace'* is Cecilia. The song comes from her album titled the *'Voice of the Feminine Spirit.'* Fitting wouldn't you say? I heard this song for the first time at a Dr. Wayne Dyer seminar held at the Unity Church in Mira Mesa."

Then I continue where I left off, after surgery from having my appendix removed

"After being in the hospital for a week, I decide that I was going to use the six or seven weeks of recovery to do some reading. I read a few John Grisham books, but was compelled to read such authors as Dr. Wayne

Dwyer, Sonia Choquette and Stuart Wilde. I discovered Paramahansa Yogananda, the founder of the Self-Realization Fellowship, in Carlsbad's book *Autobiography of a Yogi*. I read Caroline Myss' book *Sacred Contracts*, Dr. Michael Newton's *The Journey of the Soul*, Dan Millman's *The Way of the Peaceful Warrior*. I can't name them all. I was like a sponge. I wanted to know so much about spirituality. Each one provided me tidbits of information that help mold me into the person I am today."

"In the back of my mind, I keep thinking about the day that I left Greece. I know there's something bigger yet for me to do, but have no idea what that might be."

"After reviewing the Matriarchal Blessing over and over, I realize the sponge effect and the reading that I was doing is providing me knowledge of science and literature. No wonder my soul was so excited to learn about Spirituality. My faith increased day by day. I start asking questions and the universe provided the answers."

"First, I ask about the dream. What was Grandma really trying to tell me?"

Then I put the next CD in the player and play it for them. Marvin Gaye and Tammi Terrell singing, 'Ain't No Mountain High Enough.'

"This song was a hit in 1967, the same year Grandma died. It paints a picture in my mind as I hear the words, it's Grandma telling me. I realize Grandma used this song to tell me she's been with me every step of the way. It's a love song, and Grandma's teaching me to find love."

"Next, I start questioning the coin. I know it was originally given to me as a message that I'd found Papa's family. But there's a part of me thinking that there's more to it too..."

The Parable of the Coin

"The story behind the coin is revealed to me as I drive home from work one day. It's one of the many magical and mystical days of my life."

"The coin symbolized that when Papa died, I held on to him, just like I held on to the coin. I was supposed to let him go that day at his grave. Similarly, the day I lost the coin I was supposed to just let it go."

"I had lost the ability to love when he died. I held onto him and never wanted to let him go. I did the same thing with the coin. I held onto it. I never wanted to lose it. It was special because Papa sent it to me. I realize that now."

"As you might remember, I missed this coin so much, that the rest of the time I'm in the village I continually looked for it. I'm disappointed that I lost it, no different than how I felt when Papa died. I was heartbroken and felt abandoned."

"Vasil said it best, 'Don't worry about not having this coin. This coin was sent to you as a message and it brought you here to us. It was your destiny to be here, just as it was your destiny to find the coin.'"

"Losing it in the village was no surprise to any of them. It was heartbreaking for me because it was indicative of losing my grandfather that I felt the most."

"When my eyes spot the set of 1959 Greek coins at the airport in Athens, I'm astonished and amazed. What the heck, not one coin, but now a full set. But the parable related to the coins in a set is important. There were six family members who had died at the time I found the coins. Papa, Grandma, Mom, Uncle Alex, Aunt Genevieve and Margarite."

"When we lose a family member, a friend or a loved one, always let them go. It's the special memories we created that matter most. Hold on to them. The collection of those memories is all that matters."

I can hear Grandma telling me now, *"Hold on to the memories and let go of the pain."*

"And that my friends, is the parable of the coin."

"Believe it or not, the blessing is true, and I begin to see things happen in the future. Actually, I begin to listen to my inner thoughts. The next short story explains it."

Six Cents

Before I start, I ask, "How many senses do we have?"

Everyone yells out, "Five."

"Really," I say, as I bring my fingers from my right hand to my chin and grasp it as if to say, "I wonder?"

They're saying, "We only have five senses," spelling them out one by one. "Taste, touch, smell, sight, and sound."

"Yes indeed, those are our five senses."

"At the end of the story, I'm going to ask again."

"One morning as I climb into the shower a thought crosses my mind that I shouldn't drive in the fast lane on the way to work. I think, *that's an odd thought to have.* I pay no attention to it, finish my shower and leave for work."

"My commute to work is sixty-seven miles one way. As soon as I reach the highway, I climb into the fast lane. About forty miles away from home, still in the fast lane, I hit a divot in the highway. My front left tyre blows out. Narrowly missing two cars, I cross four lanes as I reach the right side of the highway."

"I get out of my car to assess the damage. There's not much rubber left on the tyre. While standing on the highway, cars are passing by. Dust flies into my face. Everyone's in a hurry. Not one person stops to help me."

"I didn't have a cell phone yet. I walk along the highway to the next ramp to call AAA for a tow. As I walk up the highway, I ask the universe what the lesson is regarding the flat tyre. I say three or four times, 'Okay, guys, what's the message with the flat tyre? What lesson are you trying to teach me now?' Because there's so much noise from the highway, I'm asking the question out loud, even yelling it, thinking I'm not being heard."

"I walk about a mile and half, no answer to my question, I make it to a payphone to make the call. The AAA operator tells me I will have to meet the tow truck driver at my car. As I walk toward my car, I stop, look up into the sky and I yell, 'Look God, universe, angels, guides, anyone who might be listening, I'm waiting for the answer to my question - what's the lesson regarding the flat tyre? What are you trying to teach me? What is I'm not hearing?'"

"Then I continue toward the car, still asking the question. About halfway there, I look down on the ground and see a nickel and a penny. I pick them up, hold them in the palm of my hand and I say, 'Okay, what's up with the six cents?'"

"Without saying another word, I smack myself on the forehead and start to laugh. I realize the answer is right in the palm of my hand, 'Listen to the sixth sense.' Had I listened and not driven in the fast lane, I never would have hit the divot in the road. But then again, I never would have learned the lesson, 'Always listen to your six cents, I mean your sixth sense.'"

Back to my original question, "How many senses do we have."

They yell, "Six."

✴✴✴

Transcend and go Beyond

"One day while driving home from work, I hear Grandma whisper in my ear, 'Yianni, look up the meaning to the family name, Meta.' By now I'm hearing messages loud and clear. I can't wait to get home."

"It was about three years after my trip. I didn't have the internet yet, so I had to consult with Webster's Dictionary. I look up the word Meta. There's multiple translations, but the one that sticks out the most is, *'To transcend and go beyond.'*"

"Webster's gives a few examples of the use of it as a prefix to words such as 'Metaphysical or metaphor.' Metaphysical by the way, I find it a fitting example because it's the study of what goes and comes from beyond. It becomes my life mantra."

"There you have it folks, short and sweet, that's the end of this short story."

"That was too short," says Simone.

"I agree, but soon after this, something happens to change the course of my life. I'll share that with you after we break for dinner."

Chapter Twenty-Four

The scars of life, painful as they are, remind me that the damage inflicted on my wounded child will remain forever in my DNA.

~ John Egreek

Everyone's in the room waiting for the next story...

"Remember a while back I told the story about my burst appendix. I forgot to tell you that I had a bout with appendicitis when I was nine. When the doctor told my parents it was my appendix, he suggests removing it when I was young. He told them if it happens when I'm older, there's a chance that it could kill me."

"My dad tells the doctor, 'We'll pass on the surgery. Let him worry about it when he's an adult. Who cares if he dies then?'"

Vasiliki says, "Your dad is an ugly human being. I wonder how a father could hate his son this much. You were young and innocent, even at nine, you poor boy. Why did the universe stick you with someone like him?"

"'Who knows, Vasiliki, maybe when he dies they'll send his spirit to the third or fourth floor to learn how evil he is,' I say with a laugh."

"However, this brings me to the next story. It's a story about forgiveness. Without going too far back and covering everything I've already shared, let me say that the three earlier stories were important for me to learn. The most powerful of course is the one related to the family name, 'Transcend and go beyond.'"

"I find it interesting yet mysterious how life can be so cruel. Vasiliki said something that I've wondered about most of my life. 'How could my father hate me so much that he'd beat me at three, wish I'd drowned at five and not care less if I die as an adult? What did I do to deserve such hatred?'"

❧❧

"There comes a time in life when I decide it's time to heal my soul. Thanks to the family name, it's time to transcend and go beyond. I heard the late Dr. Wayne Dyer speak here in San Diego in 1999. He talked about the Course in Miracles. In the course, the word 'beware' is used one time. 'Beware of the temptation to view yourself unfairly treated.' It's a life changing moment for me. I realize I've lived my whole life up to this point feeling as though life has treated me unfairly."

"I began searching the inner depths of my soul."

Vasiliki asks, "Is that how you were able to remember everything that happened to you? I'm amazed how much you remember."

"Good question Vasiliki. What does it mean to remember? I believe it means to heal. Remember, or make our Soul whole again. I believe we do this with forgiveness. Even though I will never agree with my father and everything he did to me, it's important that I forgive him. Without forgiveness, I can't make myself whole."

"Yes, but someone as hateful as your father doesn't deserve forgiveness."

"Perhaps you're right Vasiliki, or... there's work to be done. For instance, I reach the point where I stop playing *'The Dead Man's Hand.'*"

"'What's that?' asks my friend the priest."

"In 'hold-em' poker there are three types of cards. First the 'community cards,' which are four cards dealt face up, you know exactly what they are. Then there's the 'miracle card,' which you have a one in forty-six chance to draw, and last you have the 'drawing dead' cards. These are the cards that suggest it's time to fold. Country western singer

Kenny Logins said it best with his song, 'The Gambler,' when he sings about knowing when to hold, fold or run."

"I've waited my whole life for my father to say he loves me. I played the miracle card and never won."

"I hope he knows there's such a thing as Karma," says Simone.

"I don't believe he cares. He has no concept of life. He's lived the 'Poor Me,' that's been his mantra."

"I will tell you, I reach a point soon after hearing Dr. Dyer where I send my father a letter letting him out of the contract we made before I was born. The lyrics of *Amazing Grace* depict where I am today. My father's tactics were wrong and in today's society he would go to jail for what he did. But there's a valuable lesson behind his actions. He taught my heart to fear. And once I relieve him from his duties as my father, I recognize I've lived long enough feeling unfairly treated."

"It was in that first hour that I believed, it was grace that brought me peace. Soon after this, I wrote the letter that relieved him from the contract. Even though he's hated me since the very first day I was born, I'm okay with that now. He did his job, but it is grace that helped me see. I told my father he's no longer was my worst enemy but actually he's my greatest teacher. He taught me how NOT to be. I speak from my heart, from grace within."

"I tell him, 'I want to forget the past and bury it where it belongs.' Unfortunately, that's an impossible task because the scars are in my DNA. Then I end the letter by telling him that he is relieved of his duties as my father and I hope that we never do a lifetime together ever again."

"I'm curious, how did you feel after you sent the letter? Do you think he read it?" the priest asks.

"You know Father, I felt great after sending it. It didn't matter to me if he read it or even understood it. This entire process isn't about him, it's about me. I no longer get an achy feeling in my stomach when I talk about him. I no longer address him as 'my father."

Simone says, "You know Yianni, I'm really proud of what you've done. It took a long time for you to heal as an adult. But what about your wounded child?"

I step back when she says this. I have no answer. I'm at a loss for words. I just don't know what to say. I've never heard the term, "Wounded Child," and I've never thought about anyone but myself.

Barbara breaks the silence by suggesting we have some dessert.

It's baklava, but my mind is consumed with thoughts about my wounded child. I barely taste it. I want to ask Simone some questions about the wounded child, but at the time, I don't know what to ask her. Soon after we eat, I decide it's time to go home. I'm no longer excited about telling stories.

While saying goodbye, Simone comes up to me and says, "You got very quiet after I asked about your wounded child. I hope I didn't spoil your day."

"No, not at all. My mind's going a mile-a-minute trying to understand what you meant by my wounded child. I'll be just fine, but there's a wandering wounded child who needs to be healed. I had no idea."

"If I can help you in any way, please don't hesitate to ask."

"Thank you, I might just do that."

As I walk toward the door, Vasiliki says, "Yianni, when will we see you again?"

"I'm having cataract surgery next week and then going to Arizona the week after to attend my granddaughter's high-school graduation. I'll call you when I come back."

Then Christina jumps into my arms, "Mr. Yianni, please come back soon."

I kiss her on the cheeks, squeeze her tight and then set her down. As Rascal and I walk to the car, I'm thinking this might be the last time I see them.

Chapter Twenty-Five

Like a rose that blossoms in the spring,
my soul yearns to be loved.
Forgiveness is the key that heals
my older Self.
My youth is lost but not forgotten.
What Blessing will heal my
wounded child?

- JohnEgreek

Two months have passed since I left Vasiliki's house for what I thought might be the last time.

One day, the phone rings and it's Vasiliki, "Yianni, we haven't heard from you for a long time. I wanted to call to check on you."

I tell her not to worry. I've been consumed with re-branding my person, without giving a hint of what I mean.

She tells me, "We miss you terribly. The kids keep asking about you and are wondering if you have any more stories to tell."

"I thought I was done telling stories the last time, but I have one huge story to tell you. Why don't we plan to meet next week? In the meantime, I wonder if you could give me Simone's phone number. I'd like to talk with her before scheduling a time for us to meet."

"Absolutely."

We schedule to meet the following Tuesday. Then I say, "I miss you all very much. Give Christina a hug for me. Feel free to invite anyone you'd like. By the way, it's really important that Ray is there. I have something to share that I know will be important for him to hear."

"I'll do my best to make that happen." She gives me Simone's phone number, then we say goodbye.

It's time to get some insight into the wounded child, so I call Simone.

We talk in great detail, then I ask her to meet me at Vasiliki's the following Tuesday.

As I drive to Vasiliki's, a Michael Jackson song comes on the radio. I'm not a huge fan of Michael Jackson, but his song "Childhood" paints a picture in my mind as I listen to the first few lines, while pulling up in front of her house.

Simone and I arrive within seconds of each other. I wait for her to get out of her car and we walk into Vasiliki's house together.

'm barely inside when Christina runs to jump into my arms. She doesn't want to let go. Within seconds after I put her down, the rest of the family greets me with open arms. Each one of them is telling me how much they missed me. I feel really good knowing this family missed me.

A few minutes later, the Greek priest comes walking in with Ray. I greet them with a firm handshake.

After passing a few minutes with small talk, everyone's chomping at the bit to hear what's been going on. We sit in the living room and I begin telling them about the graduation and how it took me to my knees.

"Since our last meeting, the following Tuesday, I was scheduled for cataract surgery with my left eye. It sucks getting old. The day after surgery, at the follow-up with the surgeon, Dr. Lee, he tells me to wear sunglasses for the next couple of weeks so the lens in my left eye can adjust to light."

"Less than a week later, I'm driving to Arizona to visit my daughter and to attend my granddaughter's high-school graduation. It seems like just yesterday when I graduated. I'm nervous about this trip because I have no idea who they've invited to the graduation or the party the day after. I haven't seen my younger son in nearly five years since he threw me out of his life. If he's there, what will I say?"

"I drove for a little over five hours in complete silence from California through Arizona. Rascal spent most of the drive laying on my right thigh, sleeping. I'm sure he sensed I was in a different world. I kept thinking about the wounded child, wondering how to heal him."

"We made it to Natalie's house in record time. I barely remember the drive. The graduation isn't for two days. I brought my computer so I could keep up with my project coordinator position with Tom Bird."

"Natalie informed me she had to do some chores and go shopping for the graduation party. I told her not to worry about me, I'm a big boy and I can handle being left alone. Then I went to work on my computer."

"The following day I drive to Sedona to meet up with a couple of the authors in the Tom Bird writing program. When I get back to Natalie's house, I take a nap. I find myself concerned about my wounded child. My eyes are constantly drying up, so I use the eyedrops recommended by the eye doctor to keep them moist."

"Graduation day arrives the following day. I have some great conversations with my granddaughter during the early afternoon and then do some work. While working, my younger son and his wife come by. I'm too scared to come out of my room, so I continue working, hoping they will come in to say hello. That didn't happen."

"That evening my oldest son, his wife and my step-granddaughter drove me to the graduation. We spend some time catching up. We walk to the grandstands and are first greeted by my brother and his wife. Natalie asks me to sit on the end of the row next to my son's wife, Tonika. She and I have an enjoyable conversation going when my younger son comes walking up the bleachers."

"My brother and his wife are two rows down. My son and his wife stop to give them hugs and kisses. Then they greet the people sitting in front of me. I'm waiting with open arms. When they reach me, my son says, 'Naw,' puts out his hand for a handshake and says, 'This is all you get.' These are the last words he will say to me for the next two days."

"His wife is polite enough to take my offer for a hug. She tells me it's nice to see me. Unfortunately, deep inside my heart, I felt none of that was true."

"They take a seat down the row, hugging and kissing the rest of the family as they pass by, until they reach his mother and a mutual friend, Debbie."

"My daughter-in-law Tonika nestles up close to me, throws her arm over my shoulders, then says, 'Mr. John, are you all right. I know that crushed you.'"

"Thank God, I have these sunglasses. They do an excellent job of hiding and containing the tears that are flowing from my eyes. I tell her I'm fine, but my heart's broken. Humpty-Dumpty fell off the wall and there's no words that can put him back together again."

"The graduation ceremony took a little over two hours. Two hours of tears continued to accumulate under the sunglasses. I don't dare take them off to reveal my pain. I do my best to act like nothing is going on. Yet I am frozen."

"The following day is the graduation party. It starts at three and is scheduled to end at seven. This will be the first time I'll meet my granddaughter Aubrey Rose. At least so I think."

"At my daughter's house, I'm still wearing the sunglasses. Good thing, because the afternoon sun is bright. She and her girlfriend are sitting in the courtyard. I sit down to join them. A few minutes later, my ex comes walking out the door with our granddaughter, Aubrey Rose, holding hands. They walk up to us, get within five feet of me, then turn and walk away. She doesn't have the decency to tell me, 'This is your granddaughter, Aubrey Rose.'"

"I'm crushed, I'm devastated and I'm angry. The glasses hide my tears. My wounded child and I are in pain. I gain my composure and decide to go inside. My brother and his wife, along with my youngest son, his wife, her mother-in-law and mutual friend Debbie are sitting in the living room. I take a seat next to Debbie. We worked together at the powerplant years earlier, so we have that in common."

"Within seconds after sitting down, my son and his wife get up without saying a word. My eyes haven't adjusted from being outside. I make the decision to keep the sunglasses on, then explain to Debbie that I had cataract surgery and the doc told me to wear them. I'm so glad the surgery provides me the excuse to keep my eyes hidden. No one's able to see my pain."

"My son's mother-in-law begins to make small talk with me. We converse for about fifteen minutes. On three separate occasions, my ex comes in with Aubrey Rose. She marches her around like the princess that she is. She walks within five feet of me, turns around and walks her away. Nobody introduces me to Aubrey Rose. She has no idea that I'm her grandpa."

"I turn to my son's mother-in-law and I say, 'You know, I've never met Aubrey Rose. This is the first time I've seen her. I've been in the dark and only found out about her on Facebook. Nobody ever told me they were even having a child.'"

"She says, 'No, I didn't know that.'"

"I thought she'd introduce me to Aubrey Rose, but that never happened. For the next two hours, anytime I enter a room where they were, they got up and went to another room. It's obvious I'm being shunned. My daughter-in-law Tonika provides her compassion and love. She knows exactly what is going on. At one point she says, 'Mr. John, I just don't understand the dynamics of this family and what's going on.'"

"The wicked witch of the north, so called because she lives north of me, my ex, showed her true colors. Shame on her. In my mind, I'm thinking she's a spiteful bitch along with a bunch of other names, but I refrain from saying them out loud for the sake of the kids. She'll have to live with herself and be accountable for her actions in the end. How dare she be so spiteful and march Aubrey Rose around the room and never say, 'This is your grandpa.'"

I see my audience shaking their heads. Barbara and Vasiliki keep wiping the tears from their eyes. Christina's sitting close by. Ray's looking away most of the time. I'm sure he's hearing every word that I say.

"Around six in the evening, my daughter's boyfriend, Lee, comes into the living room to turn on the TV. It seems my two sons want to watch the NBA playoff game. I think this might be a chance to break the ice. My oldest son comes in and sits down next me. The youngest never comes in. Every now and then, he takes a quick look at the score and then leaves. I realize I'm cramping their style. I get up to go to the rest room. Along the way, I stop to tell my daughter-in-law Tonika and my son Roc goodbye."

"Tonika says, 'I don't blame you Mr. John. It took a lot for you to remain silent. You honored your granddaughter's graduation celebration without saying a word. I'm proud of you for that.'"

"I go to Natalie's house. Rascal is waiting for me there and he's really glad to see me. Thank God for animals. They know better than humans how to love without conditions. There was no sign of unconditional love at the party. Once inside the house, I fall to my knees and I cry like a baby. That was by far, the worst day of my life."

Vasiliki says, "Yianni, I'm so sorry for your pain."

"Thank you Vasiliki, but it's much better for me now."

As I continue...

"After the cry, I take the sunglasses off to clean my eyes, put in eyedrops and make the decision to cry no more. But my wounded child and my wounded adult are still in pain. Not crying might be an impossible task."

"I spend the rest of the evening alone, go to bed around eleven and get up at six to begin packing the car. My daughter gets up at seven and we have a cup of coffee together."

"She asks why I left the party so early."

"I do my best to tell her without showing the pain, 'The party was almost over, and it wasn't about me, it was about her. Your brothers wanted to watch the NBA game. As long as I was there, Ryan wouldn't come into the room, so I decided it would be best to leave. Sometimes things work out different than we expect them.'"

"I can't tell her the real reason I left was because I don't want to stay somewhere that I wasn't welcome. I know if I say what I want to, I'd say that her mom was a spiteful witch with a "b" and it was shameful that nobody introduced me to Aubrey Rose. I hold my words."

"A few minutes later I pack the rest of the car, load up Rascal and say goodbye."

"Even though I decided there would be no more tears, that was hard to do. Most of the way home, the tears keep flowing from eyes. My thoughts are consumed with what had transpired the last two days. Half way home, I'm yelling out loud at God. 'Why am I plagued with loneliness and why I am being treated with such cruelty. I don't understand the lesson in this God. I was brought into this world with a father who hates me and now my youngest son has thrown me away like a piece of garbage. What did I do to make him want to inflict me with so much pain? He's turned himself completely away. What have I done to deserve all of this? What karma have I created?'"

"Seconds later, I'm telling myself I've had enough of this life. I'm going to do something to change things. I'm 328 pounds, obese as my doctor will say. I'm done carrying this coat of arms that's covering my soul. I'm done with being alone. I'm going to do something different, because what I'm doing now, just isn't working for me."

"I pop a CD into my disk player with Caroline Myss' recordings related to 'Sacred Contracts.' Just before I reach home, she says something about that sticks with me. She teaches that not every lesson we encounter is necessarily for us, even though we experience it because of the nature of our relationship with another. It isn't about fixing other people, as the only one I can fix is myself. What I understand from her words is that if my younger son's lesson is to learn something in particular from our relationship, it is for him to learn. I can't make him do it or do it for him. It's his lesson, it's not mine. Hopefully one day he'll see the dynamics of what's transpired between us. Hopefully, one day he'll rise to the occasion to heal his wounded soul."

"I asked Simone to be here today to help explain what to do with my wounded child. Since she was the one to recognize my wounded child was in need, I figure she could enlighten us with her wisdom. We discussed some things on the phone last week and I know she has lots to say."

Then I turn to acknowledge Simone.

She provides the following synopsis of a wounded child.

"Since I know Yianni was born in 1950, like so many from the 50's, the fathers from that generation, more so than our mothers, were tainted by World War Two and the Korean conflict. Our dads came back into society as broken souls. Many of them were alcoholics or on their way to becoming one. More than ninety percent of them smoked. His father, being the youngest of twelve brothers and sisters, was wounded in ways one can't imagine. Most of his siblings were already out of the house and his mother was probably tired of being a mother by then. Couple that with the fact that she raised him without a father, he felt abandoned, detached from his siblings, lost, wounded, and cheated. It was easy for him to take on the life of a victim. As Yianni once said, he lived the life of the poor me."

"Oh my God, how did you pick up on all that?" I asked. "You weren't there when I told those stories."

"No, I wasn't, but since we were together last, I spent a great deal of time with Barbara and Vasiliki. They brought me up to speed and filled in the gaps. I figured you'd come calling one day."

"I believe your father, mean as he was, played the leading role in repressing your inner child. I bet he said such things as 'Kids are to be seen, but not heard from,' or 'Put food in your mouth, that way you won't be able to speak.'"

"How about this one? 'Because I said so.' He said that one more times than I can count," I added.

"He didn't let you be a kid. He expected you to act like an adult. Then to add insult to injury, he beat you at three, wished you had died at five, ostracized you from the family at six. Every step of the way, he repressed your inner child."

"Patterns took form within your unconscious mind. It started when you were three. Who knows, you might have brought some as baggage from previous lifetimes. Over time, these patterns build in your unconscious mind like an antique car rusting away in the fields. They're corrosive and your father contributed to the fears and suffering of your wounded child."

"Yes, but even so, I got past the pain," I countered.

"You think so? How old were you when you got married?"

"Twenty-one and a half."

"You couldn't wait to get out of the house I bet? At twenty-one you probably thought you were a grown-up. Unfortunately, you were most likely not emotionally ready, or even psychologically ready to be an adult. Your wife getting pregnant early on in your marriage didn't help. You didn't get to be a husband, and you definitely were not ready or equipped to be a dad. You were thrown to the wolves. Your unconscious mind was filled with anger, guilt, fear and sorrow."

Staggered by the accuracy of Simone's assessment, I reply, "I hated the fact that my wife wanted to have a baby so quick after we married. I resented her for it. I knew I wasn't ready. This is not a reflection on my daughter. I love her more than she'll ever know. But my ex-wife on the other hand... I'm not going to say it. My wounded child needs help, not more pain."

"Well, Yianni," she says with the voice of an angel, "you're a victim of your childhood. The negative patterns of your life allowed your wounded child to take charge of your life. Your father never loved you and you unfortunately were attracted to women who didn't love you either. It was your norm. You spent the greatest years of your life trying to win people over. You didn't know anything different. I bet you've been telling your story over and over to anyone that comes along. Even strangers?" she says while gesturing to everyone in the room. "I understand you suffered so much trauma and disappointment that your mind is like an eight-track tape player, playing your drama over and over in your mind."

Little Charlie interrupts, "What's an eight-track tape player?"

"You've aged us, Simone. Charlie, when we were in our teens, we didn't have CD players, we had eight-track tape players. The tapes were as big as the tape in a VCR,"

"What's a VCR?"

By now everyone in the room is laughing. The priest says, "They're like an audio cassette tape but six times the size."

Changing back to the story, I turn to Simone and say, "Yes, but I recognized these patterns when I was in my forties. I thought I healed them at that time."

"You might've, or you learned to put on a happy face. That little boy inside you is frightened. He needs healing much more than adult Yianni needed healing. He's been angry and fearful long enough."

"But I forgive my father. What more do I need to do?"

291

Simone continues, "It's important that you understand your dad didn't know he was harming you. In his own way, his ignorance drove him to be mean to you. He most likely hates you still today because of ignorance. With just one ounce of shame, he might've found some compassion toward you. Unfortunately, his ignorance is stronger than his shame."

"So, you're telling me I have more work to do?"

She reaches over to grab my hand, then says, "Yianni, forgiving your father was a big step. Even further, understanding your father is more important. This is a generational issue. Your relationship melt-down with your son is as significant as your relationship break-down with your dad. Unfortunately, you can't heal your sons. That's something they'll have to come to grips with on their own. You can only heal yourself. In doing so, you need to use the philosophy of the three A's: Awareness, Acceptance and Audacity."

"I understand the aspects of awareness and acceptance. I don't know what you mean by the use of audacity. How does this play in to healing myself?"

"Audacity is no different than the law of action. It means you have to take action and dig in to do the healing of your own self, not someone else's."

"No wonder my sons are so angry with me. We divorced before the youngest guy was one-year old. We divorced twice, first when the oldest guy was three and then again when he was five. They've evidently blamed the abandonment issues on me. Unfortunate for me, but I wasn't the one to make the decision to divorce. That decision was made by their mom."

"Even so Yianni, their wounded child is probably angry at both of you and your ex is oblivious to any of this. I would guess that she put all the blame on you. It's easy to do when you're not around."

"I'm sure of it. This explains a great deal. I'm sure the youngest guy has felt abandoned for as long as he can remember. Even in his adult years, while living relatively close to him in Arizona, I didn't go to visit him. That probably increased his wounded child abandonment issues. No wonder he doesn't want to talk to me. It's a defense mechanism to protect his wounded child, just as my gaining weight became a defense mechanism. My coat of arms as I call it."

"Yianni, your suffering was originally caused by physical abuse when your father beat you at three and it continued as he emotionally abused you with such comments as 'I wish he would've died,' after you nearly drowned. I'm sure he beat you up emotionally throughout the years, more than he physically beat you at three. This suffering became the organizing template in your mind. Because of it, you created abusive relationships, choosing the wrong women to be with. You became codependent, looking for love in all the wrong places. That's why you had such an attraction toward sexual love. It was your codependency, your addiction. As you began to recognize your codependency, fear took over, and you gained weight. It became your protection factor. Yes indeed, you built a coat of arms. Does this make sense to you?"

"Absolutely it makes sense to me. I see many of the same aspects of abandonment that my sons most likely felt when their sister came to live with me. Similar to what happened with me when I was sent to live with my grandparents and no longer lived with my brother and sister. Even though my grandparents, aunts and uncles nurtured me with their love, being away from my family made me a loner. This makes complete sense to me."

"Yianni, your abandonment issues, along with the emotional and physical abuse, have been deeply rooted into your wounded child. He feels broken, lost and left to deal with things all on his own. That's why each time a family member died, you drifted further and further away. You had no one to turn to, no one to provide you any form of love. That's why your desire for sexual love was great. It provided you with a very small dose of love. Every wounded child chooses to live with some form of addiction."

"I guess this explains why my father and my son turned to alcohol. Alcohol became their addiction," I responded.

"It most likely does. It also explains why you became obese. After realizing sexual love was not working for you, you turned to food. It became your addiction."

"Yes, it did. Food makes me feel good, unfortunately, just like sex. But it's short lived. It's twenty seconds of pleasure."

"I'm sure my sons and daughter have similar abandonment issues. But I love them from the deepest part of my soul. I didn't physically or mentally abuse them. I just withdrew from them, which most likely made their little child feel even more abandoned. My daughter was subject to the good, the bad, and the ugly from me. We argued when she lived with me. I pushed her to exceed. It was my dream that she would be more successful than me. It was my dream that all three of my kids would be more successful than me. I did my best to be a good role model for my children. I didn't drink, I didn't smoke, I didn't cuss, and I did the best that I knew how. I understand now, more than ever, that wasn't enough."

"You're sharing similar pain," Simone explained. "Their pain is miniscule compared to the pain you've been carrying. You didn't physically or mentally abuse them. You just abandoned them. At least that's how their wounded child is seeing things. Unfortunately, this is a generational issue. Remember the dream you had where your grandma took you to that building with multiple generations of people dressed in the garb of their time. And they were celebrating you being there?"

"I do, of course. It was an epic dream."

"I have a theory the celebration was because you were about to embark on a journey to heal your wounded child. That's what they were celebrating. You just didn't know it yet. But the steps you take to heal yourself, will somehow connect to the wounded children of your ancestors and descendants. There will be a domino effect that can help to heal the world. Like Neil Armstrong said when he first stepped on the moon, 'One small step for man, one giant leap for mankind.'"

"What do I do to heal my wounded child?"

"First and foremost is recognizing the existence of your wounded child. Welcome little Yianni into your daily life. Stop thinking of him as the wounded child and start thinking of him as a healthy little child. Start your morning with a hello. Have breakfast with him, then lunch, take him grocery shopping. Have dinner together. Buy some of his favorite foods. Do the dishes or the laundry together. Type on the computer together. Celebrate his existence. Make your life together an adventure."

"Hmmm, that sounds like an interesting and fun experience."

"Yes, it's a very exciting experience. But you have to take into consideration all of your little Yianni's."

"What do you mean by all of my little Yianni's Simone?"

"For instance, what about little Yianni who almost drowned? What about little Yianni whose mother was in a car accident? What about little Yianni who had to live with his mother's family instead of being with his brother and sister? What about little Yianni who was sad because Grandma didn't win 'Queen for a Day?' I could keep on going, but you get my drift. You need to heal all of them. Including the teenage Yianni's, divorced Yianni's, the lost and forgotten Yianni's. You need to heal them all."

"That's a great deal of healing Simone."

"Yes, it is Yianni. Unfortunately for you, it's sixty-seven years of Yianni's because the pain keeps stacking up. Once you stop the bleeding, then you can live a healthy life."

Then I turn to Vasiliki and say, "Why don't we break for dinner. For now, the two of us, meaning me and my little child, three-year old Yianni, can join the rest of you for dinner."

"Sounds great. We welcome you both."

❧❧

Before I tell the rest of my story, I'd like to ask a few more questions of Simone related to healing my little child.

"What other healing methods are there?"

"Yianni, you have some of the answers already. I know, because you shared some stories with me about your recent encounters with a couple of people with cancer when you suggested they use the two-chair method. You can use that with your little child."

"Duh, why didn't I think of that. Thanks for the reminder Simone."

Ray shocks everyone when he asks, "What's the two-chair method? This whole wounded child thing has peaked my interest and might explain why I'm an alcoholic."

His wife Barbara walks over to him, sits next to him and says, "Honey, I love you. You don't have be alone anymore. We are here and we all love you."

Ray breaks into tears. It's the first time he's recognized or admitted he's an alcoholic. His wife Barbara has her arms around him and she's holding him up. The rest of us sit in silence, giving them an opportunity to reunite.

A few minutes later Rays says, "Yianni, I know that day that you got up and walked away from me in the restaurant took courage. But it really opened my eyes. I have not forgotten what you said to me just before you left."

Barbara, now curious as she didn't know that we had met one day, asks, "What did he say to you?"

Ray comes clean about the encounter at the grocery store. Then he tells everyone that he'd called to ask me to meet him for lunch and that I agreed with conditions. He tells them that I promised to meet for lunch if he didn't drink before lunch and didn't drink during lunch. "Unfortunately, I ordered a beer with my lunch and Yianni got up and walked out of the restaurant. Before he left, he said, 'Alcoholism is a well-documented pathological reaction to unresolved grief.'"

Simone says, "Yes, I believe it was David Cook who said that. It's pretty accurate and deeply rooted that unresolved grief is cornerstone to the feelings of a wounded child."

Then Ray says it again, "Yianni, please explain the two-chair method."

"The two-chair method is something that I heard about in an audio series in the mid-nineties when I was listening to books on tape while driving to work. I taught it to a friend of mine, who had uterine cancer. She had been molested by an uncle when she was nine years old. Her mother didn't support or believe her when she told her, and she suppressed the pain. Over time, her dis-ease turned into cancer. I taught her to envision her uncle sitting in the opposite chair and explaining to him that although she didn't agree with him, she does forgive him. I explained that she needs to do this forgiveness from deep within her heart."

"The next step is to place her mother in a chair and do the same with her, and anyone else who may have harmed her or wounded her feelings. Then I told her to do the same with herself. What I didn't do, because I didn't know it until now, was to tell her to place her wounded child in the other chair. I used this technique around the turn of the century when I forgave my father. This technique will definitely work with the wounded child."

Ray says, "I'm going to use this technique with my wounded child and nobody is to give me a tough time if they catch me talking to my little child."

Everyone is smiling. The light from our souls has brightened the room as we hear Ray admitting he has a wounded child.

Vasiliki breaks the ice as she says, "Yianni, you haven't told us the rest of your story."

Back to the story...

"The following week after the graduation, I'm back in Arizona, in Sedona, working a 'Write Your Book in a Weekend' retreat with Tom Bird. On the first day, prior to the start of the retreat, Tom tells me his wife is a nutritionist and she's doing a study with ten people. She has included me as one of the ten. A few seconds later I introduce myself to his wife, Heidi Bird. I also meet Shifu Gagan, a branding expert who was there to write her book in a weekend and to work with Tom Bird's branding."

"What's a Shifu?" asks Bobby.

"People from India, where Gagan is from, call spiritual masters Guru. When the spiritual master is a woman, they call her Shifu."

"Within the first month after leaving the retreat I release twenty-five pounds. Things are beginning to fall into place. Soon after, during the second month, Shifu Gagan, who is a Chinese Astrology Master and Energy Healer, does a life map reading of me. I provide her with some vital statistics which include date and time of my birth, the city where I was born, San Francisco, and a little information about my family. For the next two months, she prepares a life map reading as agreed."

"In the meantime, I have weekly phone meetings with Heidi who keeps me accountable with my weight release and provides me with valuable information along with recipes for smoothies. We call what I'm doing, 'A transformation of life.'"

Barbara says, "You mean you're on a diet, right?"

"Actually, no. I'm eating more now than I ever ate before. But I'm eating mostly fruits and vegetables. I eat meat once a week. I haven't been willing to give it up completely. It's hard to do because of the Greek in me."

"I can relate to that," says the priest.

"It's a transformation of life. She has taught me to recognize, with the use of a Primary food wheel, that everything's inter-related to health, education, social life, home environment, career, creativity, spirituality, finances, relationships and physical activity. We eat certain foods based on which part of the wheel dominates us most."

"Without going into this too deep, mind you, this is a learn-as-we-go experience. Here's an example, I'll use finances. Let's say it's getting close to Christmas season and our car breaks down. We have three children, a wife, a husband and a mother to care for. The strain of the broken car puts a strain on our budget and we're thinking, 'How am I going to pay for Christmas now that the car is broken down?' With the stress eating away at us, we'll most like eat crap and continue to feel like crap."

Ray says, "That's how I feel after being drunk."

"There's a definite correlation between the two."

"Tell us more about Shifu Gagan. I want to meet her," says Christina.

"Shifu Gagan presented me with my life map reading a couple of weeks ago. It was a three-hour Zoom session that I have recorded. During the session, she was able to pinpoint every ten-year cycle of my life. She knew that at three or four years of age something traumatic happened to me. She knew that I experienced physical abuse. When I told her about the beating at three she wasn't surprised. She pinpointed the key ten-year periods of my life. It was amazing what she told me. Unfortunately, most of what she got throughout was loneliness and pain."

"She told me, 'You have lived a lonely and terrible life. The sadness in your soul was evident to me.'"

"We talked in length about my wounded child. She informs me that she's going to perform some healing. The first night she had me listen to some chakra music while she healed my lower chakras. The following morning, she called to see if I felt any different. I told her it was the first time I've woken up without a back-ache in a very long time."

"She said, 'I wasn't working with your back, but I imagine working with your lower chakras helped it to feel better. But let me ask you a question, are your ankles puffy, or numb, what's going on from your knees down?'"

"I tell her, 'Oh my God, how could you tell from that far away that my ankles are swollen? And yes, I have numbness in my feet. Since working with Heidi, I've been taking magnesium, drinking lemon water and vinegar water which has helped. I'm amazed that you could feel the numbness.'"

"Shifu Gagan says, 'Yes, that's where the pain from your wounded child has landed. When your father beat you at three, did you injure your ankles.'"

"I don't recall my exact injuries. When I dove through the glass window, I'm sure I got cuts on various parts of my body. A couple of days later, I envisioned that day, flying through the window. Normally when I ran through the open window, I did a tuck and roll when I hit the ground. After Mom replaced the window and I ran through the glass, it affected my tuck and roll. I ran away limping."

"She says, 'That's why your ankles are swollen. The accident triggered your wounded child and the pain has never left your ankles. It will take some time a, few more healings, to clear the physical aspects of your pain.'"

"Wow, that was amazing Yianni. She must be a master for sure," says our friend the Greek priest. "I've heard the masters from the East have some deep-rooted healing abilities. They say they're passed down through the generations and as we here in the West become more in tune with our souls, it's amazing how much pain in society will be gone."

Then I tell them about the next healing.

"It happens while I'm in the midst of learning about the wounded child. Shifu Gagan sent me a text message and asked if I was available for another healing."

"I sent her a message back, saying, 'Yes, but I just had a four-hour nap. I was exhausted with all of this wounded child stuff and at three in the afternoon I took a nap.'"

"She tells me, 'It's okay, I don't need you to be present during the healing. Just go on about your business. I'll start in thirty minutes.'"

"Ten minutes later I send her a text to tell her that I want to be present when she does the healing, please text me five minutes before you're going to start so I can go in the other room.'"

"Fifteen minutes later I receive a text, go into the other room, turn on the chakra music and lie flat on my back. Soon, after about seventy-five minutes that seemed like fifteen, she sends a text that says, 'done.'"

"The following morning, she calls to see how I feel. I tell her my ankles are less swollen and it feels like I'm walking on feathers."

"Then she says, 'Yianni, I've never cried when I've done a healing. I cried because your heart chakra and lower chakras were bleeding. You've been in pain your whole life. The bleeding is stopped. I closed the wounds. I'm sorry you had to go through all of this for sixty-seven years of your life. But you understand that you made the choice to live this way, don't you?'"

"What did she mean when she said you made the choice to live this way? Why would anyone choose to live a lonely life?" says Barbara.

"Because there's a higher calling in my future. It's my plight to do something for the world and I believe the life transformation is a large part of this calling. Time will tell. And that my friends, is the end of my story for now."

As my little child and I get up to walk out the door for the last time, I look behind and see many more than of my little children following close behind. I feel like my work is done with Christina's family, but now there's work to do with my own. Sharing the story of my wounded child has helped to show them that anyone can heal their wounded child and promote a more productive and healthy life.

I know I have more work ahead of me, but my little children and I will do this work together. I know they're going to be okay. If they use the knowledge and wisdom from Grandma's Secret Blessings, I know in my heart that they'll always draw an Ace and a Queen.

Seconds later I'm saying goodbye for the last time. I figure this will be the end of our time together. Then Christina runs toward me yelling out my name.

"Mr. Yianni, Mr. Yianni."

I turn and stoop down to catch her, just in time as she leaps into my arms. She hugs me tightly around the neck and then she says loud enough for everyone to hear, "Mr. Yianni, will you be my grandpa?"

"This is the Beginning, because there just never is an End"

~ JohnEgreek

❧❧

Remember

The three A's – Awareness, Acceptance, Audacity

Made in the USA
Las Vegas, NV
24 May 2024